Mel Bay Presents

Classical Guitar Pedagogy

A Handbook for Teachers

I Principles of Technique
II Principles of Pedagogy
III Musicianship

Anthony Glise
Urtext Editions

For author contact in the U.S., address:
Aevia Publications, Ltd., P.O. Box 7242
St. Joseph, MO 64507, USA
Cover photo: "Sirius," constructed 1996 by Gioachino Giussani, Anghiari (Arezzo), Italy
Photo by A. Jeannine Borngesser-Glise
Printed in the United States of America

Visit us on the Web at http://www.melbay.com — E-mail us at email@melbay.com

1 2 3 4 5 6 7 8 9 0

To my first, and finest teachers

Wyllis LeRoy Glise
and
Alma Jeannine Borngesser-Glise

and my sister and brother
Tamara Sue Glise-Filbert
and
Christopher Guy Glise

PREFACE

The primary goal in pedagogy should be to teach *why*, rather than *how*. Virtually anyone can teach "how" something is done, but few take the time to teach (or analyze) "why" we do things a certain way.

In explaining "how," students learns to duplicate, but when a similar or new situation arises, they are at a loss for what to do. They have not truly learned, they have only imitated.

Our goal should be—and I want to stress that this is the most important concept in teaching—our goal should be to teach *why* we do something a certain way. With this understood, a student will almost automatically understand how to proceed alone—even sometimes extending beyond what we ourselves understand—and finally become a self-sufficient, thinking musician. A musician who can independently analyze a situation, accurately assess the musical goals, and confidently come to terms with a solution; a solution which has an individual and rational basis, and one which enhances the music.

As a teacher, there is no greater challenge than to awaken a student to this fact.

Perhaps is it not inappropriate to add that this same aspect of teaching extends into all facets of life. The answers don't stem from understanding *"how,"* but *"why."*

If this is correct, then we as teachers hold a position of much greater importance and power than we often assume. We can positively or negatively affect—even alter—how a person thinks.

This is a severe responsibility.

Never—*never*—forget this.

A.L. Glise

CREDITS:

Magazines:

Various ideas in this book were first published by Mr. Glise in:

Anthony L. Glise, "A 'New' Left Hand Position?," *The Soundboard* IX/2 (Garden Grove, Calif., USA: Winter, 1982-83). © 1982 by A. Glise.

___"A 'New' Fingering for Beginners?," *The Soundboard* X/1 (Garden Grove: 1983). © 1982 by A. Glise.

___"Through the Back Door," *Guitar Toronto* II/6 (Toronto: March, 1983). © 1983 by A. Glise.

___"Stage Presence—A Passing Thought," *Guitar International* (London: November, 1984). © 1984 by A. Glise.

___"Musikalische Phrasierung, Teil 1," *Gitarre und Laute* VII/1 (Cologne: Jan.-Feb., 1985). © 1984 by. A. Glise.

___"Musikalische Phrasierung, Teil 2," *Gitarre und Laute* VII/2 (Cologne: March-April, 1985). © 1984 by A. Glise.

___"Musical Interpretation—A Study in Phrasing, Part 1," *The Soundboard* XIV/1 (Garden Grove: Spring, 1987). © 1986 by A. Glise.

___"Musical Interpretation—A Study in Phrasing, Part 2," *The Soundboard* XIV/2 (Garden Grove: Summer, 1987). © 1986 by A. Glise.

___"Musical Interpretation—A Study in Phrasing, Part 3," *The Soundboard* XIV/3 (Garden Grove: Fall, 1987). © 1986 by A. Glise.

___"Musical Interpretation—A Study in Phrasing, Part 4," *The Soundboard* XIV/4 (Garden Grove: Winter, 1987).

___"Stage Presence—'The Forgotten Art'," *The Soundboard* XXI/3 (Garden Grove: Winter, 1995). © 1994 by A. Glise.

Photos:

Drawings:

Publishing Acknowledgments:

I would like to thank the following publishing companies and their international representatives who kindly granted rights to reprint musical and iconographic examples. These examples were chosen because of the quality, scholarship and availability of the editions.

• Aevia Publications, Ltd.:

J.S. Bach, *Chaconne in D Minor*, BWV 1004, ed. Anthony Glise (St. Joseph/Vienna: Aevia Publications, 1997). Used by permission.

Anton Diabelli, "Andante cantabile," *Trois Sonates—Sonata in C Major* (Vienna: n.d.), *The Complete Sonatas of Sor, Giuliani and Diabelli,* ed. A. Glise (St. Joseph/Vienna: Aevia, 1997). Used by permission.

Anton Diabelli, "Andante sostenuto," *Trois Sonates—Sonata in F Major* (Vienna: n.d.), *The Complete Sonatas of Sor, Giuliani and Diabelli,* ed. A. Glise (St. Joseph/Vienna: Aevia, 1997). Used by permission.

Anton Diabelli, "Finale," *Trois Sonates—Sonata in F Major* (Vienna: n.d.), *The Complete Sonatas of Sor, Giuliani and Diabelli,* ed. A. Glise (St. Joseph/Vienna: Aevia, 1997). Used by permission.

Mauro Giuliani, "Adagio," *Sonata Op. 15* (Vienna: Richault, *ca.* 1828), *The Complete Sonatas of Sor, Giuliani and Diabelli,* ed. A. Glise (St. Joseph/Vienna: Aevia, 1997). Used by permission.

Anthony Glise, *The Child's Guitar, Vol. I* (St. Joseph,/Vienna: Aevia, 1994). Used by permission.

Anthony Glise, *Chromatic Exercises ("The Basic Seven") and Arpeggio Studies, Op. 2, A.* (St. Joseph/Vienna: Aevia, 1994). Used by permission.

Anthony Glise, *Classical Guitar Method for Adults* (St. Joseph/Vienna: Aevia, 1998). Used by permission.

Anthony Glise, "Con moto e leggerezza" from *Lullabies, Op. 5* (St. Joseph/Vienna: Aevia , 1994). Used by permission.

Anthony Glise, "Dryaden" ("Tree Spirits") from *Traum Szene (Dream Scenes), Op. 9, A* (St. Joseph/Vienna: Aevia, 1994). Used by permission.

S.L. Weiss, "Chaconne No. 3 in E Major" from *The Complete Chaconne of S.L. Weiss,* ed. Anthony Glise (St. Joseph/Vienna: Aevia, 1997). Used by permission.

- Chanterelle Verlag:

Johann Kaspar Mertz, *Tarentelle* from *Bardenklänge* (Vienna, *ca.* 1847) facsimile ed. Simon Wynberg, *The Guitar Works of J.K. Mertz, vol. III* (Heidelberg: Chanterelle, 1983). Used by permission.

- Columbia Publishing Company:

Federico Moreno-Torroba, "Allegro," *Sonatina,* ed. Andrés Segovia (Washington, D.C.: Columbia, 1966). © 1966 by Columbia Music Company. Used by permission, sole representative, Theodore Presser Publishing Company.

- Da Capo Press:

Fernando Sor, *Method for the Spanish Guitar* (Paris, 1830), trans. A. Merrick (London, 1850) (New York: facsimile ed.: Da Capo Press, 1971). Public Domain. Used by permission.

- Éditions Max Eschig:

Heitor Villa-Lobos, "Étude No. 7," *Douze Études,* ed. Andrés Segovia (Paris: Éditions Max Eschig, 1953). Used by permission.

- Ione Press Inc.:

Daniel Pinkham, "The Garden Awakes," *The Seasons Pass,* ed. John Curtis (Ione Press, Inc.,1988). Sole selling agent E.C.S. Publishing. Used by permission. Ione Press Inc., Boston, MA 02215.

- Kjos Music Company:

J.S. Bach, "Double," Lute Suite II, BWV 997, from *The Solo Lute Works of J.S. Bach*, ed. Frank Koonce (#WG100) (San Diego: Kjos Music, 1989). Used by permission, 1995.

- Mel Bay Publications:

Matteo Carcassi, "Study No. 3" from *Twenty Five Studies, Op. 60.* Included in *The Complete Carcassi Guitar Method, with Twenty-five Studies, Op. 60* (Pacific: Mel Bay Publications, 1994). Used by permission.

M. Carcassi, Ibid. "Study No. 7." Used by permission.

Fernando Sor, "Study in B Minor, Op. 35, No. 22" from *The Complete Sor Studies,* ed. David Grimes (Pacific: Mel Bay Publications, 1994). Used by permission.

Fernando Sor, "Study in B Minor, Op. 35, No. 9" from *The Complete Sor Studies,* ed. David Grimes (Pacific: Mel Bay Publications, 1994). Used by permission.

INTRODUCTION

"Classical Guitar Pedagogy" is simply the study of how to teach guitarists to teach. In spite of the vast number of active guitar teachers in the world, a book of this nature has never been inclusively compiled.

I have tried to include virtually everything a teacher would need to make his job easier. Most of the ideas in this book are consistent with accepted pedagogical practices, though some minor points have been left out, with the assumption that the teacher's common sense will fill in the gaps.

Over twenty years have passed since I began working on this book. During this time a number of my ideas were refined, not only from my own teaching and performing experiences, but from my interaction with other musicians. The names of those who contributed ideas— actively or otherwise—is far too extensive to list here, but I am nonetheless, sincerely grateful.

I would, however, like to thank Pepe Romero, whose support and understanding of technique has been a mainstay for myself and a host of other guitarists. In particular, Robert Paul Sullivan, and Dr. Julia Sutton, of the *New England Conservatory*, who provided professional and personal support, not only in the actual process of developing this book, but by instilling in me a love of scholarship and proficiency on the guitar, for which I will be eternally grateful. Benjamin Zander, the Music Director of the Boston Philharmonic, and oboist, Franc Avril, who were my first interpretive coaches, deserve my thanks. I would also like to thank the following musicians, guitarists and writers who helped proof and offered suggestions in various sections. Their insight and skill greatly facilitated the completion of this book:

USA: Tamara Glise-Filbert, G. Preston Filbert, Christopher G. Glise, Lynn Zemlin, Eve Weiss, Jim Russell, Charles Pinzino, Dr. Dave and Ruth Challener, Dr. Robert and Pamela Trent, David Brandon, Hadley Heavin, Dr. Douglas James, Margarita Valls de Quesada, David Grimes, Michael Miller, Christopher Berg, Lucinda Weaver, John Holenko, Mathew Akin, Michael Goldberg, Laurie Williamson, Douglas Back, Michael Spurgat, Gian deChiaro, Dr. Thomas Heck, Russel Brazzel, William Bay; *Australia:* Adrian Walter; *Austria:* Anthony deBedts, Angelika Bertsch, Daniella Senoner, Heinz Wallisch; *Brazil:* Fernando Araújo; *Bulgaria:* Atanas Ourkouzounov; *Finland:* Marco Jouste; *France:* Ken Sugita, Laurent DeLevoye, Fabien Degauge; *Germany:* Thomas Reuther, Thilo Schimmele, Wolfgang Rauert; *Holland:* Izhar Elias; *Italy:* Stefano Abrile, Tony Battista, Mario Bricca, Marco Battaglia, Carlo Barone, Paulo Pugliese, Claudio Maccari, Francesco Tarrento; *Russia:* Jewgenij Finkelstein.

Many thanks to my dear friends, Dr. Udo Meckenstock-Benzino and Dr. Ingrid Meckenstock-Benzino of Ingolstadt, Germany for input and clarification regarding the anatomical structure of the hands, and especially Lucinda Weaver for the tremendous research and work on the drawings in this book. As always, thanks to Richard Cocco and Robert Archigian at LaBella String Company.

When all is said and done, we learn by doing. With that in mind, I would finally like to thank my students, without whom, all of this would be pointless.

Anthony LeRoy Glise
Sainghin-en-Mélantois, France
March 8, 1997

◇ *A Special Note to Teachers*

This book was designed to be used as a college textbook for conservatory or university classes in Classical Guitar Pedagogy. If at least one chapter is studied per week, it should be possible to make it through the entire book in one semester.

At the end of each chapter (in Books II and III) there are ideas for weekly assignments. Naturally these are only suggestions, but using these or similar assignments will help students solidify their pedagogical concepts.

The most valuable technique in a pedagogy class is to have students give mock lessons to each other, focusing on ideas in each chapter. This will give them a chance to try out their teaching skills under your guidance. If you use these "mock lessons" in class it will be necessary for the "student" to "play dumb," since any guitarist studying pedagogy will already understand these ideas. Encourage them to make it difficult on each other: ask irrelevant questions, argue with the "teacher," etc. This will challenge their teaching skills, and can be painfully similar to what they will face in "real life."

I would suggest that each pedagogy class (assuming you have at least one hour per session) consist of half the time discussing the chapter, and the remainder spent giving the mock lessons (usually five to ten minutes per student is sufficient).

Finally, if you are using this book to teach such a class, please stay in touch with me! We are planning subsequent editions of this book, and your input is greatly appreciated. I can be reached through Aevia Publications, Ltd. (address on the title page).
A.L.G.

Classical Guitar Pedagogy
Anthony L. Glise
TABLE OF CONTENTS

BOOK II
PRINCIPLES OF PEDAGOGY

BOOK III
MUSICIANSHIP

CLASSICAL GUITAR PEDAGOGY

BOOK I
PRINCIPLES OF TECHNIQUE

Anthony L. Glise

Classical Guitar Pedagogy
Anthony L. Glise

BOOK I
PRINCIPLES OF TECHNIQUE

INTRODUCTION TO BOOK I

Although this is a book on pedagogy, it is essential that we consider why we physically play a certain way before we can decide how to convey this to anyone else. Because of this, a brief section on rudimentary classical guitar technique is necessary.

I would stress that this section on technique is *highly* condensed and includes only those elements of technique as is necessary to delve into our primary study: that of *teaching* the guitar. I would encourage teachers to seek out the numerous books on technique for a more in-depth study of this subject.

Throughout this writing dogmatic attitudes have been avoided in hopes that this book will be of help to all guitar teachers, regardless of their backgrounds or various schools of technique.

It is important to note that there is still considerable work to be done in the field of guitar history, which naturally includes the development of technique and pedagogy. Through continued research and performance we will hopefully standardize our pedagogical techniques which will, in-turn, help assure the future progress of the guitar.

Finally, I would like to share with you a thought that every guitar teacher should keep in mind when dealing with students:

> *"We are to admit no more causes of natural things than such as are both true and sufficient to explain their appearances.*
>
> *"To this purpose the philosophers say that Nature does nothing in vain, and more is in vain when less will serve; for Nature is pleased with simplicity, and affects not the pomp of superfluous causes."* [1]

---

1. Sir Isaac Newton, *Mathematical Principles of Natural Philosophy*, Rule I, Bk. 3, trans. Andrew Motte (Berkeley: Univ. of Calif. Press, 1962).

CHAPTER ONE
SITTING

◊ *Position of the Instrument*

Nearly every school of playing has a different approach to the subject of sitting. Yet, if we look at the matter objectively, one simple question arises: *should the player arrange his body around the instrument, or should he place the instrument where it best suits the body?* In short, since *something* has to be adjusted, should it be the player or the instrument?

This is the same problem which Dionisio Aguado tried to overcome by the use of his Tripod. Fernando Sor allegedly used a table on which he set the upper bout of the instrument. Other solutions have included supporting the guitar between the arms of a chair (suggested by François Molino in his *Method*), and the common 19th-Century practice of suspending the instrument by a ribbon tied over the neck of the player, similar to our modern guitar strap. [1]

While some of these solutions may seem a bit extreme, nearly all guitarists have come to the same conclusion: *the position of the player should be fixed, while the instrument is arranged to suit that fixed position.*

---

1. Although the 19th-Century guitar was considerably smaller than our 20th-Century instruments, this is all the more reason to look carefully at our solutions to the problem of sitting since their smaller instruments would have facilitated sitting, while our larger instruments complicate the problem.

Fig. 1. Aguado sitting with his Tripod. [2]

Fig. 2. Sor sitting with a table. [3]

2. Dionisio Aguado, *New Guitar Method* (Madrid, 1843), trans. Louise Bigwood, ed. Brian Jeffery (London: Tecla Editions, 1981), xx.

3. Fernando Sor, *Method for the Spanish Guitar* (Paris, 1830), trans. A. Merrick (London, 1850) (New York: published in facsimile by Da Capo Press, 1971), 10. Public domain.

Fig. 3. Sitting holding the guitar with the use of a ribbon. [4]

With our contemporary solution of using a footstool, the teacher must always watch that a student's back is not twisted, since this can cause excess physical stress. Much of this will be dictated by the height of the footstool, so the teacher must take care that the footstool is neither too high nor too low.

Since footstool height varies with a student's physical size, a general rule is that the footstool should be as high as the student's hand is long, from the tip of the middle finger to the wrist.

In addition, the instrument should be as "centered" as possible to the body. For example, while sitting at a piano, no one would sit at one end or the other, but in the *middle*, so that both hands have equal access to the keyboard. Likewise, for guitarists, the closer the 12th fret can be placed to the center of the player's body, the more equally the hands will be able to work and the more balanced the sitting position will be.

A fairly recent development is the use of an "A-frame" or a cushion which sits, or is strapped on to the leg of the guitarist to raise the guitar. While I have no personal objections to these devices, some newspaper critics have complained that they are æsthetically distracting on stage. As with Aguado's tripod, this can be an overcompensation

_____

4. Bennett, Alfred. *Instruction for the Spanish Guitar* (London: Chappell, n.d. *ca.* 1830-40). Public domain.

to a relatively simple problem. However some fine guitarists have found an A-frame the ideal solution.

If the guitar is centered in relation to the player's body, this means that the 12th fret will fall near the center of the body. Without the aid of a tripod or other device, this can be difficult. A simple solution (though contradictory to strict 20th-Century practice) is to move the instrument slightly to the player's right side, so that the upper bout rests on the top of the left leg. While it is more common to place the middle bout on the left leg, some guitarists have found that this position does solve the problem of centering the instrument while at the same time providing a comparable stability.

Fig. 4. Traditional 20th-Century Sitting Position.

Fig. 5. Sitting with the Guitar Centered.

◇ *Position of the Arms*

If the player's back is straight and the instrument is centered, then the arms will fall evenly on both sides of the body. To maintain this position when playing, two simple things must be done:

1. The neck of the instrument must be pushed slightly away from the player, to allow the right arm to easily reach over the instrument. This will keep the back more erect and avoid too great an arch in the right hand wrist. As we shall see later, any extreme bend in the wrists *must* be avoided! [5]

_____

5. *cf.* Chapter 2, *Anatomical Structure of the Hands,* "Position of the Wrists."

2. The angle of the guitar's neck must be neither too high, nor too low. If it is too high, a lower chair (or higher footstool) must be used to compensate. If the neck is too low, the left hand wrist will be forced to bend outwards at an uncomfortable position.

Note also that if the left leg is too high, it is very tiring to maintain this position for any length of time. In addition, this position cramps the player's insides, which can restrict breathing.

◇ *Position of the Legs*

This is not a highly debated subject, but it is an important one. It is generally accepted that the lower part of the left leg should be straight up from the footstool (approximately a 90 degree angle to the floor). The right leg may also be at 90 degrees, or brought in slightly toward the player.

It is important to note that if the right foot is brought in too close to the player, the foot will not stay flat on the floor. This causes a minimal loss of stability. For advanced students, this slight loss of stability can be advantageous, since it permits them to expressively move their bodies with the music. However, beginners should always keep the right foot flat on the floor for the sake of added stability.

◇ *Conclusion*

In short, there are several basic rules for a student's sitting position:

1. Sit comfortably.
2. There should be no excessive twisting of the player's back, neck or wrists.
3. Center the instrument.
4. Stress that students should *always* practice in this playing position!

CHAPTER TWO
ANATOMICAL FUNCTION OF THE HANDS

Particularly with older students who have played guitar for some time, it is often wise to explain why we play a certain way because of our anatomical structure. This will justify why specific finger movements are so important, and can save some considerable resistance if it's necessary to "re-work" a student's technique. This is especially true with older students who have come to you after studying with other teachers who possibly taught incorrectly.

On the rare occasions when it *is* necessary to re-structure an older student's technique, this is best done in the context of new pieces. Although exercises can be helpful, using *pieces* will obviously keep the student's interest higher and allow him to understand the actual advantages—*and applications*—of the changes. Using *new* pieces (ones that the student has never played) also makes this remedial learning less frustrating, since the student is simply re-working finger and hand movements rather than (at the same time) changing the way he has come to think about a piece he already plays.

As opposed to older students (who often find these details fascinating) younger students usually find these anatomical details pointless and confusing. They simply want to play; anatomy is one of their least concerns. Thus, with younger students, *you* should be aware of the anatomical basis of movement, but *they* should not. Simply be careful of their hand positions and finger movements since it's just as easy to teach correctly as incorrectly, but it's usually best not to trouble younger students with these anatomical details.

For us as teachers, understanding the basic anatomical function of the hands is important since it will help us define why we use certain movements in playing the guitar and will keep us aware of any movements or hand positions that could hinder progress or cause physical injury.

I should point out that hand and finger movements are some of the most complicated that exist in the entire body. First of all, virtually all these movements are inter-related. Anytime you move a finger, a *number* of muscles and tendons are activated. However, for the sake of keeping this discussion simple enough that it makes sense to us (*i.e.* non-medically trained guitarists), I will be referring to the *primary* tendons and muscles that initiate a movement. For those interested in additional study, there are numerous anatomy books that can further clarify the subject.

To give you an idea of the complexity of hand and finger movements, below is a diagram found in virtually all neurological medical books. The diagram shows a cross section of the brain and the various areas that control muscular activity of: *1)* body movement, *2)* hand movement, and *3)* facial movement. Note what a drastically large portion of this part of the brain is responsible simply for hand movement!

Fig. 1. Cross-section of the brain showing various regions which control movement.

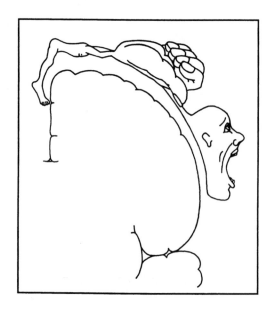

◇ *General Anatomical Terms* [1]

In teaching we must be aware of several general anatomical terms.

An *extensor* muscle or tendon is one which extends a finger (such as when you stretch out the hand so the fingers are flat). This is referred to as "extension." A *flexor* muscle or tendon is one which pulls a finger in toward the palm (such as when you make a fist). This action is referred to as "flexion." When a joint is relaxed or "at rest" (meaning no muscles or tendons are flexed or extended) the hand is said to be *"neutral."*

Ligaments are simply "bands" which hold the tendons close to the bone so that as a muscle flexes, the tendon does not spring away from the bone. Ligaments rarely concern us except in the case of accidental hand damage (such as a deep cut that might sever a ligament). Thus, ligaments will not enter our discussion.

Adduction and *abduction* are two terms that (for our purposes) refer to movement of the right hand thumb. Adduction is the movement that occurs when the thumb moves *in* toward the palm of the hand. Abduction occurs when the thumb returns, moving *away* from the palm of the hand.

Tendons simply attach to a muscle on one end and to a bone on the other. A tendon does nothing on its own; it simply moves a joint when a muscle moves.

Thus, whenever we move a finger, the following sequence of events occurs:
1) a muscle flexes or extends which
2) moves the tendon that is attached to a bone, and
3) that part of the body moves.

This is all obviously more complicated than I have just explained, especially since there are usually different groups of muscles and tendons that work together for different movements, but the above is a good basic description of what occurs when we move a joint.

---

1. For better or worse, I will be using the correct medical terms throughout this discussion. While tedious, there seems to be no other way to avoid potential confusion. Frankly, professional teachers should be at least minimally aware of this correct anatomical terminology in order to clarify hand movement to the student, to watch for potentially dangerous positions or movements *and* to be able to discuss the situation with a medical doctor should the situation arise.

In playing the guitar, we ideally try to use the simplest movement, so that only one type of muscle or tendon is used for a specific task. Keeping these movements simple and isolated to a single muscle/tendon means (besides conserving energy) the risk of damage is *highly* reduced since there is less movement and as a result, less friction and possible inflammation.

◇ *Finger Movement*

As we play guitar, we use almost exclusively the flexor tendons and muscles since these control the movements to sound the strings (for the right hand) or depress the notes (for the left hand). Thus, to avoid any unnecessary confusion, I will confine our discussion to the flexors.[2]

Throughout this discussion, keep in mind that the extensors run through the back of the hand while the flexors run through the palm of the hand. Also note that tendons run through a "sheath" which is similar to a tube. Both of these observations are important when we begin to discuss the different right hand positions and finger movement.

The flexor muscles/tendons of the hand used most often in playing are:

1. *Flexor digitorum superficialis.* This muscle/tendon predominantly controls the finger movement at the fingertip. It also assists in moving from the middle joint.
2. *Flexor digitorum profundus.* This muscle/tendon controls the finger movement from the middle joint, and assists with movement from the knuckle.
3. *Lumbrical.* This muscle/tendon controls the finger movement from the knuckle. However, the lumbrical muscle attaches to the flexor digitorum profundus *tendon* (at the base of the finger), and that tendon then continues to the lower arm. This is an important observation when we discuss which joint should be used to initiate finger movement (the middle joint or the knuckle).

Below are a series of figures that show the actual movement initiated by the different muscles/tendons, followed by a figure showing the general area where those muscles/tendons are located.

---

2. Naturally, the extensor tendons are involved in playing the guitar (especially for the left hand when a player must lift a finger away from the fingerboard), but nearly all schools of playing agree that the majority of the extensor movement in guitar playing is a result of simply *relaxing* the fingers so the hands goes into neutral position which (for the right hand) permits the finger to return after sounding the string or (for the left hand) permits the finger to raise slightly above the fingerboard to release a note.

Fig. 2. Finger Movement Initiated by the
Flexor Digitorum Profundus Muscles/Tendons.

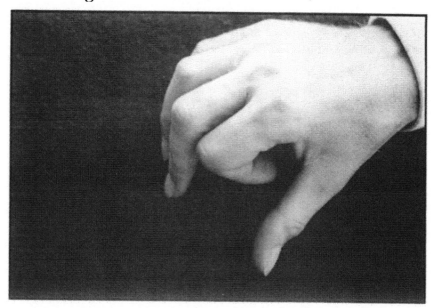

Fig. 3. General Location of the
Flexor Digitorum Profundus Muscle/Tendon. [3]

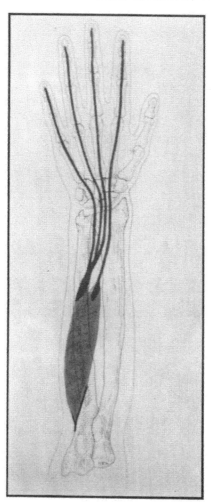

3. Note that the general muscle area is shaded, while the general tendon area (which attaches the muscle to the bone) is solid.

Fig. 4. Finger Movement Initiated by the
        Lumbrical Muscles/Tendons.

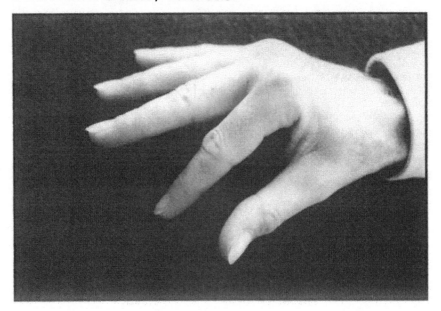

Fig. 5. General Location of the
        Lumbrical Muscles/Tendons.

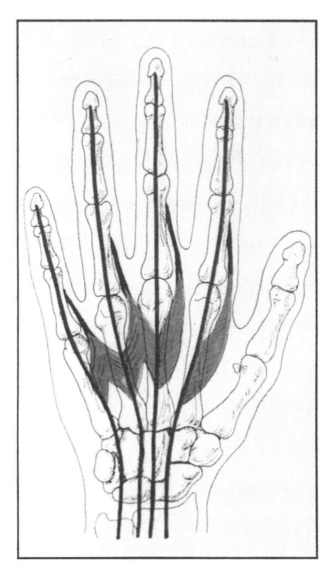

Don't be confused by the fact that, although the lumbrical muscles are located in the hand, they attach near the wrist to the flexor digitorum profundus *tendon*. This tendon then runs through the wrist to the muscle in the lower arm.

Which of these two muscles/tendons are used is somewhat debatable: some guitarists play moving predominantly from the middle joint (using the digitorum superficialis and profundus), while others move predominantly from the knuckle (using the lumbrical).

The debate boils down to one question: which joint initiates the movement when sounding the string or depressing a note—the middle joint or the knuckle? [4]

Virtually all guitarists have decided that moving from the middle joint (using the digitorum superficialis and profundus) is problematic because there is less control and less power in movements that originate from the middle joint.

The other complication is that when we move from the middle joint, there is a greater chance that the player can damage the hands. I will discuss this later in the section, "Guitar-related Injuries."

Also, when playing from the middle joint, the flexor tendons/muscles act *only* as flexors. When the finger must return (after sounding a string with the right hand or releasing a note with the left), the extensor digitorum superficialis must be used. Thus, *two* sets of muscles must be used: the *flexors* to flex the finger and the *extensors* to extend the finger so it returns to a neutral position.

Nearly all guitarists opt for moving from the knuckle (using the lumbrical tendons/muscles). This has several major advantages. When moving from the knuckle, the flexion of the finger uses the lumbrical muscles which are based in the palm of the hand. Thus, the initial movement is confined to a smaller area and is more easily controlled.

The lumbrical muscles then attach to the digitorum profundus tendons which run to a "muscle belly" in the forearm. This muscle is larger, than the flexor digitorum superficialis, which means there is a greater reserve of power. This also means it is easier to immediately relax after the movement.

---

4. This will be discussed further in the next chapter, "The Right Hand" under the subject of the *Open Hand* and *Closed Hand* schools of right hand technique.

However, when a player flexes from the middle joint (using the digitorum superficialis and profundus), virtually no muscles in the hand are used. With this movement, the tendon runs through the hand, the wrist, and to the muscle in the forearm. Because of the greater distance between the fingers and the muscle, it is much more difficult to flex and immediately relax. As a result, players need to actively use an extensor muscle to make the finger return.

Beyond all these factors, there is another *major* advantage to moving from the knuckle (thus, using the lumbrical muscle/tendon when flexing the fingers). As I said before, all the tendons/muscles that control extension run through the *back* of the hand, while all those that control flexion run through the *palm* of the hand, with one extremely rare exception: *the lumbrical.*

With the lumbrical, the tendon attaches to the muscle belly in the forearm, it runs through the arm, wrist, and through the hand on the palm side of the hand (*cf.* Fig. 5). However, between the middle joint of the finger and the first joint, the tendon curves around to the *back* (the dorsal side) of the finger!

What this all means, is when we move from the knuckle (using the lumbrical muscle/tendon), the moment that this muscle is relaxed, the finger will spring back to a neutral position. It's as if the lumbrical acts as both a flexor *and* an extensor! Thus, in using the lumbrical muscle/tendon (and moving from the knuckle), we save virtually half the energy, since the finger will (upon relaxation) *automatically* return to a neutral position by itself with little or no help from an extensor muscle.

As a result of all these factors, virtually all performing guitarists and teachers believe that moving from the knuckle (using the lumbrical muscles/tendons) is by far the best solution for both right and left hand finger movement.

◇ *The Thumb*

The movement of the thumb is essentially the same as the other right hand fingers. Virtually all performers and teachers agree that the entire thumb will move as a single unit using the *flexor pollicis brevis* (the fatty part of hand at the base of the thumb) and the *adductor pollicis* muscles/tendons.

Students usually do not have difficulty with the thumb position or movement. Simply watch that the right hand thumb extends well away from the palm of the hand (so the fingers easily follow-through as they sound the strings), and watch for over-stress. Also, be careful that the student doesn't sound the string by moving the first joint of the thumb, which occurs with some beginners.

Fig. 6. Showing the *Flexor Pollicis Brevis*
      Used to Move the Thumb.

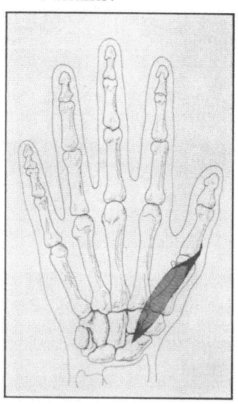

Fig. 7. Showing the *Adductor Pollicis* Tendon/Muscle
      Used to Move the Thumb.

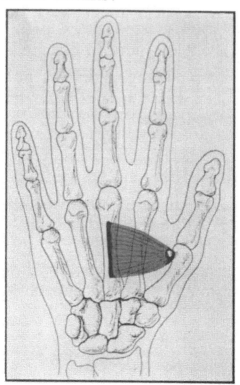

Adduction of the thumb (moving the thumb toward the palm of the hand) also uses the adductor pollicis muscle. This muscle runs from the base of the thumb across the palm and attaches to the middle finger. Because of this, adduction of the middle finger and the thumb at the same time (simultaneously playing with *p* and *m*) is normally easier.

I mention this because some intermediate students have difficulty developing a controlled motion between *p* and *i*, or *p* and *a*, but rarely *p* and *m*—because, again, *p* and *m* are attached together by the adductor pollicis muscle and the flexion tends to be easier, while using *p* with either *i* or *a* can be more difficult. This can explain why some students have such difficulty developing a smooth, even tremolo as well as performing some right hand arpeggio patterns.

In right hand technique development (especially for more advanced students) this emphasizes why it is critical to develop independence between *p* and the fingers (especially *p*—*i* and *p*—*a*). This can be done by practicing scales alternating *p*— *i*, *p*—*m*, or *p*—*a*, which we will discuss later in Book II under the subject of "Scales."

In general, technical development and potential problems in training and using the thumb are extremely rare. Simply make sure that *p* extends well away from the palm of the hand (so it doesn't hinder the follow-through of the fingers), and make sure the movement initiates from the base of the thumb.

◊ *The Left Hand*

Since virtually all guitarists agree that to depress a string, the movement initiates at the knuckle (using the lumbrical muscles), there is much less debate over left hand finger movement. *Spreading* the fingers (up and down the neck of the guitar) uses two sets of muscles: the *interossei dorsales* (between the finger bones at the back of the hand) and the *digitorum superficialis* (which are the same muscles used to initiate movement from the middle joint).

This is an additional reason that we should move (to depress a note) from the knuckle: if a guitarist moves from the knuckle (using the lumbrical) then the remaining tendons/muscles (the interossei dorsales and digitorum superficialis) can be used *exclusively* to spread the fingers.

Each set of muscles and tendons then has a specific rôle: the lumbrical (moving from the knuckle) initiates the finger movement while the digitorum superficialis (moving from the *middle* joint) and the interossei dorsales can be used to help spread the left hand fingers. However, if a player moves from the middle joint, then the digitorum superficialis must be used to both depress a note *and* help spread the fingers.

Remember that some beginners (when releasing a note with the left hand) may extend the finger very far away from the fingerboard (*i.e.* overusing the extensor tendons). Obviously this should be avoided. If the student does this, explain that the action of releasing a note should be one of simply *relaxing* the finger rather than actively pulling the finger away from the fingerboard. In extreme cases the Pulsing Exercise (described in Book II) can remedy the problem.

◇ *Position of the Wrist*

All anatomists agree (as do most guitarists) that if the wrist is straight, flexion of the lumbrical is much easier. When the wrist is moved out of neutral position (by flexion or extension) up to 90% of the potential power is lost. This fact alone justifies maintaining a straight wrist—of both hands—when playing.

Keep in mind that the tendons transverse the wrist through the *carpal tunnel*. The carpal tunnel is an area surrounded by a ligament at the wrist through which all the tendons pass as they go to various muscles in the arm. If the wrist of either hand is bent too far (either flexed or extended) the friction on the tendon as it passes through the carpal tunnel is increased which can cause injury. This leads us to the next section, Guitar-related Injuries.

◇ *Guitar-related Injuries*

Virtually all guitarist's injuries (excluding traumatic accidents) are from either *over-use* (simply practicing too much) or *misuse* (not warming up properly, playing pieces that are too difficult, improper hand positions, over stress, *etc.*). Virtually all these are clinically referred to as *"repetitive motion injuries."*

Keeping in mind this simple term—*repetitive motion injury*—can make the teacher more aware of potentially dangerous habits of students. Obviously the hands should be relaxed and the motion should be smooth. Unfortunately, there are still several repetitive motion injuries that are occasionally sustained by guitarists.

Regardless of what school of technique is being taught, there should *never* be any excessive bending or twisting of the wrists. If the wrists are bent at an extreme angle in any direction, the sheath (through which the tendons run) can collapse around the tendons (especially at the wrist) and cause friction on the tendons which can lead to inflammation of the tendon or the tendon sheath.

Explaining this to a student is simple. It's similar to bending a plastic drinking straw in half; it will collapse at the bend and at the bend there will obviously be more friction.

Moving predominantly from the middle joint poses a greater risk that the player can get *tendonitis* (inflammation of the tendon) or *tenosynovitis* (swelling of the tendon and the sheath). This, again, is because moving from the middle joint means there is potentially greater friction as the tendon moves through the sheath at the wrist, through the carpal tunnel on the way to the muscle in the forearm.

Another common guitarist's malady is *carpal tunnel syndrome* (also called "median nerve compression") which can be an additional problem for guitarists who move excessively from the middle joint or play with either wrist too arched. Since the digitorum superficialis (which assists in flexion from the middle joint) runs to the muscle belly in the lower arm, it must pass through the wrist (through the transverse carpal ligament).

If this tendon is overused, it can swell which will cause it to press against the *median nerve.* This is *extremely* debilitating and painful. The symptoms of carpal tunnel syndrome include numbness, tingling, and pain in the wrist.

This is especially dangerous for guitarists who play with the wrist (of either hand) too arched. Usually a neutral wrist position can avoid most problems, assuming that the hands remain relaxed.

The figure below shows a cross-section of the wrist. Note that the digitorum profundus (which assists in flexion from the knuckle) is nearly twice as far from the median nerve as the digitorum superficialis (which assists in flexion from the middle joint).

This is yet *another* reason to move from the knuckles (not the middle joint). Moving from the knuckle means that (since this tendon is further from the median nerve) chances are greatly reduced that there could be pressure on the median nerve which is the cause of carpal tunnel syndrome.

Fig. 8. Cross-section of the Wrist Showing the Flexor Digitorum Superficialis, Flexor Digitorum Profundus in Relation to the Median Nerve.

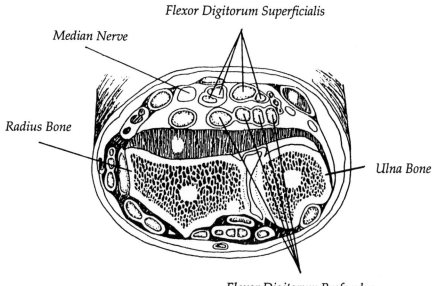

Flexor Digitorum Superficialis

Median Nerve

Radius Bone

Ulna Bone

Flexor Digitorum Profundus

Considering all these factors, it becomes obvious why nearly all professional guitarists and teachers prefer to play and teach that the finger movement initiates at the knuckle, thus utilizing the lumbrical tendons and muscles and the digitorum profundus tendons to which they attach.

Beyond the fact that it is easier to play when we move from the knuckle, the risk of physical damage is *greatly* reduced.

◊ *General Warning About Injuries*

Because teachers often have so many students, to simplify their teaching methods, they sometimes establish a list of pieces and a rigid time-frame in which these must be learned. If a student is ready for a more advanced piece, there is no problem.

However sometimes this is not the case and I can cite a number of examples when a student began playing music that was too difficult and ended up with tendonitis, or carpal tunnel syndrome. The excess physical tension that results from playing pieces that are too advanced can promote serious physical injury.

Naturally, there must be goals set for each student, and these goals require that the teacher define a program of pieces that should be learned. However, when this type of program is too structured, students are sometimes pushed into playing pieces that are too difficult.

If this occurs the student will rarely complain (since he feels like he is "making progress" because he's moving though literature). In such cases, the risk of physical injury is *very* high, and the frustration level of the student is usually equally high: he is aware of his own difficulties but doesn't understand why he is having trouble with the repertoire and other students are not.

In short, each student is different—not only musically, but *technically.* Every guitarist has specific gifts and talents and must be treated—*and taught*—as an individual.

As you teach, constantly be on guard for potentially dangerous movements or hand positions of your students. In all reality, it's fairly rare for a student to develop hand problems, but a little healthy caution can help avoid even these rare cases.

◊ *Conclusion*

The anatomy of the hand is *insanely* complex and we are obviously bound by the physical elements of our own anatomy when we play guitar. As a result, our decisions about how to play must be based on an awareness of basic anatomy.

As you teach, keep in mind how the hand functions. This will not only help you watch for any potential injuries, but it will help you organize your teaching more efficiently and develop your student's individual talents—which is the single-most important goal that lies before any teacher.

CHAPTER THREE
THE RIGHT HAND

◇ *Position and Movement of the Right Hand*

To speak of the function of one hand while excluding the other is not only difficult, but rather impractical, since only rarely do the right and left hands function independently. This is compounded by the fact that both hands utilize the same muscles and tendons, and as a result, have a very similar movement, so study of hand position and movement is actually more simplistic than it might appear.

However, both hands have a unique function, and most elementary guitar methods wisely begin the student by using the right hand alone, which helps isolate the right and left hand movements.

The position of the right hand is obviously somewhat dictated by our anatomical structure as humans. Nonetheless, the right hand position may vary a great deal, depending on the school of technique being taught.

While there are infinite variations of the right hand movement, there are basically two major schools of right hand technique: the *Closed Hand School* and the *Open Hand School*, and virtually every school of thought can be categorized as one or the other.

Closed Hand Technique [1]

This approach is most prominent in the "Andrés Segovia School" and his students. When the free stroke is used, the hand is shifted slightly more forward (toward the floor).

When the rest stroke is used, the hand shifts back (away from the floor) so that there is a sharper angle between the fingers and the strings. As a result, there are actually two different right hand positions.

This makes the use of rest and free strokes much more distinct: *rest*, being used normally for scale passages and louder notes, while *free* is used for virtually everything else. Not only will usage of both strokes be more distinct, but so will the sound: *free = lighter sound; rest = heavier sound.*

Fig. 1. Right Hand Position for Free Stroke.

---

1. Further discussion of the "Open Hand" and "Closed Hand" schools of technique will be given in Book II.

Fig. 2. Right Hand Position for Rest Stroke.

With the hand more forward (for free stroke), the fingers easily follow-through, and do not hit the lower strings. Likewise, when the hand leans back for rest stroke, the sharper angle of the fingers (in relation to the strings) makes them fall easily on the lower string.

Movement in the Closed Hand Technique varies somewhat between rest and free strokes. With free stroke, the movement initiates more from the middle joint. With rest stroke, the movement initiates at the knuckle.

This school of playing may have its origins in the flamenco style of playing, whereby the longer nails were traditionally used to achieve greater volume and a more percussive sound for the dancers to follow.

Using longer nails makes it *necessary* to angle the hand back when rest stroke is used, and angle forward when the free stroke is used (to avoid hitting the lower strings).

If this school is taught, the teacher must watch out for a common problem: if the nails are too long, the "rocking" back and forth between the rest and free stroke will become too pronounced. This can obviously cause coordination problems between the right and left hands, as well as create an instability when the player shifts from rest to free stroke or *vice versa*.

With most students it is wise to avoid having them use nails at all, until they have established a stable hand position (this may be several years). This is especially true in teaching the Closed Hand School. Sometimes, even without nails, the rocking may occur. In these cases, avoid using the rest stroke until the hand position stabilizes.

Open Hand Technique

This school of playing usually involves using shorter nails, and as a result, little or no rocking in the hand position needs to occur between rest and free strokes. The minimal difference occurs in the rest stroke.

With the rest stroke, the fingers will slightly *straighten* so that the angle of attack toward the string is lessened, but the hand position itself will remain essentially the same. Thus, the only movement between strokes is a straightening of the fingers for rest stroke, and a slightly greater curve of the fingers for free stroke.

Explaining this to a student is quite simple; place the hand on a table, directly on the fingertips. Then have the student do "push-ups" with the fingers. These two positions are essentially the same as in playing: *i.e.* down for free stroke and up for rest stroke, but the hand position itself stays basically the same.

With Open Hand Technique there is little or no difference in sound between rest and free strokes, so the player is fully responsible for the desired attack, articulation, color, *etc.*, as opposed to the sounds that can inherently result from the two different hand positions of the Closed Hand School.

Because of all these factors (and the fact that the Open Hand approach eliminates a great deal of excess movement), the Open Hand School seems to be preferred by many professional guitarists.

The major disadvantage of the Open Hand School lies in the greater amount of time it takes to learn. This reason alone probably accounts for its unpopularity with amateur players and teachers.

Fig. 3. Right Hand Position for Free Stroke.

Fig. 4. Right Hand Position for Rest Stroke.

With the Open Hand Technique, the movement for both rest and free strokes initiates at the knuckle.

The origin of this school seems to stem from the 19th-Century guitarists, notably Dionisio Aguado, Fernando Sor and Mauro Giuliani, as indicated in their writings. There has also been conjecture that many of the oral traditions of technique, which are still taught today in Central Europe (especially in Vienna and Budapest), may stem directly from these early 19th-Century guitarists.

Differences Between the Two Schools

The primary differences between these two schools of technique have to do with *which* muscles are used to initiate the finger movement. If we recall our previous anatomical discussion, we see that the Closed Hand School uses almost exclusively the *lumbrical* tendon/muscle for rest stroke, and the *digitorum superficialis* for free stroke. The Open Hand School uses mostly the *lumbrical* for both rest *and* free strokes, while the *flexors digitorum superficialis* are used primarily to *position* the fingers for rest or free stroke (*i.e.* more curved at the middle joint for free or more straight for rest).

Similarities Between the Two Schools

Both schools are concerned with the sound that is produced, and much of this depends on the angle of the nail as it strikes the string. Because this angle can be adjusted by the player, both schools of technique can produce a good tone color—the responsibility rests ultimately with the individual player.

Both schools tend to agree that playing from the left side of the nail produces the warmest tone. Still, this theory falls into debate when we consider some of the fine guitarists who have come from the French-based schools—in particular, those who have come out of the *Conservatoire du Paris*—(who, by the way, tend to be more Closed Hand players) which recommend playing off the *right* side of the nail.

Both schools also tend to agree that the first joint (that nearest the tip) remains relaxed, but does not collapse or "cave in" for an obvious reason: if the first joint collapses as a string is sounded, there is a momentary delay between the time that string is touched, and then sounded. This results in severe problems in right and left hand coordination.

While the first joint should obviously remain relaxed, permitting it to entirely collapse when sounding a string will create coordination problems between the right and left hands, and normally results in a staccato sound because of this incoordination between the hands.

◇ *Position and Movement of the Thumb*

The thumb position will dictate the position of the entire right hand. As a general rule, the thumb will extend well away from the hand. This is critical (especially with beginners), since, if the thumb is pulled too far into the hand, the fingers won't be able to follow-through without hitting the thumb and the entire finger movement will be hindered.

This is especially true if the student is being taught using an open hand position, where the follow-through for beginners is often wider.

Fig. 5. Thumb Position Viewed from Front.

This position is easily explained to the student: with the right hand fingers planted on their respective strings, looking into the hand, he should be able to see a triangle formed between *p, i* and the strings, as in Figure 6.

Fig. 6. Thumb Position from the Student's View.

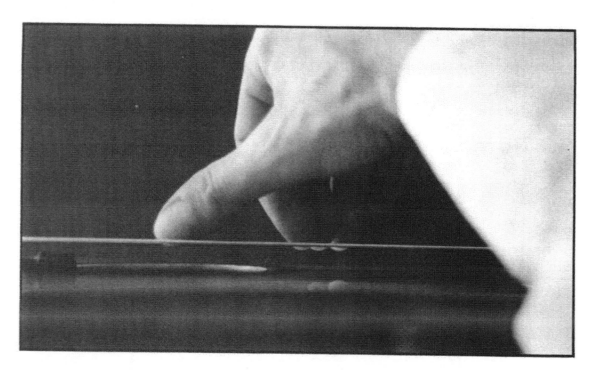

In both schools, the movement of the thumb initiates with the third joint (that nearest the palm). For free stroke, the movement is one of a small circle. The same movement is used for rest stroke but the circular movement is widened (toward the guitar) just enough to land *p* on the next string.

Remember to watch that the student is not moving from the first joint (the joint nearest the nail), and that there is no movement of the arm or hand position—all of which are common problems for beginners.

◇ *Shape of the Nails*

The shape of the nail is the most important factor in producing a good sound and will indirectly affect the right hand position. Keep in mind that everyone has a *totally* different shape of fingertip, each nail grows differently, and each nail has a different density. As a result—in spite of all the marvelous theories about how nails should be shaped—there is absolutely *no* way to generalize and say "this is correct, and this isn't."

Basically, there are two approaches to shaping the nail: *rounded* and *angled.* A rounded nail shape will normally follow the contour of the fingertip as in Figure 7. Rounded nail shape usually promotes a hand position where the wrist is more straight. The guitarist may play off the left side of the nail (which is infinitely more common) *or* the right side of the nail (as in some French-based schools), but both are an option with this shape.

An angled shape will normally have a larger surface area (at the point where the finger contacts the string) and will *not* slope back around (*cf*. Figure 8). Angled nail shape usually promotes a hand position that is slightly tilted to the player's left side. With this nail shape, the guitarist normally plays *only* off the left side of the nail.

Fig. 7. Rounded Nail Shape
     (viewing the *i* finger, from back of the hand).

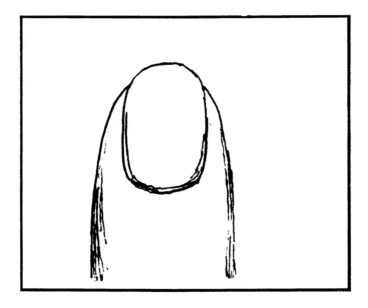

Fig. 8. Angled Nail Shape.

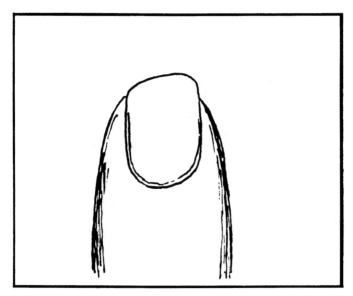

The reason that some guitarists use an angled nail shape is that it produces a very dark, warm sound. Also, some guitarists with soft, flexible nails prefer a bit more angle, because the larger nail surface on the string means that the pressure from the string is slightly displaced to a larger surface of the nail, so there is less chance of breaking the nail.

The major disadvantage to angling the nail shape *too* much, is that the string must travel over a larger surface of the nail before it is released. In short, it takes more time for the nail to release the string (though, admittedly we are talking about milliseconds). This can—in extreme cases—be the cause of right and left hand coordination problems.

Naturally the curve and length of the nail will vary depending on the school of technique, and the arch of the nail. For example, looking directly at the fingertip, notice how in Figure 9, each finger has a different arch.

Fig. 9. Various Arches In Nail Growth.

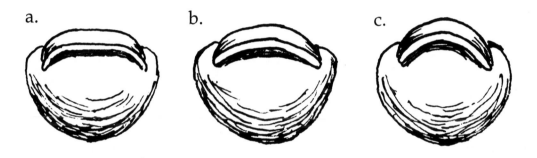

a. b. c.

In Figure 9, a—c, the arch is increasingly more distinct. Normally, the greater the arch, the more flat the nail should be filed. This will result in roughly the same amount of surface area used to release the string regardless of the natural arch of the nail; *i.e.* there will be enough surface area to produce a strong tone and timbre, but not so much that the release of the string is delayed unnecessarily (as can be the case if the nail is filed too angled).

Again, all these ideas are *very* broad generalizations, but the concepts here will give the student a basis from which to begin experimenting with his own nail shape. Beyond that, it is simply a matter of trial-and-error.

◇ *Nails* vs. *Flesh*

Using nails is somewhat confusing to beginners since they often assume that only the nail is used to sound the string. In fact, only the nail *releases* the string.

When correctly placed on the string (at the *exact* point from which the finger will play), both the nail *and* the pad of the flesh at the fingertip will touch the string at the same moment—the pad will stop the string (much like the damper pad on a piano), and the nail will be simultaneously positioned to re-strike the string.

Students must learn this exact placement as soon as they begin using nails, though two problems invariably arise: if the pad of the finger touches the string first, it will stop the string from vibrating and the sound will be very staccato. Conversely, if the nail touches the string first *without* the flesh, this causes a "rattle" from the nail touching the vibrating string.

Nearly all students will eventually play using nails, as is most common with all schools of technique. Playing with nails existed at least as early as Aguado's time, and possibly (among classical guitarists) originated with him.

Anyone who has ever played on an instrument with gut strings will attest to the fact that it is *much* easier to play without nails, since the gut has a tendency to grip the bare fingers. Thus, we may assume that Aguado was totally convinced of the advantages of the nail *cum* flesh approach (as he indicates in his *Method*), or he would not have been so eager to give up the facility of the bare fingers on gut strings.

Through the early 1900's the controversy was well documented between Emilio Pujol (who used no nails) and Andrés Segovia (who used nails).[2] The same subject was equally debated between Aguado (who used nails) and Sor (who used no nails, save for later in his career when he used a nail on his thumb, exclusively to imitate an oboe sound).

---

2. *Cf.* Emilio Pujol, *El Dilema del Sonido en la Guitarra* (Buenos Aires: Ricordi, 1956).

For the sake of historical argument, the following theory could explain Sor's opposition to the use of nails: it is possible that Sor's aversion to nails was because at that time Spanish folk guitarists used nails. Indeed, Sor was attempting to further "legitimize" the guitar as a classical instrument, and the less association with these folk guitarists (and their sound, as a result of using nails) the better.

It is also interesting to note that current research indicates that Sor's contemporary, Mauro Giuliani, *did* play with nails. Naturally, being based primarily in Vienna, Giuliani would not have had the opportunity—or the problems—of being unwittingly associated with Spanish folk guitarists. Thus, to Giuliani, playing with nails would not have been such an issue.

There is still an existing school of fine players who do not use nails, some of whom still use gut strings. Sadly, their numbers are dwindling. This school (as it exists today) stems from Francisco Tárrega and his student Emilio Pujol, both of whom played without nails. This school tends to have a more Closed Hand Technique.

Nonetheless, in spite of this fine group of no-nails players, it is best to assume that all students will eventually play using nails, since this produces the most volume (necessary for our modern concert halls) and offers the widest range of timbre changes.

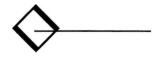

CHAPTER FOUR
THE LEFT HAND

◇ *Position of the Left Hand*

While the position of the left hand will dictate the position of the fingers, left hand position and movement is *far* more consistent than the right hand, though there are two basic schools of thought, the *Turned Hand Position* and the *Flat Hand Position.*

Turned Hand Position

In this position, the left hand is fairly stationary, with the exception of one South American School.[1] Virtually every other school of left hand technique uses the Turned Hand Position, whereby the left hand knuckles stay more-or-less parallel to the edge of the guitar neck. This Turned Hand School seems to originate from post 19th-Century technique. The fingers reach across the neck *at the same angle as the frets.*

---

1. This school of left hand technique is found almost exclusively in the teaching of Abel Carlevaro. In this school, beginners are taught different left hand positions or "angles" in relation to the neck of the instrument—*i.e.* the hand is turned toward or away from the neck, depending on the passage being played. While admittedly, there are variations in the left hand position, *for beginners*, this approach can be an overcompensation to a relatively minor problem; at worst, this can throw a student's left hand totally out of position and can cause unnecessary errors.

The other school—using a Flat Hand Position—is a slight variant of the more common position described above and seems to have its origins in the 19th-Century.

In spite of the rarity of this position today, it is an *invaluable* approach for beginners for a number of reasons that we will discuss later (*cf.* Chapter 6, "Left Hand Fingering" *The Fourth-Finger Approach*).

In the Flat Hand School, the side of the hand nearer the little finger is moved slightly closer to the neck. In other words, the left hand is kept *completely* flat, and raised directly up to the neck of the guitar.

While iconographic evidence can be misleading, it offers some support for this position. In pictures of the left hands of Sor and Aguado, we find that they both kept the part of the hand nearest the fourth finger closer to the neck.

Fig. 1. Sor's Left Hand Position. [2]

---

2. Sor; *op. cit.*, 10.

Fig. 2. Aguado's Left Hand Position. [3]

In using this position, students will find that the fourth finger is able to reach as far across the neck as the first, thus allowing for greater agility. This will also help keep the fourth finger on the tip which is a constant battle for beginners.

Using the Flat Hand Position, the player has four relatively equal fingers, rather than four fingers graded in usefulness by their size. To continually acknowledge that a shorter finger must be inferior by virtue of its size, will encourage it to develop into none other than a truly inferior member.

In Book II we will discuss several ways to develop this position early in a student's training, but for now, we need to remember two basic factors:

1. As with the right hand, the wrist should be fairly straight and flat to avoid collapsing the sheath around the tendon.
2. The left hand knuckles should be *at least* parallel to the edge of the neck (for the Turned Hand School) *or*, the fourth finger side of the hand should be slightly closer to the neck (for the Flat Hand School).

---

3. Aguado; *op. cit.*, 4.

◇ *Movement of the Left Hand Fingers*

There is little debate that the left hand movement utilizes the *lumbrical* muscles/tendons, thus moving the entire curved finger from the knuckle. There are several advantages to this consistency between the hands if this approach is also used for the right hand (as in the Open Hand School). Most obviously, the student needs to learn only one type of movement for both hands.

Additionally, as advanced players are aware, the most difficult movements with the left hand are not those of stretching the fingers *lengthwise* (up and down the neck), but of finger *independence* (moving *across* the neck).

When the lumbrical muscles/tendons are used to actually depress the string to the fingerboard (thus moving from the knuckle), the remaining side-set of tendons will be freed to help keep the fingers acting independently, both *across* the fingerboard, and *up and down* the neck. Again, this movement will be discussed further in Book II.

◊ *Conclusion*

The left hand position (*i.e.* keeping a relatively straight wrist) and movement (*i.e.* a movement originating predominately from the knuckle) means the right and left hands are actually more similar than we often think.

While the *Turned Hand* or *Flat Hand* schools of left hand position both may be used, the most important factor is relaxation.

For both hands, a smooth and relaxed movement can help insure greater control, finger independence and can help avoid damage to the muscles and tendons.

A great deal of research is still to be done on the history and development of guitar technique. Until then, we can do little more than speculate on the exact development of the different schools. We know they exist, can point out their advantages and disadvantages, but unfortunately, we can venture little beyond that point.

With that in mind, we will hopefully find ourselves much more tolerant of a differing school of technique if we remember that we are *all* trying to achieve the same end: *to play music in such a way as to be pleasing to the majority of listeners and ourselves—with conscience as our guide.*

Through this brief section on technique, we have established *why* we play as we do, from a logical and anatomical basis. The greatest challenge before us is how to teach someone *else* to play using these principles.

However, before we continue, I would like to remind you that playing the guitar does not have to be difficult, and maintaining this attitude with students will speed their progress. The more simply a subject can be explained, and an action executed, the better. Remember, when describing *anything* to a student:

"*...more is in vain when less will serve.*" [4]

---

4. Newton; *op. cit.*

CLASSICAL GUITAR PEDAGOGY

BOOK II
PRINCIPLES OF PEDAGOGY

Anthony L. Glise

BOOK II
PRINCIPLES OF
PEDAGOGY

INTRODUCTION TO BOOK II

With the questions of *"why we do what we do"* somewhat defined, we can proceed with *"how to teach someone else to do it."* But before we go into actual pedagogical practices, I feel obliged to point out several things that help make a good teacher.

• *Show Concern.* Each student chose *you* to be his teacher—*he is your* student. As a teacher, the sooner you appreciate this fact, the easier it will be for you to be concerned with his musical growth.

• *Be Involved.* Granted, this can be difficult. With current teaching practices, it is not uncommon for a teacher to have 30 or 40 students per week. Even with this number you can be involved. Have everyone meet for a party with guitars. Reading duets with 20 on each part can be as outrageously absurd as it is enjoyable.

Arranging chamber music for guitar ensemble is another option. Encourage students to go to local concerts—*not just guitar concerts*—as a group. Stage your own "Studio Competition," and so on. These activities will not only improve your relationship with students, but will expand your reputation as a teacher.

• *Don't Make It Difficult.* After all that was discussed in Book I, this may seem contradictory, but the best guitarists are those who play *naturally.* I do not necessarily mean those who are *naturally gifted,* but those who do things the way it *feels* best. If a student is sensitive to this, he will, with gentle guiding, automatically fall into a solid technique and musicianship. For students who do *not* have that sensitivity, simplicity is even more important.

• *Teach Performance.* When all is said and done, and all the finest theories applied, remember, *if something doesn't work in performance, then it's not worth teaching!* This goes for all techniques, fingerings and musical aspects of playing. The ultimate goal is to *play* the music, not simply regurgitate theories.

• *Be Positive.* No matter what a student is doing, **never** give him negative input. If something needs correcting, show him how to do it *right*—don't rave about what he's doing *wrong.* Occasionally it's necessary to "chastise" a student for not practicing and so on, but even then, do it with a sense of positive concern.

• *Maintain A Professional Attitude.* There is a confidence and trust that exists between a student and teacher that should *NEVER* be broken. Pitting students against each other or talking about one student to another student shows an *inexcusable* lack of professionalism. As you build a trust with your students, you will find them more open to new ideas and more willing to work harder.

Much the same should be stressed in talking to students about other teachers or performers. Building your own stature by degrading another professional is as destructive as it is immature, and shamefully, this is all too common among guitarists. A respect between professionals—even someone you may not agree with—will help keep *you* open to new ideas. The fact remains that you can learn something from *anyone*, and that receptiveness will be passed on to your students and enhance your own reputation.

• *Be Sensitive.* Few things will alienate a student faster than a selfish, egotistical or uncaring teacher. Each student is an individual and *must* be treated as such. In the words of Fernando Sor,

> *"...hold reasoning for a great deal,*
> *and routine for nothing."* [1]

A.L.G.

---

1. Fernando Sor, *Method for the Spanish Guitar* (Paris, 1830), trans. A. Merrick (London, 1850) (New York: published in facsimile by Da Capo Press, 1971), 48. Public domain.

CHAPTER FIVE
THE RIGHT HAND

No matter what method book is used, it is always best to start the student with the right hand alone. This way he will, from the beginning, be able to make distinct pitches, work on getting a good sound, correct finger movement, and get used to reading music with open strings, all while concentrating on the right hand alone.

Obviously, a beginning student should *not* use nails! Among other things, he will begin to feel the distance between the strings with greater facility and begin feeling the fingertips of the right hand as they contact the strings.

The only objection to this no-nail approach will be from women with long, manicured nails. This and a host of similar problems must be dealt with as the teacher sees fit. Nonetheless, in the beginning, no nails is definitely the best approach.

How quickly a student technically progresses will vary a great deal and depends on a number of factors, but the following exercises work well with all types of students, and in most cases will speed progress. Keep in mind that any exercise may be substituted for another one of a similar nature depending on specific needs, *so be flexible!*

The Scratching Exercise will help beginning students develop a sense of the correct right hand finger movement and independence.

On a table (or any flat surface), place the right hand fingers on the tips with the wrist straight, and *p* out to the side. This position should look basically the same as the right hand playing position.

Remember to keep the fingers gently curved at all times. The extent of this curve will vary from school to school, but this exercise is easily adapted to different schools of right hand technique.

Next, have the student "scratch" the surface—with one finger at a time—returning it to the original position after each scratch. Keep all fingers in contact with the surface at all times. *This includes the scratching finger.*

Keep the non-scratching fingers still. The little finger is the only one which will not be on the surface; it should hover next to *a* and move with it.

Fig. 1.   Scratching Exercise (Set Position).

Fig. 2. Scratching Exercise (Execution).

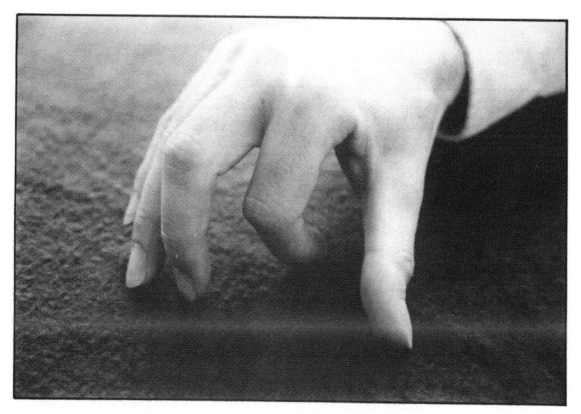

The movement should carry the finger far enough toward the wrist that it is obvious to the student that the movement is from the knuckle, though again, the exact distance of the movement will vary depending on the school of technique. The return of the finger to its original position should be slower than the initial scratch, to create a sense of relaxing, rather than an active movement.

Needless to say, this exercise is easy enough to be learned in minutes, yet it will help develop perfect right hand finger movement from the very first lesson, for students of any age or level.

With younger students, it is easy to make a game of this. Have them close their eyes as you gently touch one of their knuckles, at which time they should scratch, using that finger. As always, if a parent is involved with younger students, you can expect faster progress. This "game" can be played at home and will, from the first lesson, accustom both the student *and* parent to setting aside a specific, and subtly-monitored practice time.

◇ *Moving Exercise*

The next step is to have the student make the same scratching movement *with the right hand on the strings*. Planting each finger on its own string (*p, i, m & a* on ⑤, ③, ②, and ①, respectively), slightly move each finger slowly as if it were going to sound the note, *but do not release*.

Next, slowly relax the finger and allow the tension of the string to push the finger back to its original position.

Fig. 3.   **Moving** Exercise (Set Position).

Fig. 4.   Moving Exercise (Execution with *i*).

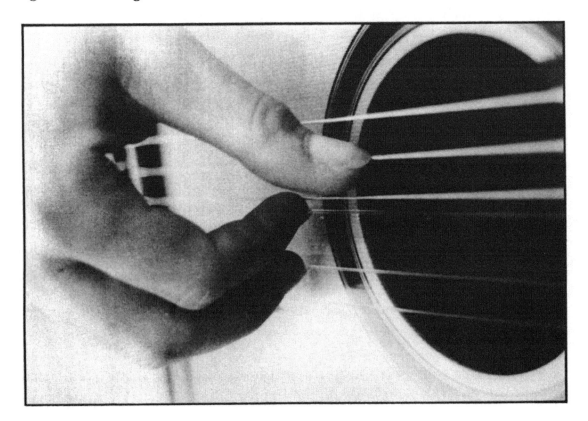

Be careful that the first joint of the active finger (the joint nearest the fingertip) stays relaxed, but does not collapse. This should be practiced one finger at a time, then in varying combinations, such as any arpeggio patterns.

When *p* is used, make sure the student feels the difference between *p* moving the string and the weight of the arm moving the string. Using the weight of the arm *can* be a legitimate way of sounding the string with *p* (for a very dark or heavy sound), but should not yet be introduced since this is too different from the way the other right hand fingers are used, and the confusion can cause the student to alter the hand position when *p* plays—which *must* be avoided!

There are several reasons for the Moving Exercise. First, the fingers will begin to feel how much pressure is needed to displace the string. Second, by leaving all the non-active fingers still (planted on their respective strings), a student can begin to feel the fingers work independently.

A danger of this exercise is, since it is isometrically based, some excess tension can be created. Also, with this gentle pulling motion, there is a tendency for the student to "dig" under the strings. However, if the Scratching Exercise is also practiced while the Moving Exercise is learned, any potential problems will be counteracted.

◇ *Releasing the String*

The next step is to teach the release of the string with the same movements practiced in the Scratching Exercise. It is a good idea to have students audibly recite the four basic movements which occur when a string is sounded.

Fig. 5. Basic Right Hand Finger Movements.

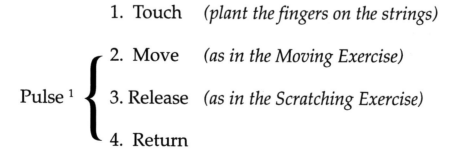

1. Touch   (*plant the fingers on the strings*)

Pulse [1] { 2. Move   (*as in the Moving Exercise*)

3. Release (*as in the Scratching Exercise*)

4. Return

---

1. The concept of "pulsing" will be discussed in the chapter "The Right and Left Hands." This is a critical element in precision playing and in developing speed, but is a concept far-beyond the grasp of most beginners.

Reciting these four steps out loud makes the student aware of the correct movements in sounding the strings. It also insures that he will practice slowly, since he will only be able to play as quickly as he can speak. In many cases, this is the *only* thing that will keep a student from trying to play too quickly!

Watch that the hand position does not change when the student alternates from *i* to *a*, since a slight "rocking" in the hand position often occurs.

In order to better understand these exercises, we should take a moment to examine these four specific movements separately.

1 Touch
At this moment, the finger plants on the string.

2 Move
"Moving the string" is the best way to describe the initial action of the fingers. The only comparable word in English is "pull," but this concept often results in a student pulling the strings *away* from the instrument (digging under the strings). It's usually much better to use the words "move" or "push."

It is interesting to note that by using the words "move" or "push," we imply that the *finger* is putting forth the effort. Another effective idea is to tell a student to *"feel the weight of the string."* This subconsciously puts the activity on the *string*, rather than the *finger*—as if the *string* were moving the *finger*. Naturally this is physically impossible, but with some students who have a tendency to exert too much force when sounding a string, this subliminal concept is highly effective.

3 Release
The best way to describe this, is to tell the student to think of his fingertip as a ball swinging on the end of a long string, and to imitate the feeling of that "swooping" motion. The direction of the release will vary depending on the specific school of technique being taught (*i.e.* moving the fingers near the palm for the closed hand school, or keeping the movement nearer the strings for the open hand school). Regardless, the Scratching and Moving Exercises will put the student on the right track no matter which school is preferred.

The amount of follow-through will vary with the school of technique (Closed Hand or Open Hand), but in either case, more follow-through than normal is usually best at this stage. This will guarantee that the movement is initiated from the knuckle, since it is *impossible* to have a wide follow-through and not move from the knuckle.

4 Return

There are essentially two ways to get the finger to return. Some schools teach that the finger should be actively pushed, or "kicked" back into position. Other schools teach that the finger immediately relaxes and simply "falls" back into position.

The latter method is by-far the best for beginners because half the energy is used—the finger simply relaxes and falls back into position. This avoids a "push/pull" effect which (for beginners) can nearly double the necessary tension.

Naturally later, especially for fast passages and scales, the fingers are sometimes gently and quickly "kicked" back into position, but for a beginner it is more important that he be able to discern the amount of power it takes to set the fingers in motion as opposed to when the fingers are "neutral," or relaxed.

Playing with *p* is exactly the same as the fingers, though in the *opposite* direction (toward the floor). In spite of this contradiction, *p* will nearly always imitate the feeling of the other fingers, and is almost never a problem.

◊ *Additional Exercises*

Once a student understands these basic movements, the following exercises may be introduced.

Using each finger on its respective string (*p*- ⑤, *i*- ③, *m*- ②, *a*-①), write out several right hand arpeggios such as those below:

	p i m a, p i m a	*sim.*
or:	p a m i, p a m i	
or:	p m i a, p m i a	
or:	p a i m, p a i m	

In the beginning, have the student practice an arpeggio by only moving the string (as in the Moving Exercise), but *not* releasing. Then later teach the release of the string using the *Individual Full Plant* then, the *Full Plant*, the *Sequential Plant* and finally *Free* (allowing some months or more between each planting technique). These various arpeggio techniques will be explained further in the section, "Arpeggios."

This is often a good time to introduce the *120 Right Hand Studies, Op. 1, A* by Mauro Giuliani. Even without using the left hand, the various right hand patterns may be easily learned. Since these studies will be with a student for his entire playing career, it is usually best to introduce them as early as possible.

◊ *Alternation*

The subject of alternating, like most other facets of playing, usually involves several steps before the student achieves the final stage. The method book chosen by the teacher will dictate when alternation is introduced. Still, if the student can be given at least several weeks (to first develop arpeggio patterns and correct right hand finger movement), alternation is much easier to learn.

In the first stage, it is usually best to have the student alternate *i* and *m*, making sure that the finger that has just played returns to hover over the string *before the next finger plays*. This insures that the fingers are moving independently.

It is naturally easier at the beginning if the alternation is confined to only one string and fortunately this is usually the case with most beginning methods. When right hand string crossings are finally introduced, the teacher *must* make sure that the alternation matches the string crossings. As we will see in the next section, "Right Hand Fingering," this is a critical factor for beginners.

The next stage in teaching alternation (sometimes a year or so later) is, rather than waiting for the finger to return before the next one plays, the student alternates the fingers so that they actually exchange position. A good explanation of this is to imagine pedaling a bicycle, or perhaps walking or ice skating.

For a moment we need to look at how right hand string crossings are best fingered for beginners. First, assume that all the right hand fingers are planted on their own strings. Every time you change from one string to another, *make sure that a finger that is already in that direction plays the next note on the next string.*

Fig. 6.   Example of "Clean" Right Hand Fingering (Ascending). [2]

In the example above, if *i* plays the D, then *m* is the closest finger in the direction of the next note, open E—if we assume all the fingers are in the order of their planted position. Remember, in writing "clean" fingerings, *always think of this in relation to where the fingers would be if they were planted on their "home strings."* Descending lines are fingered the same way.

Fig. 7.   Right Hand Fingering (Descending). [3]

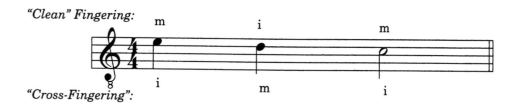

In Figure 7, all the fingerings above the staff work fine, however, the fingering below the staff of Figure 7, shows an example of cross-fingering. If *i* has just played the E, then the only finger remaining on the lower side of *i* is *p* (which is hardly appropriate for beginners), thus, *m* must reach *behind i* to play the following D on ②. This is an example of a "cross-fingering."

2. Anthony Glise, *The Child's Guitar, Vol. I,* (St. Joseph/Vienna: Aevia Publications, 1994).

3. Glise, Ibid.

As we know from playing, cross-fingerings are not necessarily bad, and after minimal practice they are no problem at all. However, cross-fingerings should be avoided for beginners! It is not that a beginner cannot easily learn to play cross-fingerings, but by using "clean fingerings" for the right hand, the student will more easily develop a sense of feeling with the right hand fingers when moving from one string to another in alternation.

Clean fingerings will also help to establish a more solid right hand position. After this, the slight complication of a cross-fingering will be even less of a problem because of the improved agility in feeling distances between the strings. Beginning exercises in most method books are usually easily re-fingered to avoid cross-fingerings, and it is *well* worth the trouble!

◇ *Conclusion*

As teachers and performers who already have considerable facility on the guitar, we often forget how complicated some things can appear to a beginner. Remember that many of the topics we automatically understand may take students weeks or months—or more—to grasp.

Be patient, keep it simple and push the student—*but gently!* For most students, it's far more traumatic to begin taking lessons than to quit, so if they've made it far enough to come to their first lesson, they're obviously serious about learning—it's up to you to keep lessons interesting enough that they will want to keep coming back each week.

- Each student choose a beginner's method and re-finger a short piece with "clean" right hand fingering.

- Teach a mock lesson to another student and explain right hand finger movement.

- Teach a mock lesson, and explain right hand finger alternation.

CHAPTER SIX
THE LEFT HAND

Although the function of the left hand was discussed in Book I, there is very little that the teacher can do to prepare the left hand before it is actually put to use, since the left hand rarely functions alone in the beginning stages.

Nearly the only thing a teacher can do is assign the Scratching Exercise using the left hand, stress the similarity between right and left hand finger movement, and wait until notes in the left hand are introduced in the method.

◊ *Left Hand Fingering—"The Fourth-Finger Approach"*

In the chapter "Left Hand Position and Movement" (Book I), we found that both Sor and Aguado used a left hand position whereby, the part of the hand nearest the little finger, is held slightly closer to the neck. In this chapter we will see how a specific manner of fingering pieces for beginners promotes this or any variant left hand position.

These fingerings (which have been commonly disregarded in modern guitar methods) distinctly help establish a beginner's left hand position. As a result, we must often change the fingerings in the method books that we use to achieve the best results for each student.

To begin with, we should look at the left hand fingerings used in modern guitar methods. To my knowledge, every 20th-Century method for guitar gives the following fingering on ① and ②.

Fig. 1.   Left Hand Fingering in 20th-Century Methods.

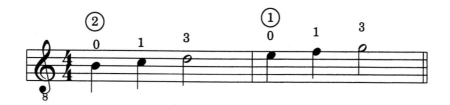

This fingering is somewhat logical since each finger plays on consecutive frets, but one problem consistently arises with beginners: as any adept teacher will agree, the lower part of the hand (that nearest the little finger), has a tendency to "drift" away from the neck of the instrument. If this is not corrected, the hand often ends up so far from the neck that it is impossible for the student to keep the third finger properly curved when playing.

In defense of the student, this is natural because the length of the third finger will tend to push the hand *away* from the neck of the guitar. Needless to say, this is an extremely serious yet common problem for beginners.

The other problem that occurs with modern fingering is that, by the time the fourth finger comes into use, the left hand position is already very established. While the left hand may be close enough to the neck for the *third* finger to be properly curved, this rarely guarantees that it will be close enough for the *fourth* finger to be properly curved.

Theoretically, since the fourth finger is shorter, *that side of the hand should be closer to the neck* so that all the fingers (*especially* the fourth) can remain curved.

If the third finger is used on the third fret (on ① and ②), a beginner will seldom achieve the proper position and as he progresses, must relearn the left hand position to properly use the fourth finger. However, if the fourth finger is used on the third fret (on ① and ②), a beginner will naturally pull that side of the hand *toward* the neck of the guitar, resulting in a nearly perfect left hand position from the very beginning.

The only argument against using the fourth finger comes from teachers who feel that using the third finger helps "stretch out" the hand. However, as any established player will attest, reaches up and down the neck are easily developed; reaches *across* the neck—*i.e.* left hand finger independence—are the most difficult. Thus, trying to "stretch" a student's left hand (especially at this stage) is absurd.

The basis for this "Fourth-Finger Approach" (as I mentioned earlier) is found in the methods and studies of, most notably, Dionisio Aguado and Fernando Sor.

As the brilliant guitar historian, Dr. Brian Jeffery, has often pointed out, much of our guitar technique thought to be inventions of the 20th-Century, goes back at least as far as Aguado and Sor, and it appears that this type of fingering (for the sake of a beginner's left hand position) originated at this time.

In his *New Guitar Method*, Lessons 3 and 4, Aguado gives the following fingering for chromatic and diatonic scales.

Fig. 2.   Aguado. Lesson 3. [1]

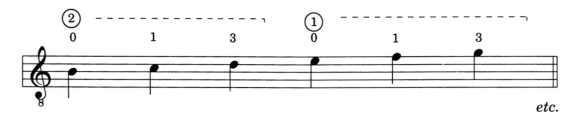

etc.

Fig. 3.   Aguado. Lesson 4. [2]

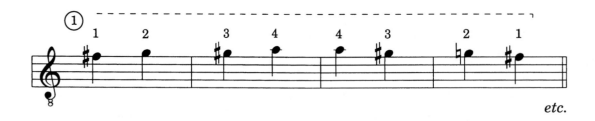

etc.

1. Dionisio Aguado, *New Guitar Method* (Madrid, 1843), trans. Louise Bigwood, ed. Brian Jeffery (London: Tecla Editions, 1981), 17. Used by permission.

2. Aguado; *op. cit.*, 18. Used by permission.

At first, the fingerings here seem to refute the Fourth-Finger Approach, until we notice that Aguado says these lessons are used for the student *"...to discover where the sounds are on the guitar..."* and to *"accustom them to plucking and stopping the strings without looking."* [3] No mention is made of anything other than the student becoming familiar with the notes. In Lesson 5, we have the first actual study in Aguado's *Method*.

Fig. 4.   Aguado. Lesson 5. [4] *(note bracketed areas)*

(N.B. fingering: Aguado, brackets: mine)

Here we find that Aguado consistently (with the exception of measures 11 and 12) uses the fourth finger on the third fret (on ① and ②).[5] Unfortunately he gives little to no reason for this fingering other than the brief explanation in Lesson 5:

> *"It seems natural to use the third finger for G and D in bars 1 and 7 [cf. Fig. 4] but it is more comfortable and more useful to use the fourth finger."* [6]

Anyone even vaguely familiar with Aguado's precision as a pedagogue would question him doing anything merely for "comfort," and as far as this fingering being "more useful," the most obvious reason is that it helps to properly develop a beginner's left hand position.

---

3. Aguado; *op. cit.*, 19. Used by permission.

4. Aguado; *loc. cit.* Used by permission.

5. In these instances, the use of the third finger is necessitated by the following note(s), which are also on the third fret, but on a different string. Thus, the third finger is used to avoid the fourth finger jumping from D to G (or *vice versa*) on adjacent strings.

6. Aguado; *loc. cit.* Used by permission.

In the studies of Fernando Sor (Op. 31 and especially Op. 60), we find the same type of left hand fingering for beginners. One of the best examples is given below.

Fig. 5.   Sor. Op. 60, no. 1.[7]

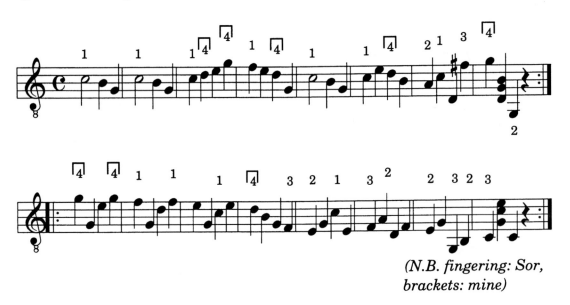

(N.B. fingering: Sor, brackets: mine)

This Fourth-Finger Approach is used consistently by Sor, though (as with Aguado), he gives no explanation for this fingering other than to say (in the preface to Op. 60) that he feels these simple studies contain *"...essential principles of technique that form the basis necessary to play the most difficult guitar music."* [8]

Since the single-most consistent element in these studies is the blatant use of the fourth finger on D and G, it is probable that Sor is, at least in part, referring to this Fourth-Finger Approach and its constructive effect on a beginner's left hand position.

It is also important to note the size of the guitars used in the 19th-Century. The majority of surviving instruments have a string length of *ca.* 62-63 centimeters. Modern instruments average between 64 (such as those built by Gioachino Giussani and Hermann Hauser) and 66.3 *cm.* (such as those by Miguel Rodriguez and José Ramírez).

---

7. Fernando Sor, *The Complete Works of Fernando Sor*, published in facsimile, ed. Brian Jeffery (London: Tecla Editions, 1982). Volumes reprinted at various dates thereafter. Used by permission.

8. Sor; *op. cit.* Used by permission.

This observation further establishes the need to use the Fourth-Finger Approach with beginners. Since reaches on 19th-Century guitars would have been *much* easier (due to the smaller scale length), it is evident that using the Fourth-Finger Approach in this period was not out of necessity, but a conscious choice. If this fingering was preferred, in spite of their smaller guitars, how much more should we be concerned, given the size of our larger instruments today?!

It appears that the Fourth-Finger Approach and its positive influence on a beginner's left hand position was well understood and practiced in the 19th-Century. Adopting this approach to our 20th-Century teaching not only helps refine our pedagogical practices, but more importantly, will help students easily acquire a correct and stable left hand position.

◇ *Suggested Assignments:*

• Re-finger one beginner's piece using the Fourth-Finger Approach.

• Teach a mock lesson to a "student" who disagrees with the Fourth-Finger Approach. Convince him that it will help establish his hand position.

CHAPTER SEVEN
THE RIGHT AND LEFT HANDS

When the student begins using both hands together, the habits of both hands—good or bad—are combined and reinforced. Therefore, a careful pace must be maintained through this critical period. This time has additional problems, since reading music becomes more involved. Still, the teacher should, as always, push forward as quickly as is prudent in order to keep the lessons more interesting.

Simple exercises are helpful, but by this time the student is often anxious to move ahead. In spite of the impatience, *be sure to have the student begin and end each practice session with a few technical exercises.* This will insure that pieces and studies are "sandwiched" between good technical habits.

I would also stress that, not only each *practice session,* but each *lesson* should begin with warm-up exercises. This will give the teacher a chance to check technical progress on a weekly basis, and will accustom the student to using warm-ups in his own practice time. Remember that the habits acquired in the lessons are the same habits that a student will carry into his own practice time at home.

In any case, the following exercises for intermediate students are very productive.

◇ *Right and Left Hand Exercises—*
"The Basic Seven" [1]

The right hand fingerings which are most common in chromatic exercises, and scales are:

1) i, m   4) a, m
2) m, i   5) i, a
3) m, a   6) a, i

A serious problem is that these patterns neglect the thumb. Especially in the Closed Hand School of right hand technique (when some hand position shifting occurs between the rest and free strokes), using only *i, m* and *a* can result in the hand leaning back (away from the floor) much further than necessary. Using *p* in the following combinations will solve this problem: [2]

1) p, i   4) m, p
2) i, p   5) p, a
3) p, m   6) a, p

• *Exercise Number 1*

Fig. 1.

etc.

---

1. The following section, "The Basic Seven" and "Arpeggios" is from: A. Glise, *The Basic Seven Chromatic Exercises and Arpeggio Studies, Op. 2, B.* (St. Joseph/Vienna: Aevia Publishing, 1993). Used by permission.

2. These various right hand finger alternation patterns will be discussed further in the next section on scales. The reason it is so important to practice *p* in conjunction with the other right hand fingers was discussed in Book I, Chapter Two, *Anatomical Function of the Hands,* "The Thumb." If you don't remember this discussion, please review the chapter—particularly the comments on practicing *p* with *i, m* and *a.*

Execution

Left Hand	*Right Hand*
each finger on its own fret (starting in VIIth position) [3]	each finger plays on its own string *or*
play: 1234/4321/1434/2434	alternate
move up to next fret and repeat	

•*Exercise Number 2*

Fig. 2.

Execution

Left Hand	*Right Hand*
Left hand fingering is: 212, 323, 434, *etc.*	alternate
At the top of the pattern, the descending pattern will be: 343, 232, 121, *etc.*	

3. Beginning these left hand patterns in the VIIth position is advantageous, since the frets are closer together. Even with intermediate students it is wise to have them begin similar studies at VII, and then work up the fingerboard, then down to the Ist position. This will gradually spread the fingers as a daily warm-up.

Notice that the accents (from the triplet pattern) will alternate between the right hand fingers (*i.e.* *m̄, i, m—ī, m, i, etc.*). This will help develop stable right hand alternation and insure that each right hand finger is accented every other time. This alternation will also indicate if one finger is weaker than another, since you will hear one finger louder than another.

•*Exercise Number 3*

Fig. 3.

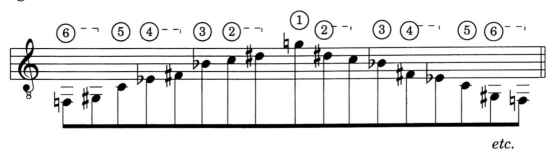

etc.

Execution

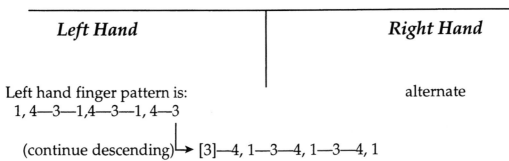

Left Hand	Right Hand
Left hand finger pattern is: 1, 4—3—1,4—3—1, 4—3	alternate

(continue descending) ⌐→ [3]—4, 1—3—4, 1—3—4, 1

A highly constructive variant of this pattern is to use 2 instead of 3. In any case, be sure to watch that the left hand stays in position without rocking between 1 and 4.

As with this, and all exercises which move *across* the neck, be sure to make sure that the left hand thumb glides slightly across the back of the neck with the fingers. This will familiarize the student with this type of movement which is so critical in playing pieces.

•Exercise Number 4

Fig. 4.

Execution

Left Hand	Right Hand
Left hand finger pattern is: 1, 2, 1, 2, 1, 2 (descending) ⟶ [2], 1, 2, 1, 2, 1	alternate

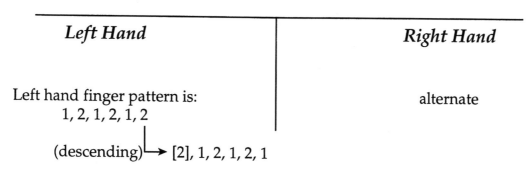

Next fret up: 2, 3, 2, 3, 2, 3
(descending is backwards)

Next fret up: 3, 4, 3, 4, 3, 4
(descending is backwards)
Move up to next fret and repeat
from the beginning.

This exercise is especially good for developing left hand finger independence and the development of the interossei and flexor digitorum superficialis muscles/tendons. As we have already discussed, independence is a primary difficulty in technical development.

This study may also be easily adapted to promote various schools of left hand technique (*i.e.* "Flat Hand" or "Angled" left hand positions).

•*Exercise Number 5*

Fig. 5.

Execution

This exercise (commonly called "The Spider" because of the way the hand looks during playing) may be altered to have more strings between the pattern; *i.e.* play the same pattern on ④ and ③, or ③ and ⑤, or ⑤ and ②, or ⑥ and ②, or ⑥ and ①. It is usually best to begin with adjacent strings (such as ② and ③, *etc.*) since this is obviously the easiest.

Be sure to watch for over-stress since this exercise is very strenuous. The independence which this exercise *should* develop is *not* rooted in power, but in left hand finger independence.

The right hand fingering for this exercise is at the discretion of the teacher, though it generally works best to make sure that as *p* plays the bottom line, at least two fingers (*ex. i* and *m*) alternate on the top line. This will help coordination between *p* and the other right hand fingers.

•*Exercise Number 6*

Fig. 6.

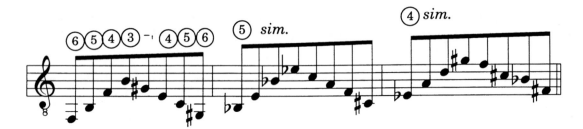

Execution

Left Hand	Right Hand
1, 2, 3, 4—1, 2, 3, 4 (repeat on ⑤ and ④) Descending is exactly backwards. Variants of this exercise may be: 1, 2, 4, 3, or; 1, 3, 4, 2, or; 1, 4, 2, 3, *etc.*	alternate or: p, i, m, a—a, m, i, p

• **Exercise Number 7**

Fig. 7.

Execution

Left Hand	Right Hand
4 1 3 1—4 2 3 2 Move up to next fret and continue. Descending is the same.	No right hand

This exercise is *very* power oriented. At no time does the right hand play. The entire pattern utilizes every ascending and descending slur possibility (with the exception of 1 to 2 which is rarely a problem).

There are two ways to execute this type of legato exercise, each with a specific goal:

1. In playing, if the student's joints consistently collapse, this exercise may be done, giving more accent to the *descending* slur.

2. If actual strength and speed are the problem, more accent should be given to the *ascending* slur.

In either case, the finger which is making the descending slur will move quickly onto the fingerboard to sound the lower note—actually "plucking" the string—(without the first joint of the active finger collapsing). Always make sure that the hand position stays secure—the motion should be confined to the fingers! The left hand position should remain the same. [4]

A Note on the "Basic Seven Exercises"

Remember to point out that both hands function essentially the same—using the same tendons and the same basic movements. A good variant of these exercises is to simply have the student *touch* the strings with both hands at exactly the same moment *(but not sound the notes)* and listen for the simultaneous "click" as the fingers of both hands instantaneously touch the string.

Taking this idea one step further, have the student touch the string with both hands (listening for the click) and "pulse," but: a) *do not release the string with the right hand,* while b) *the left hand will immediately relax after playing the note, so the string tension pushes the finger away from the fingerboard.* The right hand will also immediately relax, so the tension of the string pushes the finger back into position. This exercise will *greatly* help develop right and left hand coordination.

With this type of coordination exercise, it is best to make sure the student leaves no left hand fingers down when they are not being used. This is important because, for example, in Exercise 1, if 1 is held down while 2 plays, the student will subconsciously feel the pressure of 1 as being associated with using 2; if 1 and 2 are held down while 3 plays, that association is doubled; if 1, 2 and 3 are held down while 4 plays the problem is tripled. In other words, you are training 1, 2, and 3 to tense every time 4 plays.

An additional problem is that, in keeping fingers down, the sense of "pulsing"—which is so important in playing fast—is lost. Of course the student may be taught to release left hand pressure on the string, *but still keep the finger in contact with the string,* however most beginners will not have enough technical control to accomplish this.

---

4. Naturally a descending slur may be executed by suddenly lifting the finger (*directly* away from the fingerboard). This is normally used when a *subito piano* on the descending note is required. This is a dramatically beautiful effect, but hardly suitable for beginners. For a discussion of the *subito piano slur, cf.* Chapter Eleven, "Additional Subjects for Advanced Students."

In any case, left hand fingers that are not being used should be kept very near the strings, curved slightly and gently spread apart. Be sure to watch that the fingers "hover" over notes that they are going to play *before it is time for them to play.* This type of left hand finger preparation and positioning is admittedly difficult for beginners, but a vital aspect of left hand development.

There are a few legitimate reasons for having a student keep fingers down through these exercises. One reason is to stretch out the hand. While rare, this is occasionally necessary. Another reason is that it can help a student feel distances between notes in the left hand. For advanced students, leaving left hand fingers down creates a sense of stability—much the same as the right hand stability created through using the Full or Sequential Planting Techniques. However, a teacher needs to carefully weigh the disadvantages if prescribing this approach for beginners, since it can destroy the sense of left hand finger independence which is usually a primary concern at this stage.

◇ *Rhythmic Variants of the "Basic Seven"*

Rhythmically altering the "Basic Seven" or any other similar exercises has tremendous advantages as we will discuss later. Above all, it keeps exercises interesting for the student.

Fig. 8.   *1)* Repeat each note in groupings of 2, 3, 4, 5, 6 and 7, *etc.*

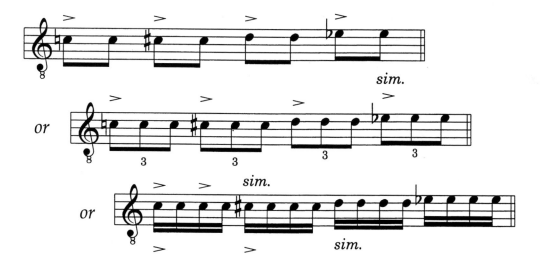

(Fig. 8, cont.)

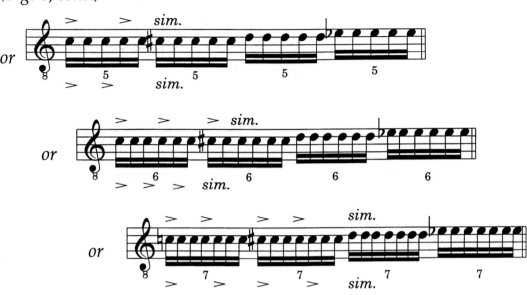

or

or

or

Fig. 9.   2) Play exercises, but accent them in groups of 2, 3, 4, 5, 6 and 7, *etc.*

or

or   *etc.*

3) Play the exercises as above, but alter the right hand patterns as given at beginning of this chapter.

In addition, using "odd fingerings" (an even fingering against an odd pattern—[such as *i, m* against triplets] or an odd fingering against an even pattern—[such as *p, i, m* against eighth notes]) will cause the accents to shift from one right hand finger to another. This will help develop greater control between the right hand fingers (*cf.* Exercise #2).

◇ *Pulsing*

Pulsing with the right hand should now be quite familiar to the student because of the Scratching, and Moving Exercises, but pulsing with the *left* hand is a very distinct movement. With the introduction of these exercises, the subject of pulsing with the left hand must be explained if the student is to make the most of the "Basic Seven" or similar exercises.

The best way to describe left hand pulsing is to take the student's arm, as though it were the neck of a guitar, and "pulse" on it with your left hand—as though you were playing and *immediately* releasing the note (but not lifting the finger off the strings). This will give the student an immediate idea of the feeling that exists with left hand finger pulsing. Make sure that he feels the pulse in both hands *at exactly the same time,* otherwise the right and left hand coordination will be inaccurate. If the left hand pulse is correctly executed, the sound will be very staccato because the finger immediately releases pressure from the string.

◇ *Scales*

As "old-fashioned" as it may sound, scales are one of the most critical studies that exist for any instrument. I have never met or heard of any major performing artist who did not practice scales with a rabid obsession. Their commitment to this study should be an example to any student, and as bizarre as it sounds, scales *can* be one of the most enjoyable facets of practicing or one of the most useless and tedious. This is because (as with any technical or musical studies) the student must understand *why* he is practicing something, and scales are no exception.

The "Basic Seven Exercises" will prepare a student for scales, the standard edition of which is the *Diatonic Major and Minor Scales,* edited by Andrés Segovia. The fingerings, shifts, and the consistent use of positions in Segovia's edition are a masterpiece of pedagogical skill. Nonetheless, there are other fine editions of scales that can be equally beneficial.

Scales can be used for a *multitude* of reasons, including:

- Developing Right Hand Finger Independence
- Developing Left Hand Finger Independence
- Developing Right and Left Hand Coordination
- Developing Legato Playing
- Developing Staccato Playing
- Developing Position Shifts
- Developing Right Hand String Crossings
- Developing Left Hand String Crossings
- Developing Speed in Either or Both Hands
- Developing Various Articulations
- Developing Various Color Shifts
- Developing Crescendos or Decrescendos
- Developing Phrasing, *etc.*

Naturally this list could continue for pages, but the importance of practicing scales, for students of *any* level, should never be underestimated.

Besides the right hand fingerings previously given (*cf.* the "Basic Seven Exercises"), students should be encouraged to practice scales in various rhythms, subdivisions and groupings as well as using different right hand fingerings.

Another essential, but often-neglected subject, is practicing right hand arpeggio fingerings with scales. For example, when a student practices arpeggios, the fingers develop a high sense of independence, but this is confined to a "right hand arpeggio position" (*i.e.* each finger on its "own" string).

I cannot overemphasize the importance of having students practice *scales* using the same right hand patterns found in arpeggio studies. This will *greatly* increase right hand finger independence and placement in scales, and develop more a consistent right hand technique—in both scales and arpeggios.

These variations will also accustom a student to irregular right hand groupings since these variations will cause the metric shifts to occur at different points in the rhythmic structure. Above all, they will help make scales more interesting and productive. The possibilities are endless, so use your imagination. When approached creatively, scales can be as enjoyable as they are technically necessary.

◇ *Arpeggios*

Along with scales and chromatic exercises, arpeggios are the most important technical exercises a student will practice throughout his entire playing career. They not only prepare a student for pieces which use arpeggio techniques, but as we shall see later, developing speed is actually a matter of developing *independence,* and arpeggios are a key factor in this process for the right hand.

The most inclusive collection of arpeggios is the *120 Right Hand Studies Op. 1, A* by Mauro Giuliani, which is available in numerous editions and I would strongly encourage teachers to begin using the Giuliani as early as possible with students.

To begin with, watch that the student's left hand stays relaxed. Since only a C major chord (I) and a G_7 chord (V_7) are used, there is a tendency for the student to "clamp" his left hand to the neck with excess tension.

There are four specific ways to practice arpeggios.

> 1) *Individual Full Plant*
> 2) *Full Plant*
> 3) *Sequential Plant*
> 4) *Free*

These different planting techniques should be given to the student *in this order,* since they progress from being very stable and requiring less independence to being less stable and requiring a great deal of independence.

To better understand these techniques, we will look at each one separately.

Individual Full Plant

The Individual Full Plant is a preparatory technique for the following three planting techniques, and has little application in actual performance.

Each finger is planted on its respective string; the arpeggio pattern is played, but after each note, the finger replants *before the next note is played.* Thus, only one finger is off the strings at any given moment; all the other fingers remain planted.

In teaching, there are tremendous advantages to the Individual Full Plant: the student's sense of finger placement is dramatically heightened and more importantly, the sense of finger independence and individual finger movement is isolated.

Again, while this planting technique has very little application to performance, for beginners, the Individual Full Plant is one of the most helpful and productive exercises for the right hand.

Full Plant

The Full Plant is exactly what the name implies; the fingers which sound the strings all plant at the beginning of each right hand pattern. For example, in a *"p, i, m, a"* arpeggio, the hand would look like in Figures 10 and 11.

Fig. 10. Full Plant (set position).

Fig. 11. Full Plant (after each finger has played).

Note that all the fingers being used will plant at the beginning of the arpeggio pattern and wait until their turn to play and, after playing, remain off the string until the pattern is repeated.

Both the Individual Full Plant and the Full Plant are especially helpful because they give beginners a chance to feel each right hand finger pulse, while the other fingers are gently held in place waiting their turn to play. This will heighten the sense of right hand finger independence and placement.

A very fine point that only the teacher needs to be aware of, is exactly *when* the planting occurs. Of course if the action of planting takes any time value, the written rhythm is altered. Therefore, the finger that starts the pattern must play *at the exact moment that all the fingers plant.* This will keep the sound as legato as possible and the written rhythm accurate. Thus, the planting of the first finger of the pattern is actually very slight, or (for advanced players) nonexistent.

Beginning students can rarely do this, and need to plant sooner in order to maintain the correct rhythm. If the sound of a beginner were actually notated, it would look something like this:

Fig. 12. Aural Notation of a Beginner's Full Plant.

With intermediate players, the planting of the first finger of the pattern is very slight since this finger will *immediately* continue its movement across the string.

Fig. 13. Aural Notation of an Intermediate Player's Full Plant.

Another fine point is to make sure that the fingers return and "hover" over their respective strings, but are not re-planted *until the pattern is completed.*

The Full Plant works well in pieces with arpeggios that ascend, and for "broken" patterns (*ex. p, m, i, a*). Descending patterns are less common in actual performance, but are still important to practice for technical development.

In performance, the Full Plant is used when an arpeggio is not intended to sustain. It also works well in pieces which have arpeggios that are at such a fast tempo that the stopping of the notes (which results from planting all the fingers at once) does not harm the character of the music (*q.v.* Villa-Lobos *Prelude IV*, section B).

Pedagogically, Sequential Planting is the most beneficial for training right hand finger independence. This is because the fingers are only *partially* responsible for their independence, while the planting takes care of the remainder of the finger independence.

In the Sequential Plant, each finger plants at the *exact* moment that the one before it plays. For example in Figure 14, as *p* plays, *i* plants; as *i* plays, *m* plants; as *m* plays, *a* plants, and so on. In this manner, the right hand fingers learn to stay one step ahead of the sound. *Remember that only one finger will be on a string at any given moment—the one that will be playing the next note.*

Fig. 14. Diagram of Sequential Plant.

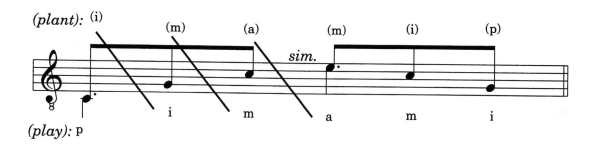

In pieces, Sequential Planting works well for ascending, descending and broken arpeggios. Thus, the Sequential Plant is perhaps the most practical, in literature, because all the notes are sustained, *except the one that will be sounded next.* Plus, there is still a sense of security from the sequential planting.

Free

The Free Technique is exactly what the name implies; *no* fingers are planted. A common problem is that this *feels* like the easiest of the four planting techniques, though it is unequivocally the most difficult to execute properly because it demands *total* finger independence.

In all the previous techniques at least one finger is planted throughout the arpeggio pattern. With the Free Technique, *no* fingers are planted, so the player is *entirely* responsible for the independence and control. All the fingers hover over their respective strings and wait for their turn to play. If student has difficulty with the Sequential Plant, it is because of a lack of finger independence. If this occurs, the student will absolutely *not* have adequate independence to properly execute the Free Technique!

In performance, the Free Technique is often used in slower tempi, which require *all* the notes to sustain. This is particularly true of arpeggios which have inner voices that must continue to resolve, such as in a chain suspension.

A Final Word on Arpeggios

While all schools of playing will usually agree that these four right hand techniques are essential in training the right hand, they sometimes disagree as to their application in performance. Remember to ask, with this or any other debatable subject: *does it help or hinder the music?* and, *does it help or hinder the player?* With these two questions in mind, a musician will confidently solve a host of technical and musical problems.

• Find one study from a method or exercise book that could substitute for one of the Basic Seven Exercises, and explain why they are similar.

• Rhythmically alter any chosen study or scale (dotting rhythms, different groupings, *etc.*).

• In a mock lesson, convince a "student" that he should practice scales. Cite specific reasons in relation to pieces that he is playing.

• In a mock lesson, demonstrate and teach each of the following arpeggio techniques:
> *Individual Full Plant*
> *Full Plant*
> *Sequential Plant*
> *Free*

CHAPTER EIGHT
THE TEACHER

> *"If you show me I will see.*
> *"If you tell me I will listen.*
> *"If you let me experience, I will learn."*
> (Ancient Chinese Proverb)

While they naturally overlap, the active rôle of a teacher falls into two categories:

1. *Teaching*
2. *Coaching*

Ideally, from the intermediate level on, lessons in both categories should be a "supervised practice time." During this time, the teacher makes technical and musical suggestions. This way, the student will begin to practice at home *the same as if he were in a lesson,* but this is as far as the similarity goes between our two categories.

From these two distinct rôles in teaching lessons, there are four discernible phases that a student will go through when he is working on a piece. These do not need to be pointed out to the student (unless the teacher feels it is necessary), but the teacher should *always* be aware of these phases. This is because each one contains specific goals and procedures that will keep the lessons more structured, and as a result more productive and enjoyable. In order, these phases are:

1. Research ⎫
2. Reading ⎬ *Teaching*
3. Memorizing ⎭
4. Polishing ➤ *Coaching*

• *Teaching* is the active process of guiding the student through the problems of becoming familiar with, and learning about the piece, finding new notes, fingerings, dynamics and timbre changes, *etc.* In other words, everything having to do with *the mechanics of getting to know the music.*

• *Coaching* is the act of helping the student discover the piece as a whole musical entity. Usually the piece is already memorized, and all the technical problems are out of the way. The student plays through the piece, while the teacher points out different ways to make the piece come alive through phrasing, articulation and so on.

At this stage, it can also be beneficial for the student to have occasional coaching sessions with a non-guitarist, since these musicians can sometimes give more objective musical insight because of their unfamiliarity with the guitar. Non-guitarists are less concerned with the guitar's idiosyncrasies, and more concerned with whether or not the music "works." These coachings can encourage a more "musical" interpretation, rather than the type of "guitaristic" interpretations which are often musically inferior.

◇ *Teaching*
Research

This is perhaps the most neglected of the four phases. Sometimes this is because of unavailability of research materials, but with the current popularity of the guitar, this problem is rapidly subsiding. Unfortunately, the other reason for neglect of this phase is a general lack of scholarship that persists in the performing arts. A teacher may simply not know where to send a student to find information. This is obviously one of the strongest arguments for a well-rounded formal education.

Research may include various things, depending on the amount of time available and the ability of the student (due to age and maturity) to carry out varying degrees of research. Nonetheless, research should *always* include the following points:

1. Look up any unfamiliar terms used in the piece.
2. Find the dates, nationality and minimal biographical information on the composer.

More advanced research projects may include the following:

1. A brief study of the composer, his style of composition, *etc.*
2. Anything having to do with the composer's personal life that might tell the player more about the music.
3. An analysis of the music. This may be only a sketch including phrasing, dynamics, *etc.*, or may be a full musical, harmonic, layer or Schenker analysis.
4. Performance practices of the historical period.
5. The social background of the piece. Who or what was it written for (royalty, friends, students, *etc.*). In particular, dances and dance-inspired music takes on an entirely new character when a student learns the basic steps of the dance. Learning a bit about the dances will also *greatly* affect decisions about the tempo, mood and articulation of the piece.
6. Make a comparative study of various recordings of the piece. If the piece is a transcription, *make sure they listen to—and study— the original as well!*

Nothing will provide more direct understanding into the nature of a piece than a few short minutes in a music library. However, as teachers we need to remember that we are not conducting a research seminar! Research should be for the sole reason of providing insight into performance of the music. As a general rule, a weekly research assignment should take no more time than a student usually practices in one day. See Appendix V ("Selected Research Source Materials") for a list of basic research sources.

I have made a habit of keeping a collection of basic research materials in my studio. I always have students come to lessons one half hour early, and while teaching one student, the next student is doing research in another room. This approach not only gives you more contact time with students, but it is a subtle way of monitoring research.

Reading

This is the stage in which the piece is actually learned—which should always be done with an eye on the previous research. The student will play through the piece to become familiar with it, study the piece, learn the notes, fingering, dynamics and begin to get an idea of how he wants to interpret the piece.

All these things must be secure in the student's reading of the piece *before memorization takes place.* Otherwise a great many problems can arise, such as second-generation interpretations copied from recordings (which perhaps were not very good to begin with), and worst of all, a misunderstanding of the music. Re-working a piece that has been learned with errors is as frustrating for the student as it is for the teacher.

In learning a piece, it is often best to apply one of the methods described in the next section, "Memorization." This will insure that the piece is learned in an organized and logical manner.

Memorization

Guitarists traditionally perform without music, so the subject of memorization is essential in any pedagogical approach and students should be encouraged to memorize anything that they will be working on for more than several lessons. Not only will this accustom them to memorizing, but it will permit them to concentrate on the technical and musical aspects of a piece without the distraction of the printed music. Naturally, the teacher needs to be careful that the written page is not left too soon, since this is how many errors creep into a piece.

There are several ways to memorize a work, and the teacher must find the one that works best for each individual student. These same methods of memorizing can, of course be applied to learning a piece.

Block Memorization

In this approach, the student must already be familiar with the piece. Looking away from the music, he plays as far as he can while being quite sure that the fingering, dynamics, *etc.*, are correct. When he can play no further, he consults the music, plays over that spot several times, and then continues from slightly before the problem spot. He should *not* go back to the beginning (which is the common tendency) since this wastes time and simply reiterates something he has already learned. When he can again go no further, the process is repeated.

This approach is quite successful, assuming that the student has a fairly good natural memory. The problem that may arise is that the transition section (the area between the memorized and unmemorized sections) must be carefully practiced so that, in the end, the student doesn't feel that the piece was memorized in sections, some being more secure than others. Needless to say, this could be a major downfall on stage.

A diagram of Block Memorization is shown below, with the numbers showing the sequence of events.

Fig. 1. Block Memorization.

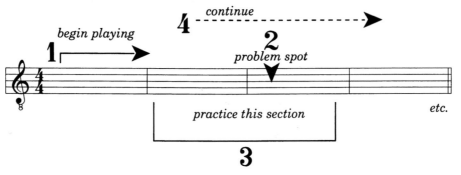

Overlap Memorization

This is the most effective method for memorizing or learning a piece. The student studies and plays over a small area and memorizes it (usually one measure is the ideal amount for beginners though an entire phrase for advanced students is more logical from a musical standpoint). Then he does the same with the second measure. Then he plays the first and second measures *together*. Next, the third measure is memorized, then played together *with the second measure only*, and so on until the entire piece is memorized.

The advantages of this method are obvious: nothing is taken for granted, since each measure is memorized and "overlapped" with the previous *and* the following measures. This eliminates the threat of any transition problems. Also, since only two measures (or areas) are played together, no time is wasted playing over areas that have already been memorized.

Fig. 2. Overlap Memorization.

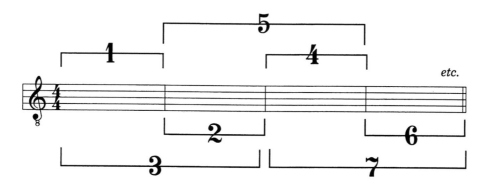

Backwards Memorization

Theoretically, the more time a student spends with a section of a piece, the better he will know it. Thus, assuming that a student normally memorizes from the beginning of a piece, the further he plays into the piece, the less secure it will be. This may be a fine point, but one worth our attention, since this can be a legitimate problem in very long pieces.

In Backwards Memorization, the student uses Overlap Memorization, but begins with the last measure first, then the next-to-last, and so on. This way, the further he plays in the piece, the more familiar he will be with the music.

This may seem like a rather extreme solution to a relatively minor problem but it is *very* successful with students who have difficulty memorizing. Backwards Memorization—*combined* with the Overlap Technique—is by far the most productive approach when a great deal of music must be memorized in a short period of time.

Sight Memorization

While I personally prefer this approach, unless a student has a near photographic memory and is very familiar with the guitar's fingerboard, this method alone will not suffice. It amounts to simply sitting down with the sheet music and memorizing it as you would a poem or a theatre script.

Note that I said this approach *alone* will not usually suffice. However, if a student studies the music he is memorizing, in addition to using one of the other memorization techniques, the results are astounding.

We are visual creatures by nature. As a result, if the student studies the music *away from the instrument*, imagining the position, fingerings, the sound and so on, the memorization process is greatly accelerated.

In doing this, the student will begin to hear what he is going to play, *before* he plays it; the music tells him *what* to play, rather than the sound telling him what he *has* played. This is exactly what Fernando Sor is referring to in his *Method*, when he makes the following observation:

> *"I make a great distinction between a musician and a note player. The former is he who, considering music as the science of sounds, regards the notes only as conventional signs representing them, and which by the sight convey the result to the mind, as letters communicate words, and words, ideas. The latter is he who considers it the science of notes, who attaches great importance to their names, the real acceptation of which is unknown to him..."* [1]

In closing, we need to briefly discuss the process that occurs in memorizing. When we memorize, we are trying to recall one or more things: the sound, the fingering and position, or in some cases, we may try to envision the actual page of music.

Normally, it is usually best to stress the importance of trying to recall as many of these items as possible. However, this type of recall does *not* work well in performance, since it does not allow the performer to "let go" of the music.

In performance we "sing" inside, and it comes out of the instrument; the recall is nearly all aural. This will be discussed further in Book III, but for the purpose of basic memorization, the most successful approach is for the student to recall the sound as well as the fingering, hand positions, *etc.* In short, he should recall aural, visual and tactile details of a piece.

The teacher must remember that this stage is *very* analytical, and for that reason, as the piece is being memorized, the Coaching stage should begin. If not, the piece can stay in this analytical phase and have no more life than a rock.

---

1. Sor, *Method; op. cit.,* 18.

This stage of teaching is often the most enjoyable because you are dealing with your student as a *musician* rather than a mere *technician*, sharing your ideas about the music rather than simply making sure all the notes are correct, and so on.

At this stage, supporting and gently guiding a student's musical individuality is a key factor—*even if you may disagree with some of the interpretive decisions!* Remember, we are not attempting to make musical "clones" out of our students, we are attempting to shape individual musicians.

The main reason for this phase is to literally polish the piece, making it an intrinsic part of the student's musical awareness. There are several steps that can promote this:

1. *Play The Piece Slowly.* If the student cannot play it slowly, he won't be able to play it up to tempo. This will help expose any problems that might slip by at a faster tempo. It will also force the student to listen to his musical decisions.

2. *Concentrate On Everything.* A very high level of concentration is required at this stage by the teacher (to catch any previously undetected problems), and by the student (to solidify the piece in his mind). He should think about the sound, the fingering, how the fingers feel and look when they play a given passage, and so on.

3. *Make Accuracy An Obsession.* Naturally you can go overboard with this, but be very picky. If a mistake occurs, have him slow down the tempo and play over that small area a number of times correctly. I have found that seven times in a row (correctly) will tell a teacher if the student has actually corrected a problem, or simply made it through by "dumb luck." Remember that ideally (especially at this stage), *a lesson should be supervised practice time.* If a student gets in the habit of correcting mistakes in this manner, his own practice time at home will be infinitely more productive.

4. *Alter The Rhythm.* Sometimes a student will get a piece to a level of proficiency, and seem unable to progress any further. Have him practice the piece one phrase at a time, dotting the rhythm in both directions. This forces the fingers to react faster than normal. For example, if a written area looks like Figure 3, have a student practice it as in Figure 4.

Fig. 3.   Original Measure.

Fig. 4.   Original Measure Altered for Practice.

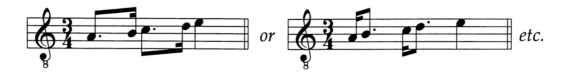

Naturally, there are many ways to alter rhythms, such as grouping the notes into triplets, groups of five, *etc.*—such as we discussed in the chapter on the "Basic Seven Exercises." The decision as to how a student should practice a given section is up to the insightful guidance of the teacher, but remember that rhythmic alteration is one of the most productive practice techniques.

5. Play Lines. Since music is almost always made up of lines (even from one chord to another), playing the lines separately will help solidify a student's conception of the piece.

In playing one line at a time, it is essential that the original fingering for both hands be used, to reinforce the fingering when all the lines are again played together. In more complicated works (especially fugues), an excellent exercise is to play one line only with the right hand, while still fingering *all* the lines with the left hand.

There are numerous ways to practice like this, such as *playing* one line while *singing* another, and so on. These methods can be difficult, but are well worth the time and effort.

6. Play Arpeggios As Chords. For example, the study in Figure 5 may be played as block chords as shown in Figure 6. This can help with memorization, as well as solidifying left hand movement throughout the piece.

Fig. 5. Carcassi, "Study No. 3," Op. 60. [2]

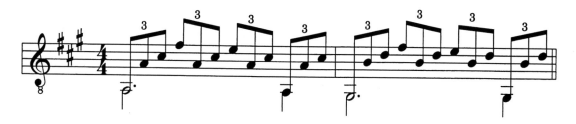

Fig. 6. Study Altered as a Chordal Study.

7. Play The Piece Mentally. One of the most beneficial, yet neglected ways to practice is to mentally perform a piece *without the guitar.* The student should be able to sit quietly, with eyes closed, and mentally "see," "feel," and "hear" himself play the entire piece. If a student is able to do this—*through an entire piece*—then the piece is truly "learned." This will be discussed at length in Book III, but for now, suffice it to say that this type of mental practicing is of paramount importance in preparing for a recital.

8. Practice Slowly. This may seem obvious, but make sure that the student practices slowly. For some reason younger students often have the idea that if they can't hear the mistakes, there are none, and the way to not hear the mistakes is to play faster. Of course this is absurd, but it is a common problem. Make sure students practice slowly!

2. M. Carcassi, "Study No. 3," from *The Complete Carcassi Guitar Method, with Twenty Five Studies, Op. 60* (Pacific: Mel Bay Publishing, 1994). Used by permission.

• Make a list of eight research books to have on hand in your studio and defend your choices. Be sure to include: one music dictionary, one music history book, one book on performance practice and one book on performing dance music. The rest are up to you. [3]

• In a mock lesson, teach one memorization technique.

• In a mock lesson, teach one piece, then (pretending several weeks have passed) *coach* the same piece.

---

3. If you have difficulty compiling a list, check Appendix V ("Selected Secondary Research Source Materials") for a basic list of books. Also ask the head music librarian at your music school, since he will be familiar with any new releases.

CHAPTER NINE
PRACTICING

> *"Practice Makes Perfect..."*
> (An ancient lie invented
> by a non-musician)

I would like to dispel, at the outset, a terrifying fallacy:
"Practice Makes Perfect."

This idea exists in every language with which I am familiar. In German, it's *Übung macht den Meister* ("Practice makes the master")—in French it's *C'est en forgeant qu'on devient forgeron* ("It's in the forging that one becomes a blacksmith")—in Italian, it's *Vale piu la pratica che la grammatica* ("Better to practice than study the grammar"). This is probably the most blatant untruth in music—or for that matter, in *life*.

Practice does **not** make perfect: *practice makes **permanent!***

How a student practices—well or badly—will become the inescapable characteristic of his playing. If he practices well, yes, perhaps he will approach "perfection," but just as surely, if he practices poorly, he will play poorly, and the *more* he practices, the more consistently he will continue in either direction.

Helping students develop good practice habits is probably the single most important trait you can give them. We can probably all think of guitarists at a local, and even international level, who are less than gifted teachers. In spite of their deficits as pedagogues, they consistently produce well-rounded, "talented" students, and the simple reason is that they have inspired their students to work well on their own.

As J.S. Bach said, *"I have worked hard; anyone who works equally as hard will accomplish equally as much."*

I will admit that the miracle of Bach is matched only by his Baroque humility, but he is correct: much of what we try to teach in the studio is a matter of physical mechanics, and a majority of that mechanical skill can only be developed by the student on his own. If *any* student maintains a correct and regimented practice routine, he will improve— in spite of himself *or* the teacher!

There are two basic ways that we practice. The first is to *"Practice"* and the second is to *"Practice Performing."* These are two highly distinct methods of practicing, and the student (and the teacher) needs to constantly be aware of which one is occurring in both lessons and practice time.

◇ *Practicing*

"Practicing," in the strict sense of the word, is the process of working through a piece to learn it. However, it often becomes simply a matter of the student "playing through a piece" (which is actually practicing performing!).

Because of this, it is important to stress to the student that when one *practices*, it is a matter of isolating sections, phrases, even separate notes, and obsessively working and reworking these areas over and over from a technical and musical standpoint—*not* simply playing through the piece. As a general rule, the key word is *isolation;* picking out small areas, analyzing them and practicing them outside of the piece.

In isolated practicing, a small section (a phrase, measure, *etc.*), is taken out of the piece, and worked separately from a technical *and* musical standpoint. It is easy to teach students to make up studies around certain technical elements in a piece, such as by taking a specific scale or left hand movement (from the piece) and moving it up and down the neck *etc.*

Various right hand patterns from the piece may also be practiced separately, or perhaps using the same right hand pattern on different strings, *etc.* Any variation will help solidify the original in the student's mind, and the options are endless.

The mental attitude that the student must adopt for this type of practice is one of absolute analytical obsession. He hears everything, sees everything, feels everything, thinks through every move, every sound and constantly questions every single musical result that he gets from the instrument. It's as if the student becomes two people: a "player" and a "listener," both sitting there at the same time. The student becomes his own hypercritical teacher.

This is why, in lectures and masterclasses, I am constantly telling teachers that *a lesson must be a supervised practice time.* This way, a student will learn to become his own teacher for the other 6 days a week that he does *not* have the teacher looking over his shoulder, and more importantly, *he will learn to analyze and solve problems on his own.*

The mindset in "practicing" involves using predominantly the left side of the brain (the analytical and logical side), while performing (*i.e.* thinking only of the abstract sound) is predominantly a right brain function.

It is interesting to note that different languages have been tracked to the different sides of the brain; Germanic languages (including English) are predominantly "left brain" languages, while the romantic languages (such as French, Italian and Spanish) are more "right brain" oriented. We will discuss these aspects further in the chapter "Temporal Modes in Music" in Book III, but with students, the main thing to stress is the distinct difference between *practicing* and *practicing performing.*

Remember that practicing is not simply a matter of running through the piece. It is conscious, active work. While perhaps a bit severe, the brilliant Viennese-based pianist, Anthony deBedts often tells his students, "*After practicing for one hour, you should have worked so hard that your brain hurts! If it doesn't, you're not working hard enough!*"

While Maestro deBedts' genius as a performer and teacher may be too extreme for many students, it is a valid and very true observation. True practicing is far more mental work than physical.

This type of practice is what most students are doing when they *think* they are "practicing." It consists of running the piece—beginning to end—without stops. However, until the piece is actually being polished for performance, this is a relatively useless type of practice that only reinforces bad habits and solidifies mistakes in a piece.

Naturally, this type of practice *is* necessary when preparing for a concert. Otherwise the piece may never develop a sense of musical unity, but running a piece—beginning to end—is not the sort of practice that truly "works" a piece.

However, when a student *is* ready to begin "practicing performing," an entirely different mental attitude is necessary. As opposed to the critical listening used when "practicing," when "practicing performing," the player only "sings" inside and "runs the piece" from beginning to end.

The player must imagine that he is simply listening to the music, as if it were being played by someone else, although the concentration should be so obsessively high, that (as Pepe Romero once told me), "...*if a fly lands on your nose, you don't see it.*" **Nothing exists but the sound.**

I would like to temper this with a word of caution: there is no other way to make a performance "live"—to make it truly come to life—except for the player to totally lose himself in the music. Nonetheless, because accidents do sometimes happen in concert, this is a very dangerous mental state to be in.

If a mistake occurs on stage, and the player is very "locked in" to the performance, then it can be difficult to suddenly shift back into the *technical* mindset, and recover from the error. However, if the piece has been truly practiced (as defined above) *and* practiced mentally (*cf.* the chapter, "Mental Control Over the Sound"), then this type of "recovery" is usually not a major problem.

In this phase of practicing for a performance, if an error does happen, *the student should not stop!* He should consider it an opportunity to practice "recovering" from the error—as if he were actually on stage. This will familiarize him with the sort of split-second decisions that are necessary if a similar mistake happens on stage.

I have found, when helping students arrange a daily practice schedule, that the teacher must specifically define which sections of the practice time are actually "practice" and which are "practicing performing." [1] This will help clarify the difference in the student's mind and result in a more economical and constructive practice time.

Mechanically, how one practices efficiently (when actually "practicing"—as opposed to "practicing for a performance") requires a regimented system. I have found it best to encourage students to practice using exactly the same methods we already discussed in Chapter 8, "Teaching," using the Block Memorization or Overlap Memorization techniques, but applying these same techniques to *learning* the piece.

The only basic difference in applying these memorization techniques to *learning* a piece (as opposed to memorizing a piece) is that the player will look at the music constantly as he practices. More often than not, after practicing a piece using one of these methods, even less-than-average students will learn the piece with considerable facility and, once practiced correctly, the piece will be easily memorized.

---

1. *cf.* Appendix 2, "Sample Lessons Outline" for an example of a student's daily practice schedule.

• Write out a sample practice schedule for a beginning student. Be sure to consciously note the difference between practice time that should be spent "practicing" and practice time that is spent "practicing performing."

• In a mock lesson, teach a student one of the memorization techniques *(Block, Overlap, Backwards, Backwards-Overlap and Sight Memorization.)*, and explain the way these can also be used in practicing and learning a piece.

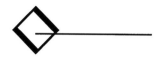

CHAPTER TEN
ADDITIONAL SUBJECTS FOR
INTERMEDIATE STUDENTS

This chapter contains a number of subjects which are of concern to advanced beginners and intermediate students. These should always be introduced in the context of pieces which the student is learning. For that reason, in this stage of repertoire development, the teacher must find pieces which gradually utilize these various techniques.

The most important thing is to make sure the music is interesting for the student, while at the same time, being sure that every single piece that is studied has a specific technical and/or musical goal, *and make sure the student understands what that goal is.* Often we blithely assume that a student will recognize the technical or musical goal of a piece and, frankly, this is rarely the case. Making goals clear to the student will obviously help them recognize how to systematically learn a piece and will help them appreciate the finer aspects of your teaching skills.

Also—do *not* assume that simply because a certain method or collection of studies is published, that it has been logically designed. Trust your own judgement and experience. Often our own understanding of the guitar surpasses that of many "famous" editors, who occasionally publish illogical, poorly-arranged and *horribly* fingered editions. *Use your own judgement!*

◇ *Bars*

Developing bar chords should not be introduced too early, since bars are contrary to a basic premise of left hand technique, *i.e.* keeping the left hand fingers on the tips. There are a number of works by 19th-Century composers which use an F Major chord, with ① and ② barred on the first fret (for notes F and C respectively) which can be a good introduction to bar chords.

Also, teach bar chords progressively! For example, begin by barring two strings (such as in an F chord), then three strings (such as a D chord in second position, barring the A on ③ and the F♯ on ①) and so on.

Always stress that barring is essentially the same thing as using the fingers separately; it is *not* a matter of "clamping" the fingers tightly, but a matter of *accurate finger placement directly behind the fret.* Once a student understands the basic concept of barring, it will usually happen on it's own within a few weeks.

◇ *Vibrato*

Before teaching any type of vibrato, make sure that the student's left hand position is stable. Using vibrato—even for some advanced students—can cause left hand finger inaccuracy, because of the rocking motion that occurs. Also, in spite of the frequent use of vibrato in modern performance, remind the student that through the Renaissance, vibrato was considered an ornament. Even today, vibrato could be used more selectively than it is.

There are three basic types of vibrato: *arm vibrato, wrist vibrato* and *finger vibrato.* In reality, most players use these in combination with each other, but we will study each one as a separate technique. These different types of vibrato should be taught in the order below and obviously practiced with each finger.

Arm Vibrato

There are three easy steps in teaching a good Arm Vibrato:

1. Have the student play the following passage, striking only the first note, and slurring all the other notes by using a glissando (with the same left hand finger). Make certain that the passage is rhythmically even, and that the motion includes moving the entire arm—not just the hand at the wrist.

Fig. 1.   Preparatory Glissando for
          Developing Arm Vibrato.

gliss.   etc.

It is usually best to use this specific note on ③, because this string at the seventh fret is very flaccid, making a vibrato more audible and easier to execute.

2. Next, have the student make the same movement, but let the finger slide only *within* the seventh fret. Make sure that the arm still moves along with the hand. The finger will still slide on the string, as will the thumb behind the neck.

3. Finally, have the student hold the left hand finger and thumb still, but move the hand and arm back and forth (in exactly the same motion, as in steps 1 and 2), but *without* permitting the finger (or thumb) to slide. At this stage he will have a perfectly controlled vibrato.

In the beginning, the arm movement will often be too wide, so be sure and watch for an overemphasis of this movement, but otherwise the steps above provide a simple, yet highly effective approach to teaching the arm vibrato.

Wrist Vibrato

The Wrist Vibrato should be reserved for more advanced students since it throws the left hand slightly out of position. In practice, it is usually reserved for faster passages, since this type of vibrato can be executed more quickly than the Arm Vibrato and the vibrato itself can be faster.

In teaching the Wrist Vibrato, have the student practice steps 2 and 3 above, but keeping the arm still. The *hand* will "rock" back and forth slightly at the wrist, up and down the length of the neck. This is similar to the vibrato commonly used by violinists.

Finger Vibrato

The Finger Vibrato is more common in electric guitar technique than classical. However, on occasion—particularly at the end of slow phrases with sustained notes, when a slow, wide vibrato is desired—this can be *very* effective.

In this, the finger actually pulls and pushes the string across the neck (*parallel* with the fret). To teach Finger Vibrato, have the student play a slow chromatic exercise, "bending" each note as he goes. Be sure to watch that the first joint of the vibrating finger does not collapse, which is a common problem.

Final Observations on Vibrato

With all three forms of vibrato, the result should be a controlled, even sound. For this reason, it is wise to have the student practice the vibrato very rhythmically—such as in a strict 16th note pattern, with a metronome. This will avoid a "frantic" sounding vibrato, which can result if the student uncontrollably "shakes" the note.

At first, the vibrato should be restricted to one or two notes per piece. This will avoid problems such as altering the hand position or fouling finger placement. More advanced students should watch that vibrato is used carefully in fast scales and fast position shifts! In these cases, missed notes are often because a student is beginning the vibrato too soon (before landing securely on the first note after a shift) which causes the shift to be unstable.

◊ *Developing Speed*
Right Hand Speed Development

The most common question that arises with intermediate students, is how to develop speed in playing. The simple answer is not to work toward *speed*, but toward *complete finger independence and control*.

To illustrate this to a student, have him play one note as fast as possible with the same right hand finger (*not* alternating). Explain that, theoretically, whatever speed he can play with one finger, he *should* be able to double that speed by alternating two fingers—*if* the fingers are working independently of one another. Only rarely will a student be able to do this, and you will have gently made your point.

As we have already found, right hand finger independence is best developed through arpeggios, however, in addition to this, scales, chromatic exercises and sections from pieces are helpful.

Break Speed in Speed Development

With a metronome, have the student play through a scale or exercise, and after each comfortable playing, move the metronome up one notch. Start slowly, and at some point, the student will hit a tempo that suddenly feels very insecure. This is much the same as a break in the voice of an untrained singer, moving from the chest voice to falsetto. The break will vary from player to player, but it is *always* there and until it is overcome, it is painfully obvious.

The solution to this "break speed" is to move the metronome down (one notch *below* the break) and work with *that* speed. When it feels comfortable, move one notch *above* the break. *The trick is to work* **around** *the break.*

There are two schools of thought concerning what happens when this break is overcome. The first states that by working around the break, it can be totally erased—*it will no longer exist.*

The second states, perhaps more logically, that the break will always exist, but by practicing around it, a player can smooth the break point to where *it will be unnoticeable.* This is exactly the same as a singer learning to move undetected from a chest voice to a falsetto.

The problem with teaching the second theory is the implication that—as the tempo increases—the player will go slightly "out of control" (at the break speed), and this is *not* what is intended. Instead, it is a sort of "technical overdrive" that a player carefully shifts in to. Above all, it is rigidly controlled.

Additional Aids in Developing Right Hand Speed

One of the most beneficial exercises for developing speed in the right hand is to practice scales staccato. For example, play the left hand pattern, 1, 2, 3, 4, on the same string, on consecutive frets (as in Exercise Number 1 from "The Basic Seven Exercises"). Alternate with the right hand, but play each note very staccato by sounding the string and *immediately* replant the next right hand finger on the string, *but do not immediately play.* Then at the same time that the left hand plants the next finger, sound the string and again replant the next right hand finger to stop the sound. This insures that the right hand fingers are staying ahead of the left. A step-by-step diagram is given below.

Fig. 2.   Diagram of Staccato Right Hand Exercise for Developing Speed.

Left Hand	Right Hand
touch the string	touch the string
pulse	pulse (sound the string)
keep fingers down	*immediately* replant the next finger that will play
repeat (from "pulse")	repeat (from "pulse")

Left Hand Speed Development

Normally there is less problem with left hand speed, though again, if the problem arises, it is usually an indication of an independence problem rather than one of actual speed development. Nonetheless, the following exercise is very effective.

Using the same or a similar left hand pattern as in Exercise Number 1 of the "Basic Seven Exercises," have the student practice the following sequence.

Fig. 3.   Diagram of Left Hand Staccato Exercise for Developing Speed.

Left Hand	Right Hand
touch the string	touch the string
pulse *(immediately release)*	pulse (sound the string, but do *not* immediately re-plant the next finger)
repeat (from "touch")	repeat (from "touch")

Remember to keep the left hand finger on the string after the pulse; simply release the pressure so that the tension of the string will *immediately* push the finger off of the fingerboard. The sound will be similar to the right hand staccato, but in this case, the staccato will result from the left hand finger instantaneously releasing pressure from the string.

If necessary, this exercise may be practiced without using the right hand. However, more often than not, right and left hand coordination is actually a greater problem than simply left hand speed development.

Another highly effective exercise for left hand speed development is the slurring exercise (Number 7 of "The Basic Seven Exercises"). Although this is rare, if the teacher determines that strength and speed *are* actually the problem, the student should practice this exercise, giving more force to the *ascending* slur. This will cause a more defined left hand finger movement, resulting in more control which, in-turn, will help develop greater speed.

◊ *Accuracy in Fast Passages*

A number of suggestions for increasing right and left hand accuracy are listed in Appendix I, "Trouble-Shooting Checklist for Teachers." However I want to briefly mention a few of the most important, yet neglected practice techniques for working on fast passages.

Naturally small sections should always be isolated and practiced slowly outside of pieces—particularly in difficult passages—but beyond this, students should be taught to "target" notes. This consists of beginning the passage, and stopping on each separate note. Practicing this way will insure that each note, and each movement *to* each note is stable.

For example, Figure 4 shows the complete passage, while Figure 5 shows several versions of how the passage might be practiced, "targeting" each note in the given passage.

Fig. 4.   Original Passage.

Fig. 5. Targeting Each Note in the Passage.

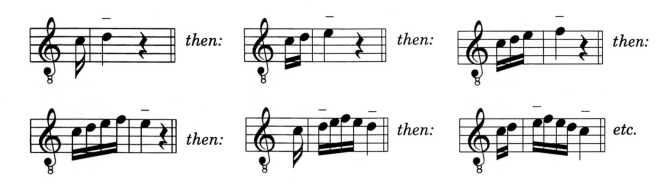

Often a passage sounds unstable because one or more notes are insecure. Practicing in this manner insures that the movement of each shift, and fingering (of both hands) is secure because each is isolated, thus exposing any potential problems.

This method of targeting notes has an additional advantage because each version (as the student gradually adds one note at a time to the practiced passage) results in a different series of accents, by virtue of the natural rhythmic grouping of each version (note marcato markings in Figure 5).

Unstable passages often sound that way because of one simple problem: one or more notes are being "skimmed" over, and thus, do not match the color, dynamics, phrasing or articulation of the surrounding notes. This is nearly always because of one of the following factors:

      1) inaccurate right and left hand coordination,
      2) an unstable shift from one position to another,
      3) incorrect finger placement of either hand.

Targeting notes as in Figure 5, will expose any actual or potential problems in passages, and will easily remedy unstable notes with minimal practice.

I will readily admit that this type of practicing is tedious and *highly* technical. However, in defense of this type of "intensive" practicing to avoid "wrong notes," I would like to mention a concept that I stress in virtually every masterclass I've ever given:

Invariably in a masterclass someone makes a mistake as they are playing. When I ask what happened, the response is virtually always the same: "....I played a wrong note." "But how is that truly possible?", I ask, "the guitar has all the notes *already there*—even the one that *should* have been played was already there..."

My point is (admittedly somewhat existential...), there *are* no wrong notes on the guitar. When a note is played that shouldn't have been played, it's not a matter of a "wrong note," but a wrong finger or hand movement that *resulted* in that note.

Yes, I suppose objectively we can play "wrong notes" on the guitar, but they are—at the core—a *result* of wrong finger or hand movements. When these incorrect movements are isolated and corrected, the "wrong notes" simply don't occur.

As teachers, we walk a thin line between training musicianship and technical precision. Teaching our students to recognize which one needs more attention than another in a given situation is a tremendous challenge. However, when precision *is* the goal, this type of intense practicing can be highly beneficial.

◇ *Tremolo*

Developing a good tremolo is no different than any other right hand technique, though it is one which often concerns students. As with any specific technical problem, if it is isolated from the piece and practiced separately, the results are more satisfactory.

The first thing a student must understand is that a tremolo should not, ideally, sound like separate notes. It should be a smooth, virtually continuous sound—almost a "hum." However, because of the physical movement, an uneven rhythm may occur.

The easiest way to develop a smooth tremolo, is to practice the pattern (*p, a, m, i*) *all on one string*. This can be done while playing a chromatic scale (which will also help with right and left hand coordination).

Practicing this way will keep the fingers from planting on the string too soon, which is the main cause of a tremolo sounding uneven.

Fig. 6.   Chromatic Exercise for Developing Tremolo.

Another useful exercise, is to play a left hand pattern that does not fit into the four notes of the right hand tremolo pattern, shown in Figure 7.

Fig. 7.   Exercise for Developing Tremolo.

p a mi   p a mi   p a mi   sim.   etc. until beat one is
                                         again "c," then repeat
                                         scale on each half step

Practicing tremolo as in Figure 7 has many advantages. First, each finger is alternately accented, because the left hand pattern fits into a metric grouping of three, while the right hand pattern is in four (*cf.* accents). This can help prevent one finger from inadvertently sounding louder than the others when the tremolo is performed, which is a common problem. Another advantage to this type of exercise is that it trains the right hand fingers to act more independently, and will ultimately result in a smoother tremolo.

Obviously the triplet pattern may also be practiced with three notes per triplet as in Figure 8.

Fig. 8.   Exercise for Developing Tremolo.

p a m i p a m i p a m i   sim.

This approach has the same advantages as we have often discussed: *i.e.* an even fingering *(p, i, m, a)* against an uneven series of notes *(triplets)*, which alternately accents each finger *(N.B.* accents).

Although rare, in cases where the right hand fingers are not playing soon enough, it is important to have the student practice the above exercises very staccato (on the top melody line only). In short, planting the next finger that will play sooner, but waiting a moment before sounding the string.

In cases where the student is planting on the string too soon (but *playing* too late), the student should practice the above exercises very legato. Again, this is the most common problem, and results in the tremolo sounding very "choppy."

Tremolo is an important technique, not only because of the amount of popular literature requiring this technique, but because it is a *marvelous* right hand exercise for finger independence and for right and left hand finger coordination.

- Find a series of beginner's pieces that use bars:
    - a) across two strings,
    - b) across three strings,
    - c) across four strings,
    - d) across five strings,
    - e) and across six strings.

Try and find pieces that are progressively more difficult, since this is how the situation would arise "in real life" in the studio.

- In a mock lesson, teach the three different vibrato techniques.

- Rhythmically alter a passage from a beginner's piece. Explain to a "student" why you did it that way and how it will help him fix a technical problem.

- In a mock lesson, teach the tremolo technique.

CHAPTER ELEVEN
ADDITIONAL SUBJECTS FOR
ADVANCED STUDENTS

There are obviously hundreds of subjects that you will need to address with more advanced students. Realistically, some of these techniques are so rare that they apply only to a few pieces and by the time a student is this far along, he will probably already be familiar with most of these techniques.

However, the items below appear with some frequency in advanced literature, and you should learn to recognize them and be familiar with teaching them. Naturally, this chapter barely scratches the surface of the various advanced techniques found in our concert literature. Those given below are listed alphabetically, since there is no specific order in which they must be taught. These techniques should be taught in the context of pieces.

◇ *Advanced Bar Techniques*

There are several types of bars used in advanced literature that are very different from a normal bar. While these are fairly rare, when they are needed, there is usually no other fingering that will work, and—although these techniques can be difficult to master—they can simplify an otherwise terribly complicated fingering.

A Hinge Bar is exactly what the name implies. The first finger (of the left hand) acts like a hinge of a door as it opens or closes. Rather than barring all the strings at once, the lower part of the first finger (the part nearest the hand) plays the first note. Although the first finger is stretched out in a barring position, the rest of the first finger *does not touch the strings* (which allows the lower strings to be played open). Then, usually on the very next note, the rest of the first finger plays the bar as normal—usually while the first note is still being sustained.

This movement can also be reversed so that a bass note is sustained, then a melody note is played. Theoretically, this movement can be reversed for either the melody or bass (either sustaining *or* releasing a note), so practically speaking, there are actually four different ways to use a Hinge Bar which are shown in the following figures:

1) Sustaining a melody, then next playing a bass with the Hinge Bar,
2) Sustaining a bass, then next playing a melody with the Hinge Bar,
3) Sustaining a melody, then releasing a bass with the Hinge Bar,

and,

4) Sustaining a bass, then releasing a melody with the Hinge Bar.

Fig. 1. A. Diabelli, "Andante cantabile," from *Sonata in C, Op. 29, No. 1.*[1] Sustaining a Melody, Then Playing a Bass with the Hinge Bar.

In this figure, the C in the melody (measure 2, beat 1) (barred on I) must be sustained, while the E grace note in the bass is "hinged" in a slur to the F in the bass.

---

1. Anton Diabelli, "Andante cantabile," *Sonata in C Major, Op. 29* (Vienna: n.d.), *The Complete Sonatas of Sor Giuliani and Diabelli,* ed. Anthony Glise (St. Joseph/Vienna: Aevia Publishing, 1997). Used by permission.

Fig. 2.   M. Giuliani, "Allegro spiritoso," from *Sonata in C Major,*
             Op. 15.[2] Sustaining a Bass, Then Playing a Melody with the
             Hinge Bar.

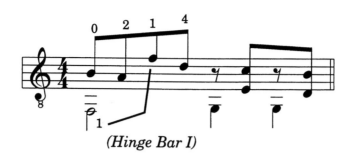

(Hinge Bar I)

In the previous figure, using a Hinge Bar permits the player to
sustain the F in the bass (while playing the B in the melody open), and
then (1 beat later) the bar is "hinged" to play the F in the melody while
still sustaining the bass note.

Fig. 3.   M. Giuliani, "Andante," No. 5 from *The Complete Bagatelles,*
             Op. 73.[3] Sustaining a Melody, Then Playing a Bass with the
             Hinge Bar *and* Sustaining a Bass, Then, Playing a Melody
             with the Hinge Bar.

(Hinge Bar III)

(Hinge Bar II)

The previous example is extremely rare, since two consecutive
measures use a different type of Hinge Bar. In the first measure, using
the Hinge Bar permits the player to play the last D of measure 1 with a
Hinge Bar and then (on beat one of measure 2), play the barred G chord.

2. Mauro Giuliani, "Allegro spiritoso," *Sonata in C Major, Op. 15* (Vienna: Richault, *ca.* 1828), *The Complete Sonatas of Sor Giuliani and Diabelli*, ed. Anthony Glise (St. Joseph/Vienna: Aevia Publishing, 1997). Used by permission.

3. Mauro Giuliani, "Andante," *Bagatelle, Op. 73* (Vienna: Pietro Merchetti, *ca.* 1819), ed. Anthony Glise, Anthony Glise Critical Editions, *Mauro Giuliani, The Complete Bagatelles, Op. 73* (Cincinnati: Willis Music Co., 1989). Used by permission.

This is a good example of using a Hinge Bar to help with the phrasing. Since the D is actually an anacrusis to the following G chord, the correct phrasing is more evident to the listener, because there is no break in the sound between the D and the following chord. There would be a break in sound if the D were played with a separate finger, then "jumped" to the bar chord. Using a Hinge Bar solves this phrasing problem.

Avoiding a jump in the left hand fingers (across strings) is one of the most practical reasons to use a Hinge Bar and, as in this case, can help solve an interrelated problem between fingering and phrasing.

In the second measure, using a Hinge Bar permits the player to sustain the bass notes (F♯, A) while the next note in the melody (C♯) is played using a Hinge Bar. This is a tremendous piece for students, since Hinge Bars are rare to begin with, and to have two back-to-back is virtually unheard of.

Figure 6 shows another common usage of a Hinge Bar: sustaining a melody note while releasing a bass note. This type of Hinge Bar is often found in 19th-Century literature.

Fig. 4.   A. Diabelli, "Finale," from *Sonata in F Major, Op. 29, No. 3.* [4]
Sustaining a Melody, Then Releasing a Bass with the
Hinge Bar.

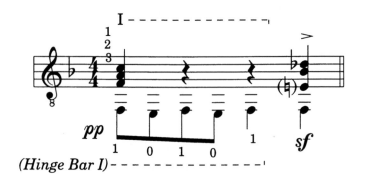

In this figure, the F chord (on beat one) is usually sustained [in spite of the written rest], but the player must play the bass line F, E, F, E, *etc.* Here, the bar is "hinged" (at the fingertip) so that it is possible to play this bass line while at the same time sustain all the upper notes in the F chord.

---

4. Anton Diabelli, "Finale," *Sonata in F Major, Op. 29, No. 3* (Vienna: *n.d.*), *The Complete Sonatas of Sor Giuliani and Diabelli,* ed. Anthony Glise (St. Joseph/Vienna: Aevia Publishing, 1997). Used by permission.

Fig. 5.   A. Glise "Dryaden" from *Traum Szenen, Op. 9, A.* [5]
Sustaining a Bass, Then Releasing a Melody Note Using a
Hinge Bar.

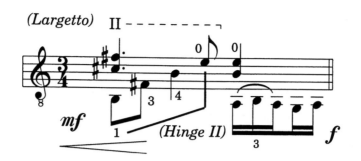

In this figure, because all the bass notes should sustain while the open E is being played (on beat 1.5), the guitarist plays the full bar, then simply holds the upper part of the bar (that part nearest the fingertip) which allows the bass notes to sustain. He then (on beat 1.5), lifts the lower end of the bar to play the open E, while still sustaining the bass notes, B, F♯ and B.

The reason a player usually opts to use a Hinge Bar is to simplify an otherwise very complicated fingering, or to achieve a specific phrasing. Naturally there are other ways to circumvent some of the fingering problems presented above, but often a Hinge Bar is the easiest and most logical solution to a problematic fingering.

The Hinge Bar is a fairly rare technique, and should obviously be reserved for more advanced students and literature that truly requires this solution. However, if you truly need it, virtually nothing will take the place of a Hinge Bar.

Split Bar

A Split Bar is a *very* advanced and rare technique—even more rare than the Hinge Bar. Using this technique, the lower part of the first finger (the part nearest the hand) plays on one fret, while the upper part of the first finger (at the fingertip) plays on another fret. Usually the lower part of 1 plays the lower fret, while the upper part of 1 plays the next highest fret. Obviously, this is used only one fret to the next.

---

5. Anthony Glise, "Dryaden," ("Tree Spirits") from *Traum Szenen (Dream Scenes), Op. 9, A* (St. Joseph/Vienna: Aevia Publications, 1994). Used by permission.

In theory, it is possible for the frets to be reversed (the fingertip playing a lower fret, while the lower part of the finger plays the upper fret), though I have never seen an instance where this is truly an advantage. Nonetheless, particularly with some contemporary music which can make such extreme demands on the player, this could be an option.

Fig. 6.　S.L. Weiss, "Allegro," from *Prelude, Fugue & Allegro.* [6]
　　　　A Split Bar Between Frets VIII and VII.

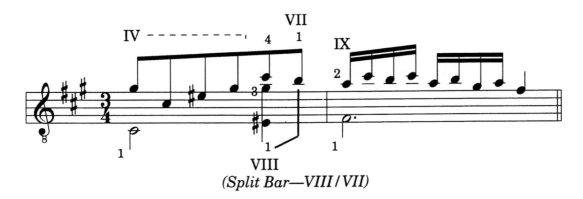

(Split Bar—VIII / VII)

In this instance, the E♯ (on fret VIII) in the bass and the following B in the melody (on fret VII), are both played with a Split Bar which avoids "jumping" fingers across the strings. *Both notes are played with the same first finger bar.* Especially at this tempo *(allegro)*, this is virtually the only solution to an otherwise very difficult fingering.

As I said before, using these specialized bar techniques should be reserved for advanced students, and should be applied directly to literature rather than simply learned theoretically. However, when such a technique is necessary, it is often the *only* logical solution to an otherwise *ghastly* fingering.

◇ *Appagado*

We are all familiar with the appagado effect (*étouffé* in French), where the hand leans on the strings at the bridge to create a dampened *pizzicato* sound. In pieces, make sure that the student leans only the lower side of the hand (the fatty part of the hand below the little finger) on the strings.

---

6. S.L. Weiss, "Allegro," from *Prelude, Fugue and Allegro* (Kassel, *ca.* 1719 [?]), ed. Anthony Glise, Anthony Glise Critical Editions (Cincinnati: Willis Music Co., 1992). Used by permission.

It is also crucial that the hand be placed at the saddle of the bridge so the hand covers all the strings evenly, otherwise some strings will sound more dampened or more resonant than the others and the appagado will sound "unbalanced."

In teaching the appagado, have the student first play a diatonic or chromatic scale, all appagado—not only with *p* (which is normally how appagado is played)—but also alternating. Alternation with appagado is fairly rare, but occasionally necessary because an appagado line may move quickly across several strings which makes it impractical to play only with *p*.

Once the student has found the sound he wants (the combination between dampened and resonant), have him practice the shift *to* the appagado position—*but play only the first note of the appagado.* Shifting into the appagado playing position is usually the only real difficulty in the context of literature. Next have him practice the entire section—slightly before the appagado, through that section, then slightly further into the normal right hand position. The important thing is to practice moving *in and out of the appagado playing position.*

The appagado appears in literature such as the B section of *Asturias* by Isaac Albéniz, the *Sonatina* by Torroba, and a great deal of other Spanish and contemporary literature.

◇ *Arpeggiating Chords*

In classical guitar, virtually anytime that we have a chord, we have the option of playing it arpeggiated. This is a beautiful effect, but it is precisely that: *an effect.* Remind students that if a piece has too many arpeggiated chords, it can sound overly-romantic, or in German, *"schmaltzig"* ("greasy").

Still, arpeggiating chords is something all guitarists do and teaching this effect can be divided into three basic stages.

1) Have the student play a block chord "straight," *i.e.* with no arpeggiation.
2) Next, have him play the chord as if it were written as a notated arpeggio *i.e.* each note as a sixteenth.
3) Next, have him play all the notes in the chord as grace notes *except the last note of the arpeggio.*

The exercise below is helpful because, played exactly in tempo, it allows the student to feel the rhythmic placement of an arpeggiated chord. Naturally this exercise can be adapted to use a simple chord progression, such as a C major followed by G₇, as in the Giuliani *120 Right Hand Studies.*

Fig. 7.   Exercise for Teaching Arpeggiated Chords. [7]

The most important question in arpeggiation with more advanced students is where to place the beat in the arpeggio. Often students will assume that the *first* note of the arpeggio is on the beat. With very rare exception, *this is wrong!* The *last* note of the arpeggio should be heard exactly on the beat, which means the arpeggio itself must begin slightly before the beat (*cf.* Figure 7, grace notes).

If the last note is not played on the beat, the tempo will have to be altered in order to fit all the other notes in, *or,* the next beat (after the arpeggiated chord) will have to come in early to make up for the timing difference (which makes the music sound disjunct and out of time).

In chamber music this placement is especially important because each player is listening for each beat, and playing *directly* on the beat. The *last* note of the guitarist's arpeggio must be placed exactly on the beat or the rhythmic precision between the instruments is destroyed.

Virtually anytime you are coaching an ensemble with guitar, if there are problems in keeping the group together (particularly at the end of a phrase, when guitarists often arpeggiate a chord) check to see where the guitarist is placing the last beat of the arpeggiated chord. It's often—*very often*—the guitarist who is making the problem.

---

7. Anthony Glise, *Classical Guitar Method for Adults* (St. Joseph/Vienna: Aevia Publications, 1998). Used by permission.

This is a technique used almost exclusively in Baroque literature at the end of a phrase when a full chord is being played (often across all six strings). It is similar to the same technique used by Baroque harpsichordists at the end of some phrases. In performance practice of the Baroque period, they often arpeggiated a cadential chord back and forth a few times *ad libitum.*

Fig. 8.   S.L. Weiss, *Chaconne No. 3 in E.* Cadential Chord (written). [8]

Fig. 9.   Cadential Chord (possible interpretation).

Note that the arpeggiated chord is not measured (*i.e.* does not stay in a meter), and normally there is a gradual ritard through the arpeggio. Some guitarists also prefer to play the last note of a descending Cadential Arpeggio with *p,* which is at the discretion of the player.

Execution of the Cadential Arpeggio is simple: the last finger of the arpeggio (at the top note), is simply pulled across all the strings—backwards—to the last note in the bass. Be sure that student moves *the*

8. S.L. Weiss, "Chaconne No. 3 in E Major" from *The Complete Chaconne of S.L. Weiss* (Kassel? *ca.* 1720), ed. Anthony Glise, (St. Joseph/Vienna: Aevia Publications, 1997). Used by permission.

entire arm toward the bass note. Do not keep the hand in position! The entire arm must move the set hand position toward the bass note so that the angle of the nail is the same for each string. This will insure that the timbre stays the same for each note throughout the arpeggiation.

This technique is found in some contemporary literature, but again, it is most common in music from the Baroque Period (particularly German and French) as a cadential ornament. As a result, the use of this technique is entirely at the discretion of the player, but it should be used sparingly, since it is such a distinctive sound.

◊ *Harmonics*
Natural Harmonics

When teaching harmonics, stress to the student that the left hand will simply touch the string directly *above* the fret (not behind it, as when playing a normal note), and to release the left hand fairly quickly to allow the string to vibrate.

There are hundreds of pieces in the repertoire (even some for beginners) that use natural harmonics at XIIth, VIIth, and Vth positions. Other pieces use the harmonics at IX, IV and III, *etc.*, though these are more advanced, and include *Prelude IV* (Villa-Lobos) *Grande Sonate Eroica* (Giuliani), *Sonata No. 4 in C Major*, "Allegro non troppo" (Sor), the *Complete Bagatelles, Op. 43, No. 3* (Sor), *etc.*

With harmonics that are "unstable," (*i.e.* any of those which are not on frets XII, VII and V) it can help to play the harmonic a bit more *ponticello.* This will set the string in motion more forcefully (because the string is more taunt at the bridge) and produces a clearer pitch.

Notation of harmonics, as we all know, is a nightmare. We have never found a notational system for harmonics that pleases everyone, and the debate continues: should an editor write the actual pitch or write where the left hand finger plays, or write where the left hand finger plays and above the note write the actual pitch that will be produced?

Because we still haven't come to a mutual consensus on these questions, you will simply have to explain each situation to your students in the context of specific pieces.

Although artificial harmonics are more difficult to execute, the notation is much clearer because it is nearly always a melody (written in the actual notes that the left hand plays), and the composer or editor simply writes *"artificial harmonics"* above the notes (often using the traditional diamond-head notes).

In teaching artificial harmonics, have the student first play the section (playing the notes normally) then later add the right hand (playing the notes as harmonics twelve frets above the left hand notes).

If the notes in the left hand are secure, the student can simply watch where the right hand is and will easily find the correct placement.

Because the melody in harmonics is usually above a bass line (which is played normally), the harmonics are touched with *i* and plucked with *a*. This leaves *p* free to play the bass, and *m* free to play any middle voices.

Occasionally we find artificial harmonics in the bass. In this case the sound is usually more "solid" if *p* is used to sound the string while using *i* to touch the harmonic node. This leaves *a* and *m* free to play any additional voices.

Standard repertoire with artificial harmonics includes *Valses Poéticos*, "Melódico" (E. Granados), *El Testament d'Amelia (arr.* Llobet), as well as numerous other Spanish folk songs arranged by Llobet.

◊ *Left Hand Split Trills*

This is more a stylistic choice than a technical one, but I know several professionals who use this type of trill. The trill itself is played normally, but the left hand fingering alternates between two fingers on the upper note.

Fig. 10. Left Hand Split Trill (execution).

In theory, a Left Hand Split Trill has the advantage of allowing the player to articulate the trill more quickly. However, realistically, a trill is such a basic left hand movement for an advanced player that it rarely justifies such an extreme solution.

Another specialized trill is the *Cross-String Trill*. This involves playing the two notes on separate strings. The problem with this is that *both* of the notes will sustain which destroys the crisp articulation that we normally want in a trill.

Because of this distinctive articulation, a Cross-String Trill is inappropriate in the "historically correct" interpretation of most periods. However in some literature, at the discretion of the player (such as in pieces which have the "harp effect," like the Mudarra *Fantasia in A*), the Cross-String Trill can be a fun effect that complements the inherent nature of the piece—but it is *very* much only an effect, and in actual use is not terribly practical.

◇ *Playing With The Flesh*

Occasionally a darker—almost *pizzicato* sound—is desired, but not as extreme as a true appagado. If the nails are filed evenly and fairly short, it is possible to tilt the hand back (similar to the right hand position used in the Closed Hand School for rest stroke), but in this case, play free stroke so that *only* the flesh of the right hand fingers sounds the strings.

Sounding the string with only the flesh of the right hand fingers produces a dark timbre that is similar to an appagado sound, but much more resonant. However, because of the extreme alteration of the right hand position, this technique is usually only used in slow pieces or in situations when the right hand will stay in this position through a fairly long section.

Playing with the flesh is similar to the other techniques of timbre changes *(ponticello, tasto, etc.)* and can be taught or used in virtually any piece at the discretion of the player.

◇ *Rest Stroke Melodies in Arpeggios*

This appears to be an invention of the 20th-Century. I have never found any mention of this technique in any of the hundreds of 18th or 19th-Century guitar manuals that exist, though it is used by virtually all guitarists today.

In this, the right hand fingers play an arpeggio (free stroke, as normal), but the very top melody line is played using rest stroke. This can be a solution to the problem of making sure that a melody is audible (and depending on the school of right hand technique) the melody line will often have a slightly different timbre, which also helps the listener identify the melody.

Stress to the student that he *should* be able to bring out these various lines without needing to use this technique. However, this is a common 20th-Century technique and should be learned as soon as it is applicable in the literature.

Usually (as in Figure 11), the melody is played with *a*, though this is not always the case. Often *p* is played rest stroke in a free arpeggio, as well as any other finger (such as *m* or *i)* to bring out a middle voice, accent, *etc.* In Figure 11, the marcato markings show which notes are played with a rest stroke.

Fig. 11. F. Sor, "Study in B Minor," *Op. 35, No. 2.* [9]
Arpeggio with Melody Played Rest Stroke.

etc.

◇ *Right Hand Cross Alternation*

In very fast scales, errors can occur if the right hand fingering is not "clean" as we discussed in Chapter Five ("Right Hand Fingering"). This happens because, with a continued alternation (*i.e.: i, m, i, m)*, an uncomfortable string crossing may occur automatically. A common solution is to find a place where one right hand finger can be repeated when crossing to a lower string.

In the example below, the string crossing occurs at the asterisk. However, because the next note is on a lower string, repeating the same finger (*m),* then continuing the alternation solves the problem.

---

9. Fernando Sor, "Study in B minor," Op. 35, No. 2 from *The Complete Sor Studies*, ed. David Grimes (Pacific: Mel Bay Publications, 1994). Used by permission.

Fig. 12. J.S. Bach, *Chaconne in D Minor.* [10]
Right Hand Cross Alternation.

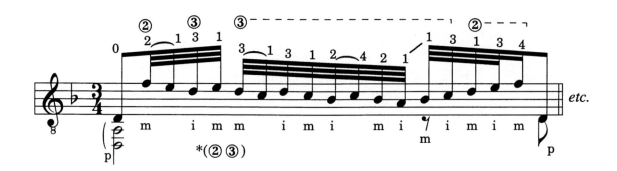

Particularly when scales are played rest stroke (as is common with fast scales), the Right Hand Cross Alternation offers a simple solution, because the finger (just having played) is already resting on the lower string.

Another solution to uncomfortable string crossings is to slur two notes in the scale, as in Figure 13. Sometimes this is inappropriate, or will alter the phrasing, but this can be another solution to right hand string crossing problems.

Fig. 13. J.S. Bach, *Chaconne in D Minor.* [11]
Slurring to Avoid a Right Hand Cross Fingering.

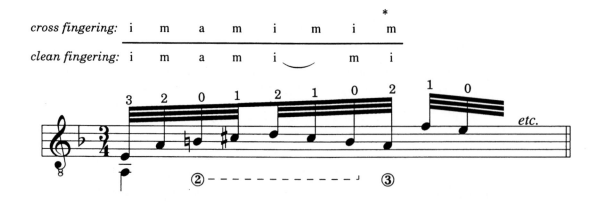

10. J.S. Bach, *Chaconne in D Minor*, BWV 1004, (St. Joseph/Vienna: Aevia Publications, 1997). Used by permission.

11. Bach, *Ibid.* Used by permission.

Note the upper right hand fingering has an uncomfortable string crossing at the asterisk since *m* has to reach backwards to play the A on ③. In the fingering below the staff, this is corrected by inserting a slur, which keeps the alternation consistent *(i.e.: i, m, i, m, etc.)*. A cross-fingering, especially at such a fast tempo, should be avoided if at all possible.

◊ *Right Hand String Crossing With P*

In some pieces, a right hand arpeggio lies much better if *p* is used in a middle voice, as well as in the bass. This can avoid having an uncomfortable repetition of one of the fingers in the middle voice of an arpeggio. This is one of the most common uses of a Right Hand String Crossing With *P*. It can also help place "weighted" beats, since *p* normally produces a stronger sound.

Both instances are found in the following example by Mertz. Here, *p* is used in the bass line *and* the middle of the arpeggio to avoid using *i* for consecutive notes on ③ *(N.B.* bracketed areas). Using a Right Hand String Crossing with *P* also helps the player bring out the "weighted" beat. In this case, where *p* crosses to play a middle voice, that voice is on a downbeat. At such a fast tempo, this helps the listener recognize the rhythmic drive of the inner voice.

Fig. 14. J.K. Mertz, *Tarentelle.* [12] String Crossing with *P*.

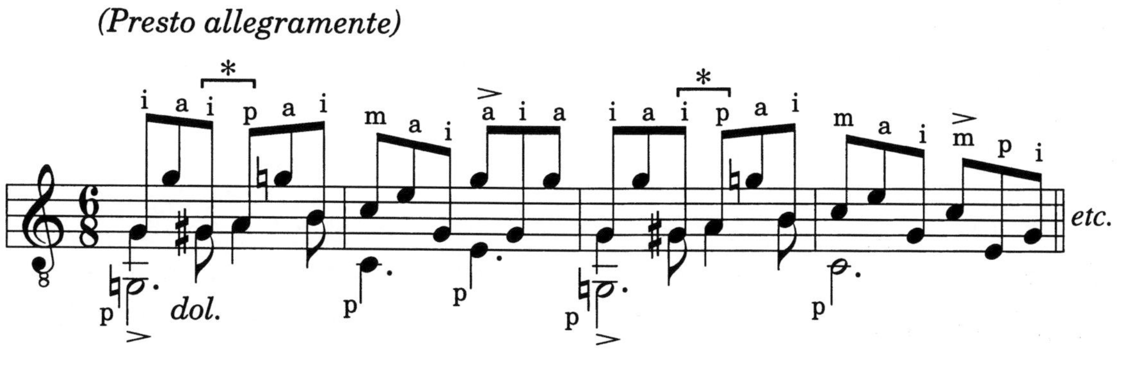

As with many of the techniques in this chapter, if a student is playing such advanced-level literature, he may already have strong opinions about solutions to problems such as this. However, in many instances, the Right Hand String Crossing With *P* can be a tremendous solution.

---

12. Johann Kasper Mertz, *Tarentelle* from *Bardenklänge* (Vienna, *ca.* 1847) facsimile ed. Simon Wynberg in *The Guitar Works of J.K. Mertz*, vol. III (Heidelberg: Chanterelle Verlag, 1983). Used by permission.

◇ *Subito Piano Slurs*

This is a technique used exclusively when the second note of a slur is to be played *subito piano*. Rather than making the slur "plucked," as a normal slur, the slurring finger is lifted *directly away from the fingerboard*—i.e. it does not pluck the string.

Fig. 15. S.L. Weiss. Capriccio in D Minor.[13]
      Subito Piano Slur (*N.B.* asterisk at slur).

As with many of the techniques in this chapter, the use of the Subito Piano Slur is an interpretive decision and its use is at the sole discretion of the player. Still, this is a subtle yet beautiful effect that creates a gentle "hush," or *morendo* in the line. It should be used sparingly and it can be totally useless in a large concert hall because the second note of the slur is very quiet. However in smaller halls and in recording, this is a *tremendous* dramatic effect.

◇ *Tamboura*

The tamboura effect is when the left hand holds a chord, and the entire right hand thumb actually hits the strings briskly to sound the chord. The result is a percussive effect, but the listener still hears distinct pitches.

If the player wants to hear more of a percussive sound, the right hand should bounce more slowly off the strings after the hit, *or*, hit the strings more *tasto*, which will dampen the pitches even more. If the player want to hear more of the pitches, the right hand thumb should bounce quickly away from the strings to let them resonate, *or*, hit the strings more *ponticello*.

---

13. S.L. Weiss, *Capriccio* (Kassel [?] *ca.* 1719 [?]), ed. A. Glise, Anthony Glise Critical Editions (Cincinnati: Willis Music Co., 1991). Used by permission.

If there is a specific note that the player wants to hear over the tamboura sound, it is possible to let the nail of *p* hit that string while the flesh of the thumb hits the remainder of the strings. The nail hitting the strings will bring out a distinct pitch in the melody, while still giving the dampened tamboura sound on the other strings.

The tamboura effect is found in many contemporary and Spanish pieces, such as the *Grande Jota* (Francisco Tárrega).

◊ *Timbre Changes Using Opposition*
and Complementary Movement with the Wrist or Arm

As with many instruments (such as violin, piano, *etc.*) players often use movement in the arm or wrist to alter the attack or color of a note. This effect is normally used on guitar only by extremely advanced players.

Because this is specifically related to the way we change timbre on the guitar (*i.e.* using the traditional shifting of the hand position toward the bridge or fingerboard for *ponticello* or *tasto*), we will discuss this special technique in Chapter Seventeen—*Physical Control Over the Sound* ("Timbre").

Keep in mind that using Opposition or Complementary Movement is an *extremely* advanced technique that should be taught and used only by very advanced players, since it drastically alters the right hand position. Nonetheless, this produces some *marvelous* colors that we rarely hear on the instrument.

◊ *Conclusion*

This brief section covers some of the more common special effects and techniques that will be used by your advanced students. There are obviously *many* other effects but they are so rare that they do not warrant attention for the general classical guitar student.

Keep in mind, these effects should always be taught in the context of the repertoire, thus it may be necessary for you to seek out various pieces that use these effects.

◇ *Suggested Assignments:*

  • Each student in the pedagogy class should find a piece with one of the aforementioned advanced techniques, and in a mock lesson, teach it to another student. Note that many of these effects are found at the student level in the *Method* by Matteo Carcassi. [14]

---

14. If you opt to use the Carcassi Method with your students, please check the edition carefully! Unfortunately, there are numerous editions of this work that are not only embarrassingly unfaithful to the original, but many of these bastardized editions indiscriminately add incorrect and damaging pedagogical concepts. The best approach is to get an urtext edition of the Carcassi, compare it with modern editions and (for the sake of readability) use that selected modern edition with your students.

CHAPTER TWELVE
PERFORMING

> *"The tone of the text should preferably be expressed in your eyes. Your hair and mouth can help you at this, as well as your neck and chin as you raise or bow your head...*
>
> *"Thus you move and play your instrument in the spirit that the music demands."*
>
> Sylvestro Ganassi (1542) [1]

There are so many facets to performing that to attempt an all-inclusive series of essays in this book would be impossible. Performing is as much an *attitude* as it is an *activity*, and something that must be experienced over and over to learn. This is especially true because each of us reacts differently on stage, and there is no absolute "correct," or "incorrect" stage presence.

Still, there are common traits that we all share on stage, and many of these *can* be taught. Frankly, a good performance by one of your students is the best advertisement that you can have. It says that you are successful as a teacher and coach. It says that you know how to get the most out of your students. That kind of teacher is rare—rare enough that you can easily expand that reputation into a solid teaching career.

---

1. Sylvestro Ganassi, *Regala Rubertini* (Venice, 1542-43), ed. Hildemarie Peter, trans. Daphne and Steven Silvester (Berlin: Robert Lienau, 1977), 9.

Stage Presence is a subject that is often ignored. In fact, there are virtually no articles on stage presence in any major music dictionary and it is seldom discussed in lessons.

The reason for this neglect seems to lie in the fact that stage presence is not purely a musical subject; it has nothing to do with the sound or the music, yet stage presence involves a great deal more than simply "existing" on stage. It is a critical element in communicating with an audience and for that reason it *must* be taught as part of a student's formal training.

The current ignorance of stage presence seems to have grown, not from our musical-performance heritage, but from our digital-recording mindset. Since most of us listen to recordings far more often than we go to live concerts, we habitually use only one of our senses (hearing) when we listen to music. As a result, stage presence (which is almost exclusively visual) has become a terribly neglected subject, and only until we consider the importance of stage presence will the effects of this inexcusable neglect become apparent.

In a study on verbal and non-verbal communication we find the following information:

Fig. 1. Statistics on Verbal/Non-Verbal Communication. [2]

Form of Communication results in:	*percentage of perceived message.*
communication through words:	7%
communication through vocal intonation & inflection:	38%
communication through facial expression & posture:	55%

---

2. Albert Mehrabian, Cited in *The Denver Post*, August, 25, 1970. *et al.*

Some 40 years earlier, the great violinist Carl Flesch made a fascinating parallel between communicating with words and communicating with music: *"The difference between the interpreter of word and of tone, lies, fundamentally, only in the materials which he has to shape, the concrete word or the abstract tone."* [3]

Assuming Flesch's statement to be valid, we can, with some certainty, apply Mehrabian's three categories to performance as in Figure 2.

Fig. 2.   Statistics applied to Performance.

Form of Communication results in:	*percentage of perceived message.*
aural music:	7%
musical interpretation:	38%
stage presence:	55%

Even if we accept these figures as only partially applicable to performance, we find that non-aural communication on stage is a prominent factor. Another study goes so far as to theorize that: *"...judgements from visual cues are more accurate than judgements from vocal [i.e. audible] cues."* [4]

Again, Maestro Flesch says basically the same thing: *"The first impression which a personality makes on us is essentially influenced by its externals as well as by the tone of voice. The moment a violinist appears on the concert stage, his appearance alone gives the public an impression of his human and artistic being."* [5]

A similar observation was made by Igor Stravinsky, who stated: *"One sees music. An experienced eye follows and judges, sometimes unconsciously, the performer's least gesture."* [6]

---

3. Carl Flesch, *The Art of Violin Playing, Vol. II* (New York: Carl Fischer, 1930), 70.

4. K.L. Burns and E.G. Geiter, "Significance of Vocal and Visual Channels in the Decoding of Emotional Meaning," *The Journal of Communications*, vol. 23 (1973), 118-2.

5. Flesch; *loc. cit.*

6. Igor Stravinsky, *Poetics of Music* (New York: Vintage Books, 1956), 51.

In short, our aural senses are not the only ones tantalized (or in some cases, abused) during a live performance. We truly do "see" music. In recognizing this critical fact, we are left with two problems: *what* to communicate, and *how* to do it.

What to Communicate
Music—7%

This question is easily answered once we define the rôle of the performer—a subject that branches directly into the study of æsthetics. This will be discussed further in the section "The Middle Man," in Book III, but in short, Plato gives us the best answer: we are to "interpret the interpreters," or for our purposes: *to communicate to the audience that which we feel the composer intended.*

How to Communicate—Interpretation and Stage Presence
Interpretation—38%

Again, this will be discussed further in Book III, but a simple answer of how to communicate to the audience is that we must understand the historical and theoretical basis of the piece *and* be technically capable of including those elements in our performance. This does not simply mean didactically hitting all the notes, but also applying an individual sense of interpretation.

Stage Presence—55%

How a performer communicates beyond the music and subsequent interpretation is done *via* stage presence. In the opening quote by Ganassi, we find this can be done with physical movements "...in the spirit which the music demands." Similar references abound, such as that by Friedrich Wilhelm Marpurg: *"I know a great composer* [C.P.E. Bach?] *on whose face one can see depicted everything that his music expresses as he plays at the keyboard."* [7]

The above description is an example of a positive stage presence: a player so drawn into the performance, that he conveys a deep sense of personal interaction with the music. Through this, an audience is caught up in the involvement and has little choice but to become equally involved.

---

7. Friedrich Wilhelm Marpurg, *Der Critischer Musicus an der Spree* (Berlin, 9 September, 1749), quoted in C.P.E. Bach, *Essay on the True Art of Playing Keyboard Instruments* (Berlin, 1759), ed. trans. William J. Mitchell (New York: Norton, 1949), 152.

This is most easily conveyed, as we have seen, by physical movements of the body, which complement the musical events in the piece. This suggestion, however, must be tempered with a warning by C.P.E. Bach who says, *"Ugly grimaces are, of course, inappropriate and harmful; but fitting expressions help the listener to understand our meaning."* [8]

I seriously doubt that there are any of us who have not seen a perfectly acceptable recital enter the realm of the macabre from the player's transmission of terror to the audience. If a performer's *negative* mindset can be transmitted to the audience, it is logical to assume that a *positive* mindset, or "presence," will also be transmitted. This brings us to a vital element neglected in the above statistics: *the attitude of the performer.*

If we acknowledge the deep, even spiritual quality of music, then our motives and attitudes are intrinsic to stage presence, since it is from these that our stage presence will emerge. As the great Russian actor, Konstantin Stanislavsky noted, *"You may play well or you may play badly; the important thing is that you should play truly."* [9]

Without this communication in performance, audiences will drift slowly away from the concert hall, choosing the equally lifeless (though infinitely more convenient) performances of the recording industry.

I do not mean to sound opposed to the recording industry. It certainly has its place, but it is *not* the same place as that of a live performance. A recording should be considered a documentation of one performance at a given moment. Sadly, it has become (*via* editing, *etc.*) an example of absolute perfection; a marvelous perfection, not necessarily contrary to a live performance, but a perfection by which, erroneously, live performances are judged!

In concert, the most exciting performances are those where the player—often with a split-second decision—will try a new phrasing, articulation or dynamic, which can alter the entire interpretation of a piece. This instantaneous risk can be extremely dangerous, but—if the player is willing to take that chance—it can result in *tremendous* performances. This is due, in part, to the fact that as his metabolism is sped up (from performance stress, adrenaline, *etc.*), a performer is often more sensitive to ideas that had not occurred to him before. Having the

---

8. Bach; *loc. cit.*

9. Konstantin Stanislavsky, *An Actor Prepares*, trans. Elizabeth Reynolds Hapgood (New York: Theatre Arts, 1939), 14.

courage to trust and act on those fleeting bursts of enlightenment on stage is something which only the finest players consistently achieve.

In recording, one *rarely* takes this sort of risk. It's not that recording is devoid of exciting playing, but usually by the time you sit down in front of the microphone, you have gone over the literature thousands of times, made virtually every musical and technical decision, and previewed these decisions with your producer (who, in turn, has made decisions as to possible edit spots, *etc.*). The goal in this situation is 100% consistency. An exacting consistency that, on stage, can result in sterile, boring performances.

While flawless, pristine recordings have raised our expectations of a live performance to an artificial level, worse yet, it has nearly obliterated the element that we normally seek from live concerts: *a spontaneous magic,* which any discerning ear will testify, is nearly impossible to capture in the studio.

Additionally, recordings cannot convey the *attitude* of a performer and it is from this attitude that stage presence will emerge. In short, there are two extreme ends of the spectrum when it comes to a performer's attitude.

The first, and most common attitude is found under the banner of "Knock 'em Dead!" It is a performance more suitably billed as a boxing match than a recital. Unfortunately, a number of guitarists take this attitude; those recitals are little more than a display of technical gymnastics.

While there is nothing wrong with a few pieces chosen to show technical prowess, a current and rather tiresome mode has emerged whereby entire guitar recitals consist of nothing more than "encores." This type of programming, as Flesch states, "*...allows the auditor no time for reflection, it simply carries him away... His art is more calculated to impress the masses than to move the individual.*" [10]

The opposite idea is the passive "Pied Piper" approach—a type of "charm-them-into-Nirvana" approach. While this is perhaps more conducive to a high sense of art, it can produce a weak—even shy—stage presence. In short, both attitudes can be helpful and both can be harmful. It is up to you to see that your students maintain a proper stage presence with regard to "*...the spirit which the music demands.*"

---

10. Flesch; *op. cit.,* 70.

-138-

As a teacher you must help students to develop their own sense of stage presence; to be able to tastefully move with the music, and to build an attitude that is balanced between grotesquely overt and embarrassingly timid. Have them practice with each other—perhaps even writing brief—and tactful—"reviews." *But work with them!* They are not likely to learn this from anyone but you.

In closing, it is interesting to note that the passive and active attitudes from which stage presence will emerge, are similar to the crook and staff held by the ancient Egyptian Pharaohs. The idea was, if Pharaoh could not gently shepherd his flock with the crook, he would beat them into reverent submission with the staff!

Every performer must decide what proportion of either attitude is best to produce the most effective stage presence. However, we would be wise to remember the problems Pharaoh encountered from his constant use of the staff.

◊ *Suggested Assignments:*

   • Each student play through a short piece as if in a recital (complete with entrances, bowing, *etc.*) and the others write a brief and tactful "review" of the performance. Concentrate on elements of stage presence.

   • The entire pedagogy class should go to a professional concert together (not a student recital) and write a brief review of that performer's stage presence. Discuss these reviews and also compare these with any reviews that may appear in the newspaper.

   • With regard to this professional recital, write another section (after your "review") discussing how your perception of the music was affected (positively or negatively) by the performer's stage presence.

CHAPTER THIRTEEN
ON STAGE

"The applause! Delight! The wonder of our stage!" [1]
Ben Jonson (1573-1637)

◇ *Stage Etiquette*

Realistically, the ultimate goal for most students is to perform. While only a handful of your students will probably ever aspire to an actual performing career, *all* should have the experience of performing now and then, at least in a semi-formal setting.

This may include playing in a studio class, church service or other similar functions. Students should be encouraged to perform as often as possible, since this gives a specific deadline to work toward in preparing pieces. As a result, proper stage etiquette is a vital element of pedagogy, and *must* be addressed in the lessons.

A majority of our modern stage etiquette is descended from social etiquette as it developed through the 18th and 19th-Centuries. While some of these "rules" may seem overly pompous, they are still recog-

---

1. Ben Jonson "To the Memory of My Beloved, the Author, Mr. William Shakespeare" *Seventeenth Century Verse and Prose* (New York: MacMillan, 1971), p. 163.

nized as valid among professional concert presenters, performers and the educated audience. In general, there are two types of performances: *Formal* and *Informal.*

Formal Performances (After Dinner) [2]
Women's Dress

Normally, a long evening gown is worn. A black gown is traditional, although this is less observed in recent times. For a concerto performance, a neutral color is best. This will distinguish the soloist from the background of orchestral players who are normally dressed in black.

Sleeveless dresses are generally avoided for several reasons. First, the player's arm is apt to stick to the guitar, which is uncomfortable and makes shifting the arm (when moving to play *ponticello* or *tasto*) more difficult. Secondly, as one perspires (which we *all* do from performance stress), there is nothing to catch the perspiration, which can be as distracting for the audience as it is for the player.

Also, take some care with the cut of the dress! Women performers can obviously encounter "problems" with a low-cut dress as they make their final bow. Naturally, avoid any jewelry that might rattle on the guitar while playing.

It has become more common for women to wear dress slacks in formal performances. This can be a good solution to the combined problem of a dress and a footstool. With the vast array of women's styles, slacks do not necessarily detract from the formality of the performance or the femininity of the player.

Shoes should *always* be flats. Even for the most experienced, high-heels are worn so infrequently today that they can be treacherous when a performer is "under the influence" of adrenaline. High-heels also *greatly* complicate navigating a footstool and will totally alter the sitting position.

---

2. At the risk of over-stating the obvious, make sure that your students give a dress rehearsal, *wearing the exact clothes that they will be wearing in the performance.* The slick material of a tuxedo, the different feel of dress shoes, *etc.,* can be terribly disorienting, and a full dress rehearsal can alleviate these very avoidable problems.

A dinner tuxedo (named for the Tuxedo Club in New York in the early 1900's) or tails (originally named because of their resemblance to a swallow's tail) are traditional. Tails are used almost exclusively for concerto performances, though either is acceptable for solo recitals and chamber performances.

A bow tie or cravat (a type of 19th-Century scarf) is standard with either type of tuxedo. If a bow tie is worn, the student should discreetly check through the performance to make sure that it is straight. As a guitarist leans on the instrument, the tie is often pushed sideways which looks, at best, ridiculous.

Although seldom observed in the last 75 years, originally, if women were present, a white tie or cravat was worn. If exclusively men were present, such as in the case of a gentlemen's dinner (a rarity in modern society) a black tie was worn. More recently, a white tie was required in any circumstances with tails, and a black *or* white tie with a dinner tux.

In modern times, virtually all these rules are ignored and any color is acceptable for either tux or tails—but use some judgement—a purple and orange paisley bow tie might be acceptable at a high school prom, but on the concert stage see that students maintain at least some level of common sense and dignity.

A vest or cummerbund is appropriate, but never at the same time. Remember that a cummerbund should be tight enough to stay in place, but loose enough that it doesn't cramp the player's insides. Anyone who has ever worn a cummerbund which is too tight will confirm that the literal German translation of "Kummerbund" ("grief band") can be quite accurate!

Shoes are always black for a formal performance, and remember to make sure that socks are long enough to cover the player's leg when the foot is on the footstool.

With regards to perspiring on stage, I, and a number of performers I know, have acquired the habit of wearing a tight (but comfortable) short-sleeve T-shirt under the tuxedo shirt. This will trap the perspiration and more importantly keep the perspiration from dripping down the side of the player which can be terribly distracting in performance.

For women who have a similar problem with perspiration. A man's T-shirt may be appropriate, depending on the cut of the dress. If not, there are "pads" used in theatre that fit comfortably in the underarm of a dress.

Finally, remember to be careful of tie tacks and tuxedo shirt studs! They make nasty gouges in the back of a guitar!

Informal Performances (Before Dinner)
Women's Dress

A calf-length skirt of a neutral color is acceptable, but remember that your foot will be raised on a footstool, so for obvious reasons, be careful of dress length. Problematically, a long dress for an informal performance may look "over done," but a shorter, more casual skirt (particularly with the footstool) can be problematic, depending on the sitting position of the player. Again, dress slacks are becoming more and more common, and while less traditional, seem to be preferred by most professional women players who I know.

Men's Dress

Either a dinner tuxedo or suit and a four-in-hand tie is expected. Traditionally, brown shoes are worn before dinner, but black shoes are always worn after dinner and with a tuxedo. Remind the student that if a suit is worn, the belt color should match the shoe color.

General Comments on Concert Dress

In general, try to dress one step (more formally) above that which the average audience member will wear. For example, in a student recital if the audience wears jeans, wear a suit. If the average audience member wears a suit, the performer should wear a dinner tuxedo. If they wear a tuxedo, the performer should wear tails. The same is true for women's dress; always dress one step above the audience.

Also, while this is a fine point, check the material from which the concert dress is made. While silk or man-made fibers can look marvelous, they tend to not "breathe," and under stage lights, can turn the performer into a lump of sweating flesh. Also, watch the cut of the garment. It should be tight enough to look tailored (whether or not it is), but loose enough for the player to move freely.

Remember, how a player looks, is how the audience will expect him to play. If he looks good, they will expect the same from the performance—and *vice-versa*.

On and Off Stage

In professional concerts, there is usually someone called a "spotter" backstage to tell the performer when to go on. Whether or not this is the case, when cued, the player should walk on stage at a normal pace while watching the chair, turn to the audience, smile, bow, sit, take a moment to concentrate, and begin.

Remember that the moment a player walks on stage, he tells the audience a great deal about himself. His gait, manners and confidence—or lack thereof—will be conveyed immediately, so be sure to work with students on how they carry themselves as they make an entrance or exit.

In many cases "buying" a few lessons with a professional dancer or actor can help students better understand how to simply walk gracefully on and off the stage. This is especially important for us as guitarists, since we must carry the instrument with us, which we rarely do in "real life." In any case, I would strongly encourage such lessons to any student who is serious about making a career on stage.

After each piece, stand, smile (perhaps say "thank you" or something similar while nodding to the audience) bow, nod a few more times, turn, and (while watching the exit) walk off stage.

Keeping a firm gaze on either the chair (during an entrance) or the exit (when leaving the stage), will give a confident sense of direction which is a major part of the overall communication with an audience.

Encores

When backstage, count to five, slowly, return to the stage, bow, announce the encore, sit and begin. If no encore is planned, the player should leave the instrument backstage, return to center stage, bow and exit. Leaving the instrument backstage is a subtle way for the performer to tell the audience that he is truly finished.

As a general rule, if the performer can count to ten and the audience is still applauding, either play another encore or at least return to stage to acknowledge the applause.

In short the student must always remember: *bow and smile*. Stress that this is the player's acknowledgment of thanks to the audience; an acknowledgment that the audience expects and appreciates.

Between pieces, the guitarist should stand and bow. This is the traditional courteous response (for *all* soloists) to applause—plus it gives the performer a chance to surreptitiously stretch.

Talking from the Stage

It has become more common for recitalists to talk to the audience between pieces. Assuming you are in a country where you speak the language, this can be very effective and will personalize the performer to the audience. Performers should have a fairly well-planned "speech"— *and keep it brief!*

This type of presentation may include the composer's biographical data, a bit about the style or historical information about the piece, *etc.* In any case, it should be kept short and the performer **MUST TALK LOUDLY!**

It should be added that managers tend to disapprove of performers talking on stage. This is partially because they are afraid that a performer may accidently say something offensive or "stupid." The other reason is because it is difficult to speak on stage immediately after playing.

When a player is totally focused on a performance, the right side of the brain is "switched on." Speaking is a function that operates predominantly from the left side of the brain. Frankly, it is difficult to quickly "switch gears" from performing to speaking, because of the different spheres of the brain that dominate these two different activities. However, I personally enjoy speaking from the stage—and my managers have yet to figure out a way to stop me!

After the Performance

This is difficult to tactfully convey to a student, but after a performance, he should be prepared for some unprofessional and absurdly inane questions from admirers. While this can be frustrating, the student must remember: an audience member came backstage to talk as a friendly gesture. Behind those innocent gaffs, is a sincere interest in the music and the player. The performer has an obligation to present himself in a professional and honorable manner. A performer must *always* show the utmost courtesy and respect.

The best way to instill this unassuming manner in a student (beyond your own example) is to remind him of one simple fact: the audience is there to listen to the *music*, played by the *performer—in that order!* **The music comes first.** If at *any* time a player feels it's the other way around, he is headed for some egotistical problems that have destroyed many careers and alienated audiences.

We are *far* beyond the days when audiences, managers or even fellow musicians would tolerate the childish outbursts of "the artist," and simply accept such behavior as "eccentric." Admittedly, on stage, we are under more stress than most people *ever* experience. However, a performer simply has to learn how to cope with that pressure—and coping with it does *not* include having temper tantrums or acting like a spoiled, egotistical moron. As a teacher you have a responsibility to see that your students maintain a balanced ego. If a musician cannot control that one simple aspect of his personality, he is in the wrong business.

◇ *Stage Fright*

When anyone is nervous, the blood draws from the extremities (hands, feet, *etc.*) to the center of the body. This is part of the "fight or flight" mechanism instilled in us by nature. This trait was an important survival element for our ancestors as they were trying to outrun lions and tigers and bears (*"oh my..."*). It meant that, if caught—with the blood drawn into the center of the body—the chances of bleeding to death from a wound to the extremities was lessened.

For better or worse, we still have this physical reaction when we are nervous. What this means for us as performers, is that the blood draws to the center of the body and the hands get cold before a concert. This is especially true since backstages are usually cold to begin with. Remember to tell the student to keep the fingers warm, (mittens or gloves are not a bad idea) and keep the fingers moving.

Everyone gets nervous before they play. As a student becomes more familiar with this feeling, he will usually grow to enjoy the feeling of excitement and intense focus. Ironically, once a performer is accustomed to the excitement of performing, if he goes for a period of time without climbing on stage, he may actually go into a mild state of depression. In short, at first performing is very disturbing, but once it becomes more routine, there is nothing on earth that will substitute for that feeling!

The best remedy for stage fright is simply being well-prepared. From there, one can maintain a stoic attitude that, since everything was carefully prepared, there is every reason to believe that the performance will go smoothly—and quite frankly, it nearly always does.

If at all possible, it is best to *mentally* overcome stage fright. Below are a few examples of auto-suggestion which, when repeated over and over in the player's mind, can lessen the fears sometimes associated with performing.

1. *The moment I walk on stage, I am in control.*
2. *I know the works being performed better than anyone in the audience—because it is me who is playing.*
3. *The audience is here because they want to be here—they are on my side.*
4. *I am performing because I **enjoy** performing.*

There are several minimally-disruptive solutions for performers who *truly* need help overcoming severe stage fright. I recommend these with *great* reservation because of the potential dependence on such solutions. Still, these can help some players who would otherwise avoid performing:

Carl Flesch recommended a small glass of wine a half an hour before a performance for players with extreme stage fright. Late 20th-Century solutions include doctor-prescribed "Beta-blockers" (*ca.* 5-20 *mg.*). Beta-blockers are a medicine commonly used for high blood pressure and migraine headaches. Numerous clinical studies have been conducted on musicians and other performing artists, and have established the effectiveness of Beta-blockers in treating stage fright.[3]

Acupuncture has also proven *highly* effective. If the player can locate an acupuncturist, the points used most often for stage fright are: *Chung-wan* (0022-5184), *Tsu-san-li* (6398-0005-6849) and *Yin-t'ang* (0603-1016). This approach is much more frequent in Europe, though many chiropractors in the U.S. are also trained in acupuncture.

---

3. *Cf.* Daroff, Robert, Frishman, Lederman and Stewart, "Beta-Blockers: Beyond Cardiology," *Patient Care,* vol. 27/11 (June, 15, 1993). *N.B.* This is a brilliant article written for doctors. If your personal physician is hesitant to prescribe Beta-blockers, and/or unaware of the current usage of this medication for performing artists, I *highly* recommend that you give him a copy of this writing.

As bizarre as this sounds, recent studies have established that the natural potassium in bananas can alleviate situational stress. The effective amount varies from person to person. Generally, one to three bananas are eaten an hour or two before the concert, but each performer must experiment to find the correct "dosage." [4]

Naturally this is not advised for singers, as the bananas can cause excess phlegm. Also note that (at least for myself, not being a fan of bananas), simply having the taste of bananas in your mouth through a performance may be distracting. Still, this is another solution to stage nerves which is preferred by several concert artists I know.

A similar approach is to take a calcium and magnesium tablet several hours before the performance. While this approach has not yet been studied, the effects would presumably be the same as the bananas, without the taste.

Needless to say, no medicinal solution to stage fright should ever be self-administered, and while these solutions may be helpful in severe cases of stage fright, they all have a major drawback, since they slightly lessen the "intensity of the moment."

Often this intensity—the "nervousness"—is what gives a player the "edge" or heightened awareness in a performance. When that feeling is diminished by any means, the performer is losing one of his most valuable assets on stage.

Remind your students that, ultimately, we perform because we enjoy it and are good at it. If you can stress this single aspect to your students, they will begin to live up to that positive expectation, and truly begin to savor the feeling of being on stage.

Pre-Performance Routine

One of the things that will help a student become more comfortable with performing is developing a pre-performance routine. This is a highly regimented series of activities that the player can go through on the day of the concert. This will provide a sense of security because it is a familiar routine.

---

4. *Cf.* Toddi Gutner, "High Anxiety," *Forbes Magazine*, vol. 148/7 (Sept., 1991), pp. 166-68.

It is, however, absolutely essential that these activities can be done in any unfamiliar town, or country, otherwise, if the routine is broken the sense of security is lost.

Below is a rough schedule which I keep the day of a performance:

1. Get up.
2. Shower.
3. Eat a light breakfast.
4. Practice:
    a. technical exercises,
    b. play the first few measures of the first piece I will be performing, then play the last few measures, [5]
    c. go to the next piece and repeat "b" above with each piece,
    d. at the end of the "abridged program" bow, *etc.*, as if it were the actual performance.
5. Eat a light lunch.

For the rest of the day I read, walk, eat, sleep, go to a movie—anything I want. At performance time:

1. Shower and dress.
2. Arrive backstage about 45 minutes before curtain time to warm up, check lighting, *etc.*
3. Perform.

While this type of routine might seem overly strict, it is one of the most important things that a performer can do to feel at home in a strange city or country, and to help instill a sense of calmness on the day of a performance.

◇ *Media*

It has become more common for students to secure media appearances. This is especially true since nearly all local stations (radio and TV) often have "open forum" talk shows, and program directors are usually very amiable to featuring local talent, which obviously can be used to promote recitals.

---

5. I, as well as most performers I know, tend to avoid playing through entire pieces the day of a concert, because, once warmed up, the first run-through tends to be the best. It's obviously preferable to save that for the stage.

While there is no official routine for securing media appearances, in general, as soon as a recital is contracted, the student should call, or if possible, visit the station. Keep any meetings brief, and bring all the information they might need. This includes a press release, biography, press photos and a CD or at least a high-quality recording of the player (a cassette is acceptable, though a DAT or analog reel-to-reel is usually preferred by radio stations).

Television stations normally slate guests one or two months in advance; radio stations normally slate only a few weeks in advance, but plan far enough ahead that they have time to comfortably slate an appearance. Remember, they are doing the player a favor. The media is the single-most important ally in securing an audience. The publicity is vital, and the experience is priceless!

Because usually at least three-fourths of the airtime will be talking, it is a good idea to have a cue sheet prepared for the show host (this is in addition to the traditional press materials already mentioned above). A cue sheet will give the host specific questions to ask, and, more importantly, will avoid questions which are irrelevant, perhaps embarrassing, or on occasion, idiotic.

A cue sheet should be easy to read, and target the most critical information that a TV or radio host might need to consult at a glance. For players who have a name that is out of the ordinary, it is extremely important to give the phonetic spelling for pronunciation. Also, the type should be large enough to be easily read at a slight distance, since a cue sheet is often either laid on a table (several feet away from the host), or shot onto a "prompter" (a small screen off the set).

A major advantage to a cue sheet is that it can be photocopied, and the updated information simply filled in for each separate recital, which can save considerable time and effort in a touring situation.

The student should always have several pieces ready to play, and know *exactly* how long they last! This is not as important for radio, but for television it is absolutely essential, since TV airtime is so structured.

Insofar as dress, for radio, virtually anything goes. Radio hosts tend to be marvelously casual people, since only their voices go out to the public. This is one of the true joys of radio: *visual anonymity*. The host for one radio program I did a few years ago wore a swim suit. I wouldn't suggest quite such casual attire, but have the student dress comfortably. Dressing for television spots is more rigid:

1. Wear neutral or "gem" colors, since they show up more clearly on camera.

2. Do not wear hard patterns (such as plaids or checks), since these can create a dizzying optical illusion on older cameras.

Fig. 3.   Sample Cue Sheet for Radio/Television Appearances.

Aevia Publicity, Ltd.

MEDIA CUE SHEET
ANTHONY GLISE—Classical Guitarist
[Pronounced   gl'ice (like "ice")]

•CAREER: Background (formal training, etc.)

•ADDITIONAL ACTIVITIES:
     (publications, residencies, hobbies, etc.)

•RECORDINGS: (mention record label)

•PAST CONCERTS:

•AMUSING STORIES: (on stage, on tour, etc.)

•UP-COMING LOCAL CONCERT:
     Date:
     Time:
     Place:
     Entrance fee:
     Contact Phone#:

[Updated 1.1.97—© 1997 by Aevia Publicity, Ltd. Permission granted for reprint in whole or in part. Destroy previous listings.]

Press

Performers need reviews to get recitals, and need recitals to get reviews. This paradoxical "tourne en rond" is a true curse of the business. Thus, *anytime* a student has a recital, have him contact the local newspapers, music critics and even the smaller "underground" newspapers. These smaller papers are often very open to doing feature interviews which can help tremendously.

Frankly, radio and TV are more fun, but they are fleeting moments. A newspaper, on the other hand, will lay on someone's kitchen table all day. Normally, the press can actually do more good in publicizing a concert.

Also, be sure when visiting any media organization to have the student leave behind a press release and p.r. photo (B/W 8x10 glossy) for the recital. A sample release is given below, and should always include *"who, what, when, where, how much it costs and a contact phone number."*

Fig. 4. Sample Press Release.

Aevia Publicity, Ltd.

—FOR IMMEDIATE RELEASE—

• American-born classical guitarist Anthony Glise will give a solo guitar concert on *[date]* _____ at *[time]* _____, at *[location]* _____.

• Glise is a product of the New England Conservatory (Boston), and the Konservatorium der Stadt (Vienna) with additional study at Harvard, the University of Vienna, Université de Lille (France) and the Academy for the Study of 19th-Century Music (Italy) where he periodically teaches.

• The only American-born guitarist to win First Prize at the International Toscanini Competition (Italy), he has been awarded additional diplomas in France, Hungary and Italy. Glise frequently performs throughout Europe and the U.S. and records for Dorian Recordings in New York.

• A Pulitzer Prize Nominee for composition, his compositions have been premiered in the U.S., France, Italy, Hungary, Austria and Bulgaria.

• Glise currently lives and teaches part-time in the Black Forest region of Germany and the Flandres region of Northern France.

• The concert will feature works by Giuliani, Weiss, Brescianello, Pinkham and Diabelli as well as one of Glise's original compositions.

[END]

Date:
Time:
Place:
Entrance Fee:
Contact Phone:

[Updated 1.1.97—© 1997 by Aevia Publicity, Ltd. Permission granted for reprint in whole or in part. Destroy previous listings.]

A Final Note on Critics

You should explain to your students the following about critics. Not only because they need to understand this bizarre aspect of the business, but because it can save some severe "heartbreaks" if they happen to get a less-than-rave review.

There are two types of critics: those who "criticize," and those who "critique." Those who criticize are more concerned with expounding on their self-assumed knowledge; writing "cute," though often derogatory articles, often at the expense of minor problems which may occur in a performance.

Those who "critique," will objectively document a performance, giving details and perhaps even personal observances—which are valid, since they were also part of the audience. Unfortunately, this type of critic is all too rare. Not only because this requires a vast education and familiarity with the music, but it also requires an objectivity of which few people can boast.[6]

Remind students that:

1. Good, bad or indifferent, a review is still only *one person's opinion.*
2. If a critic doesn't like a performance, think about what might be done differently the next time.
3. If a critic loves a performance, don't take it too seriously.
4. Finally, reviews are a valuable source of information.
   a) Read them,
   b) put them in the scrap book for the grandchildren,
   c) *and forget them!*

---

6. An example of a *brilliant* critic is George Bernard Shaw. A collection of his complete reviews are published in the books below. I would highly recommend these writings as an example of what a good critic looks for in concert performances. Shaw, George, Bernard, *Shaw's Music* (three vols.), ed. Dan Laurence (London: The Bodley Head, 1981).

◊ *Suggested Assignments:*

- In a mock lesson, teach a student to walk on stage, bow, *etc.*

- Make a list of "auto-suggestion" phrases that you and your students might find "comforting" before going on stage and discuss them in class. Remember we *all* get nervous before performances—it's a normal part of the business, so be objective when listening to others' ideas.

- Write a press release and a media cue sheet for yourself and critique them in class together.

CHAPTER FOURTEEN
TEACHING CHILDREN

> *"Naught, yet enough had I when but a youth,*
> *Joy in illusion, yearning toward the truth."* [1]
> J. Wolfgang von Goethe
> (1749-1832)

For nearly all guitar majors just graduating from a university or conservatory, teaching will be the primary means of income. There are always cocktail parties, weddings, and occasional recitals where you can make extra money playing, but teaching is usually the main source of income for guitarists.

This may be privately (in the teacher's home), in a music store or sometimes, as part of the "extension" or "continuing education department" at a college. It's *extremely* rare for a graduating student to fall directly into a tenured post at a university or conservatory.

Because of this, a vast number of the students you get—especially at the beginning—will be children.

---

1. J. Wolfgang von Goethe, *Faust* "Prelude on the Stage," *Great Books of the Western World,* trans. Geo. Madison Priest (London: Encyclopædia Britannica, 1952), p. 5.

One word of warning: If you do not enjoy working with children, *do not take any as students.* The "damage" that can be done to a child with impatience, poor pedagogical practices, *etc.*, can totally destroy a child's innate love of music—not to mention the damage to your own teaching reputation.

On the other hand, children can be a *tremendous* thrill to teach! Every small bit of progress is a major leap for them. They are fascinated and excited with every aspect of the instrument, and often form strong emotional ties with the teacher.

Working with children can also help considerably if you start feeling "teacher burn-out." The excitement, blatant honesty and utter joy that a child experiences through music is contagious and I know several teachers who—after years of teaching in conservatories and universities—simply quit in order to work exclusively with children.

Teaching music—and especially guitar—to children is rapidly becoming one of the most open and profitable fields in the business. A number of conservatories in Europe have even founded degree programs that are designed specifically for teachers of children.

In short, there is a great need for guitar teachers who enjoy working with children, but if you *don't* enjoy working with children, *don't do it.*

Technical Aspects

Obviously the size of a child is an important consideration. There are numerous companies who build three-fourths, half and even quarter-sized guitars. Stress to the parents the importance of the correct size of instrument for the student.

Unfortunately, sometimes the parents will have already bought a guitar or have one that has been in the family. If they insist on using a larger guitar, have the student use a capo on the second or even fourth fret. [2]

A capo doesn't solve the problems of sitting and string spacing that may be too wide for smaller hands. There's simply no solution to

---

2. These frets are usually best because many guitars have markers or "dots" (at the frets 3, 5, 7, *etc.*) and placing the capo on II or IV will keep the dots in the same respective position.

these problems aside from buying another guitar. However, a capo will help with the left hand placement and position if a larger guitar is used.

Some guitar teachers, at the beginning of each semester, use the first lesson to meet with new students and parents at a music store to either help pick out the new guitar, or to at least show parents what to look for when they go shopping for an instrument. This can solve a host of problems at the beginning and help form a stronger bond between you and the parents.

If you are fortunate enough to assist in choosing the guitar, a general rule is, when the guitar is stood on the floor next to the student, the head of the guitar should be roughly as high as the child's waist or a little higher. Obviously the action of the instrument should be set so it plays easily. Medium or high gauge strings are best. Stress to the parents that a footstool and small chair (without arms) is *absolutely* necessary for practicing at home. [3]

"Classical" Guitar

Often parents—and children—will expect lessons in chords, and more popular styles of playing from the beginning. Stress that regardless of the style, the technique of playing is the same for *all* styles, and that the easiest and fastest way to develop a solid technique is by studying classical guitar.

In these cases, after the student has learned all the diatonic notes in the first position, the teacher may opt to continue with classical or change to folk style for chords, *etc.* In any case, after the second year or so (when the hand positions have totally stabilized), the student should be introduced to chords. This is important, not only for them to have fun playing songs, *etc.*, but it will also help develop the student's understanding of music theory.

Several teachers I know have arrangements with rock guitar teachers, and trade students back-and-forth. This can give you access to many students who would not normally study classical, but who do recognize the need for the technical precision that classical promotes.

---

3. A majority of teachers I know who take younger students have found that a higher string gauge is preferable with small guitars.

In spite of what one might think, if the action of the instrument is set fairly low, most smaller guitars (half-sized, or quarter-sized) tend to be play easier and sound better if they are strung with high gauge strings. If a smaller guitar is strung with light-gauge strings, the student will have a tendency to "pull" the strings because the strings are so loose. This naturally results in a poor right hand movement.

I would *strongly* suggest trying any of the following strings on the smaller guitars of your younger students: *LaBella, 2001, High Tension* or *LaBella, 2001, Extra High Tension* or *Savarez Yellow Label*.

This can also give you a good outlet for students who later want to study other styles that you may not want to teach.

Parents

Keep in mind that you must often gently educate the parents as well as the child! Because guitar is so popular, parents with some minimal background in guitar (which nowadays is virtually everyone) may have already decided what and how the child should learn to play. Deal with this tactfully! Remember, while their ideas may be totally off-base, parents are allies since they are the ones who make sure the child practices.

After a short time it's not uncommon for brothers and sisters—and even the parents—to become so interested in the guitar that they begin taking lessons as well.

Once a month invite parents to sit in on the lessons, ask questions, *etc.* This can help understanding tremendously, plus, for very young students it will give them a chance to "show off" in a slightly formal setting—similar to older students playing in studio class. This type of involvement is critical, and insures greater progress.

Recitals

All students should perform. Once or twice a year you should have a studio recital for all your students, and this includes the children. Beyond the obvious advantages of having a deadline to work toward, the chance to let the parents see progress, *etc.* Recitals also give the students a chance to meet each other, which can be a tremendous motivation.

The most important thing is to make sure the child plays a piece that is easy enough that there is virtually no chance of error. This can mean playing a one-line melody that lasts five seconds, but that's o.k. It is still performing, and the experience *must* be positive.

In preparing for a studio recital, have the student go through the entire "performance" every week for at least one month prior to the performance date. This includes practicing the entrance, bows, *etc.* It's not a bad idea to have him do it first thing when he comes in for a lesson. Granted the hands won't be warmed up, but that is precisely why this is good—it will familiarize him with the feeling of playing "cold"—a feeling that is very similar to what happens on stage when one is slightly nervous.

I've also found it enjoyable to have all the students write their own program notes. I've had several so young that they couldn't read, which meant reading them biographical information and letting them paraphrase it in their own words, but let *them* actually do it.

This accustoms the student (even the youngest) to doing "research," and at the very least makes for some outrageous program notes! For example, below are some program notes written by very young children from one of my studio recitals several years ago.

• *Torneo* by Gaspar Sanz. Sanz was from Spain. He played guitar and got real good and wrote a lot of stuff.

• *Au Claire de la Lune.* anon. This is a folk song from France. It's really pretty. It means in the moon light. We don't know who wrote it so you have to say that it's anonymous. That means we don't know who wrote it.

• *Minuett* by S. L. Weiss This is a really cool piece. It was a dance that people did when George Washington was alive. But he's dead. So is Weiss.

Special Suggestions for Children

1) Help the child design his own practice schedule. While the schedule should be "arranged" by the teacher, if the child helps design the schedule rather than simply being told, "do this..." he will almost always practice more.

In helping young students design their own practice schedule, I often suggest that they practice 30 minutes total per day, in two, 15 minute segments. At the end of each 15 minute segment, they are "assigned" to go have a cookie or some other "prize."

2) Have the child practice with a timer, such as a standard kitchen timer, but make sure that the timer is kept in another room, since the "ticking" can be a distraction. It can be a good idea to have them also set the timer to signal the end of the break (usually 5 minutes is enough). Otherwise they often "forget" to go back and finish the practice session.

3) Teach the child not the system. There are a number of good methods for children (*cf.* Appendix III "Suggested Methods, Studies and Pieces for Students") but these nearly always need to be adapted to each student. If a method moves too quickly, assign supplementary pieces until his technique "catches up" with the method, then continue. Although rare, if a method moves too slowly, feel free to jump ahead, but make sure the progress is logical.

4) Don't be afraid of going over the student's head! Make explanations very clear, but children will grasp things much more easily and profoundly than you might imagine.

5) Use group lessons. While this can be a little extra work for you, if you have several children of roughly the same age and level, once a month or so have them all meet for a "group lesson." This is similar to the studio classes you will give for older students. Simply having them play through the same piece—together—will help develop their sense of ensemble, plus the chance to meet other students is often highly motivating.

How you charge for these lessons varies. Some teachers actually use these group lessons as a once-a-month lesson (if you do this, be sure and explain this in your "contract" with the parents). Some teachers charge an extra fee while some use group lessons as a make-up lesson.

It's really up to the teacher, but again, I strongly encourage this type of lesson for the social interaction, sense of camaraderie and as a motivating factor with your younger students.

6) Finally, make it interesting! Don't just "teach." Tell stories, make it exciting, play games, talk about the composers, *etc.* If you can win the loyalty of the student, and at the same time make it fun, I guarantee, he will practice.

If you find yourself in the midst of working with a number of children, I would strongly suggest taking some additional classes on musical development for children. There are some tremendous pedagogical techniques and methods exclusively for children that, sadly, are never addressed at the university level.

Because teaching children is so specialized it often demands some extra training that is beyond the scope of this book. If this field seems interesting to you, seek out some extra training. It doesn't take much, but it can be a great help. Working with children can be *highly* gratifying for the teacher who has the ability—and courage—to tackle the job.

◇ *Suggested Assignments:*

• Each student find and critique one child's classical guitar method. Watch for cross-fingerings, the Fourth-Finger Approach and most importantly, see if you believe the method progresses logically.

• Find and/or make up one game for children that would help in teaching rhythm, note reading, *etc.* If you have trouble with this, talk to a music education major—they normally know of hundreds of such books.

• Find (or arrange yourself) some simple music for beginners that would be appropriate for use in an ensemble or group lesson with your younger students. Keep in mind this does not have to be actual "chamber music" with different parts—all the students *could* play the same part while you (or an older student) provide the accompaniment.

CHAPTER FIFTEEN
ARRANGING A PRIVATE STUDIO

> *"Men learn as they teach."* [1]
> Seneca (*ca.* 4 B.C.—65 A.D.)

There are a number of simple things that can make your life easier if you decide to set up your own private teaching studio. Many of these ideas are scattered throughout this book, but this is such an important subject that I wanted to use a separate chapter to address these ideas.

◇ *Contracts*

While this is nothing that you should consider "legally enforceable," a contract signed by your private students (or their parents) can help clarify a number of important items. Included in this agreement should be:

• *Payment of Lesson Fee.* Most free-lance teachers prefer to receive payment in advance at the beginning of each month. If this is done, be sure to keep an eye out for the months which have an extra week or weeks with holidays. Naturally, always give the student a dated receipt.

---

1. Seneca [Lucius Annæus], "Epistolæ" VII, viii, *Seneca—Letters from a Stoic [Epistulæ Morales ad Lucilium]*, trans. Robin Campbell (Harmondsworth: Penguin, 1969), p. 43.

- *Absentee Policy.* Normally if a student calls 24 hours in advance the lesson can be rescheduled. Otherwise the teacher should be under no obligation to make up the lesson, and the student forfeits the pre-paid lesson fee. If the teacher cancels a lesson, the lessons should be made up or the fee refunded.

It is often a good idea to set aside one day a week in which no lessons are scheduled and use this day to make up any lessons that have been missed. This is important if you are away for several weeks, such as on a concert tour. Otherwise you can exhaust yourself trying to "catch up" on missed lessons.

- *List Any Additional Required Items.* This may include the method book, footstool, an extra set of strings, a notebook in which to write assignments, *etc.*

- *Your Phone Number.* I admit this is dangerous, but unless you have an answering service or are teaching at a music store who can take messages for you, this is necessary. Now and then you may have a student call at 2:00 A.M. with questions, but this is rare.

◇ *Keep Good Records*

If you are teaching free-lance, there are two essential categories in bookkeeping : 1) *records of lessons,* and 2) *records of money.*

Lessons should be documented in some sort of "sign-in book." This is simply a folder which lists each day, and the student's name. When students come for lessons, the first thing you should do is have them sign-in under the proper date. This can help clarify matters if there is a question about the number of lessons given, *etc.* This can also help considerably insofar as keeping track of make-up lessons.

Money must always be documented! This is necessary, not only so that you can budget your income, but for tax purposes.

On the nasty subject of taxes, under current taxation laws, if you teach in a portion of your house, *that is used exclusively for teaching,* you may write-off a portion of the home upkeep from your taxes as a business expenditure (this includes a percentage of your rent, electricity and heating bills). In addition, any materials that you buy, which are directly used in your teaching (thus, are a necessary business expense) may also be written-off your income tax.

Keep in mind that tax laws in the U.S. change almost every year. I would strongly suggest that you find a good tax advisor. I can personally assure you, that the small fee that they charge can save you a great deal of money, and a *considerable* number of headaches.

Do *not* assume that because there are no formal records of your income, that the tax bureau will not find out about "outside income" (including playing "gigs," *etc.*). When you list "Musician" as your profession on income tax forms, this automatically signals the IRS (or in their terms, "flags" them) that you are a potential tax evader, and your odds of being audited dramatically increase.

Keep pristine records and if you are audited, you'll be fine. Otherwise, you could get hit with some hefty back-taxes, as well as penalties. Most tax advisors will accompany you to an audit (free of charge) if you are audited for a year in which they prepared your taxes. This is another reason I would *strongly* advise having a tax consultant.

◇ *Health Insurance*

While we are discussing one of the most unpleasant aspects of free-lance teaching—*i.e.* taxes—we should briefly discuss the other most unpleasant aspect of free-lance work: *i.e.* health insurance.

As opposed to most Western European countries (where everyone is covered by a health program from the moment they're born, to the moment they die), in the U.S., this is not the case.

Most health insurance programs are available only through association with an employer who pays a portion of the insurance premium for their employees. As a free-lance teacher/musician (under the current U.S. system), the bad news is, you're going to have to take care of this yourself.

There are, however many health programs available. Check with existing guitar foundations, the local musicians union (this can be a good reason for joining the local union, *etc.*). Many universities also offer health programs to their alumni who work free-lance.

Again, there are many programs that are affordable and *insurance is absolutely necessary!* With the current cost of health care in the U.S., an accident—even a minor one—could totally wipe out your savings, and leave you in a catastrophic financial situation.

Also, begin thinking about retirement savings. This may seem premature, but a *little* saved in a normal bank account or an IRA, can make a *tremendous* difference in financial security later—*assuming you begin saving early!* [2]

◊ *Teaching in a Music Store*

Teaching in a local music store can solve a number of problems. First, music stores often have people simply come in off the street looking for guitar teachers. While this can mean that you have an immediate flow of students, it can also mean that you may have to teach styles other than classical—or convince the student that he should start with classical. Each teacher must decide how he will deal with these situations.

However, teaching in a music store *also* means that you have basic secretarial service—they will often take your phone calls and relay messages to students. They keep your studio space clean, and the minimal "rent" that you pay for the studio space can (under the current law) be written off your taxes. That may not sound like much, but if you have 30 students a week, and pay $2 per lesson for studio space, that means a write-off of $60 per week—or, over a 9 month session—$2,100 per year. Small amounts add up, *so keep good records!*

For using their studio space, a music store usually charges a minimal fee—two or three dollars per hour. From their stand point, this is a good service, since the students who study in their store are more likely to buy from them. In short, it's a good compromise for both you and the store.

Obviously, let the music store know what method, music, strings, *etc.* you will be using with your students. This helps them turn a profit and is a great convenience to have these items immediately on-hand.

In Europe there is an unwritten agreement between an established teacher and a music store. Anytime a student buys something (at the suggestion of the teacher), 10—20% of the retail cost of that item is paid (by the store) directly to the teacher. In the U.S. this is considered an illegal "kick-back," and frowned upon. However—if you end up teaching in Europe—this practice is normal and is considered an accepted part of the teaching profession.

---

2. A recent article in *The Wall Street Journal* (*cf. The Wall Street Journal*, August 1, 1995, p. 1.) documented that, if a person saves $3,900. per year in a normal bank account, from age 25, (with the current interest rates as of 1995), he will (with accrued interest) have saved one million dollars by the age of 65.

Once every month or two, it is a good idea to have older students gather for a studio class. You can use this time to explain general things such as transcribing lute tablature, stage presence, find an article in a guitar magazine and discuss this subject, *etc.*

These activities are the single-most important thing that you can do to build a sense of camaraderie among your students, which in-turn heightens your reputation, and guarantees that you will have more students.

Studio classes may also be used as a time for your older students to simply spend time together, reading through chamber music, going to concerts together, *etc.* Again, all this will help develop your reputation and result in a steady flow of students.

Studio recitals are a totally different matter. These are an open recital where your students play in public, for each other and respective parents, friends, *etc.* Depending on the number of students you have, you may need to divide your class in half, and have the recital last two evenings. If so, be sure to mix beginners with advanced players for both recitals. This gives students (and visitors) a chance to see the full range of your teaching.

Make sure that you go to the trouble of actually printing a program for the recital—*and include program notes written by the students themselves.* This means that the program may be several pages long, but this is important for a number of reasons:

First, it distinguishes you from the majority of guitar teachers (without formal training) who *a)* rarely have studio recitals and *b)* who do not include this minimal type of research as part of their teaching. Second, this also gives parents and visitors a chance to see the type of quality teaching that you do and a printed program gives them something to document that their child played in a "real" recital. This sort of "incentive" can make a tremendous difference in keeping parents happy.

Naturally make sure that all students play pieces that are easy enough that there is virtually no chance of error, and for at least a month prior to the recital, have the student (in his private lesson) go through the entire program he will play. This includes the entrance, bowing, playing, the exit, *etc.* All this must be routine by the time of the recital.

I would like to point out that, for some unknown reason, we in the U.S. have adopted the mentality that free-lance teaching is inferior to teaching in a college, university or conservatory. It's as if teaching in an institution is "serious teaching" and teaching privately or in a music store is for those who "can't make it" otherwise.

First, let me say that this attitude exists *only* in the U.S. and England. In Europe, a free-lance teacher not only has the recognized title of "Professor," but in many cases is considered *superior* to someone teaching in a formal institution. A free-lance musician commands a sense of mystique and eccentric non-conformity that is *highly* respected in Europe. As I said, this is unfortunately *not* the case in the U.S. or England.

However, if you do want to teach in a school, and have a fairly strong command of a foreign language, the option of teaching in Europe can be a good move. The pay scale, benefits and "job satisfaction" often exceed the possibilities in the States. This is especially true for guitarists who have just finished a degree and want to find work in a music school instead of free-lance teaching. [3]

Financially—especially in the U.S.—a teacher can be better-off to teach privately. While admittedly teaching in a formal institution has a slightly higher level of job security and the prestige may be higher, the pay is often less than it would be if a teacher worked free-lance.

If a teacher is good, and has some instinct for business, he can earn a *tremendous* income as a free-lance teacher.

---

3. For musicians interested in studying or teaching overseas, I suggest consulting:

A. Glise, *Handbook for American Musicians Overseas with Dictionary of Contemporary Musical Terms* (St. Joseph/Vienna: Aevia Publications, 1997) [in English, French, German and Italian].

This explains numerous aspects of studying and working as a musician overseas, including the various degree programs, teaching options, visa requirements, *etc.*

◊ *Suggested Assignments:*

• Make a sample "contract" to be given to your private students. Be sure to include lesson fee, payment schedule, absentee policy, additional requirements (method book, extra set of strings, *etc.*). If you plan on using studio classes or "group lessons" (*cf.* Chapter 13, "Teaching Children") be sure to include an explanation of this.

• Make a sample sign-in sheet for your private students.

• Contact an HMO or health insurance organization and ask for information on programs for self-employed workers (*i.e.* free-lance musicians). This may not arrive until after the end of the course, but find out what you can about the options in health care for free-lance musicians. [4]

• Go to your local bank, explain your situation as a free-lance musician, and ask about the options for a long-term IRA or similar savings program. Get all the documentation, flyers, *etc.* that they have and discuss these items in class.

---

4. I should point out that there are *tremendous* differences between HMOs in the U.S.—some with potentially terrifying consequences should you require long-term health care. As of the writing of this book, there have been a number of legal allegations and charges against some of the largest HMOs.

Presumably as these matters are sorted out in court, this type of private health care will become more secure. However, until then *check the services offered by an HMO very carefully!* For a basic primer on what to look for, I strongly recommend the following article:

Ellyn Spragins, "Beware Your HMO," *Newsweek,* October 23, 1995, p. 54-56.

CLASSICAL GUITAR PEDAGOGY

BOOK III
MUSICIANSHIP

Anthony LeRoy Glise

INTRODUCTION TO BOOK III

There are few subjects more difficult to write about than that of musicianship and æsthetics. Yet among guitarists, there are no subjects in greater need of attention. We often seem unaware of the tremendous difference that a study of aesthetics and musicianship can make in our playing.

A major reason for this is that audiences (including ourselves) often leave their "musical ears" in the concert hall lobby when they attend a guitar recital. They allow themselves to fall into the trap of being amazed that the guitar ("...since, after all, it is a 'folk' instrument" [sic]), is capable of playing such pretty, complicated music.

Sarcasm aside, this painfully unenlightened attitude is common among many trained musicians and listeners. They are either unaware of the musical potential of the guitar or simply do not recognize true musicianship. The former is embarrassing, the latter, *terrifying!* Worse yet, guitarists have a habit of living up to these ghastly expectations.

To attempt to address all the æsthetic, musical and interpretive needs of guitarists in a single volume of essays is absurd; many of these concepts can only be understood subjectively and this writing barely scratches the surface. Nonetheless, this volume does contain some basic ideas on æsthetics, interpretation and musicianship which I have found helpful in my own teaching and personal development. Naturally a student's technical level and maturity will dictate the extent to which these subjects can be taught.

With these obstacles in mind, I make no apologies for ideas which have been omitted, but I feel confident that the following essays are worthwhile, and well within the grasp of most serious students.

A.L.G.

CHAPTER SIXTEEN

THE MIDDLE-MAN—An Introduction to Æsthetics [1]

Socrates.   And you rhapsodists are the interpreters of the poets?
Ion.   There again you are right.
Socrates.   Then you are the interpreters of interpreters?
Ion.   Precisely. [2]

◇ *The Artist*

An important factor in teaching musicianship is that it must be done from day one. If a teacher waits until the later lessons, or until a piece is technically conquered, it is already too late. The student will be so concerned with only technical aspects, that musicianship will become a secondary concern. At worst, a piece will be nothing more than a mechanical regurgitation of the ink from the page.

The distinction is that the notes should merely be the means through which the composer chooses to tell the performer (Plato's "middle-man") what he is trying to say (*via* the music), so the performer can, in turn, tell the audience.

---

1. Note that this chapter gives an example of some basic æsthetic concepts. Depending on the level and maturity of a given student, similar discussions can be highly motivating (on a periodic basis) and gently initiate your students into this tremendous realm of our art. Similar æsthetic ideas can be a constructive topic for discussion in studio classes.

2. Plato, "Ion" *The Dialogues of Plato,* 4th ed., 4 vols., trans. B[enjamin] Jowett (London: Oxford University Press, 1953) I, 109.

Many forms of art eliminate this middle-man. These are the non-temporal arts—those created only once. Painting, for example, goes directly from the artist to the audience, as does sculpture, literature, and all the other non-temporal arts. In these art forms, the artist deals *directly* with his audience.

The advantages to this are obvious: the artist gives the audience an exact, finished product. But there are disadvantages. What if the audience changes as a result of new artistic tastes, the passage of time, *etc.*? Surely we do not believe that we view a Renaissance painting in the same way as its original owners!

So it is obvious that the non-temporal arts cannot adjust themselves to changes in audience. However, the audience *is* able to experience exactly what the artist wanted at that moment in time.

Conversely, the temporal arts (music, dance, theatre, *etc.*) must be "brought back to life" in a performance. This requires a "middle-man"—in our case, the performer.

Music is a medium through which the composer chooses to convey an idea. In coaching a student, ask what that piece would look like if the composer had decided to use canvas and oils as the medium to convey the same idea.

What would a piece look like if it were a painting, a dance, or even a place? Is this place light; is there a breeze; are there others around? These ideas are essential, and can give the student an immediate point of reference or "mood" that he can recall each time he plays the work.

This sort of visualization can also be extremely helpful in overcoming stage fright, since it psychologically puts a performer in "familiar territory," and lessens the unfamiliarity of being on stage.

Visualization also helps a player to "let go" and become part of the audience, listening along with them. As we will discuss later, this is one of the key factors that promotes a loss of temporal awareness. That loss is *essential* in concert and helps create the "magic" which we want in a concert.

To further understand the medium of music, we must attempt a rough definition of it. Dialectically, this is easier if we look at what music is *not:*

1. Music is not always sound.
We as performers use silence (often with great effect), and composers do the same. Silence is, so to speak, the blank canvas which nearly all music requires as a basis. Naturally there are rests within the music, but this silence can also act as the "frame" around our picture of sound (a little before and a little after) to help create the proper mood.

2. Music is not always silence.
Naturally music consists primarily of sound.

Both these maxims leave us nowhere—they are too objective, so in our search for a definition, we need to be more subjective, more personal in our observations. The above maxims deal only with the *physical* properties of music, while those below deal with our *response* to the music.

3. Music is not always "pleasant."
Many compositions consist of a great deal of tension. In fact, one basic definition of music could be: "a series of audible events consisting of tension and release," although this hardly covers all the necessary aspects we need.

4. Music is not always unpleasant.
This perhaps goes without saying, since most of us were originally drawn to music by its sweetness.

Here we have the problem: while everyone will agree when music has sound or silence, and that music is audibly oriented, many will disagree on whether a particular piece is pleasant or unpleasant, but regardless of each personal view, each person will have some *opinion.* Recognition of this individual opinion is a key factor in defining æsthetics.

To clarify, music, as well as all Art evokes a feeling, an emotion, or (on a strictly personal level) an opinion. This is the only solid maxim of which we can be absolutely certain. Therefore, a relatively safe definition of music is: *An organized aural event that evokes a feeling.*

Put more simply, the creator (in our case, the composer) tells the artist to do something—which he in-turn tells the audience, all of which is intended to make the audience feel something. Granted, the response that an artist *wants* from an audience may not be the same one which he *gets*, but this is irrelevant. What *is* necessary is that the response *exists*.

Our problem with this definition is found in the question, "...*then why isn't everything art?*" In our definition, we will find that the stimuli (music, painting, *etc.*) *must be organized by the artist*. There needs to be some sort of intentional setup. Even the justification for "chance music," such as John Cage's *Fontana Mix*, falls under this definition, because, in its conception, it was *planned* to be *unplanned*.

A bit of a paradox, but wholly legitimate. In fact, if we concede that all things were created by an intelligence, or "God" ("created" implying an intentional act), then perhaps it is safe to say that everything is Art, although this is a subject best left to theologians.

The remaining question of "what constitutes *good* art?" is more easily dealt with if we remember our first maxim (Art is a response to a stimulus organized by the creator). A simple answer is that good Art produces a response *that is most like what the artist intended*.

Then what about the premier performance of, for example, Beethoven's First Symphony, which was initially so negatively received? Is it possible that this work was not good Art then, and later became good Art? In other words, since we have already implied that the true quality of a work is dependent upon the reaction of the audience, how do we account for disastrous premieres of great works of Art?

This is somewhat clarified by accepting a basic quality in humans—*subjective adaptation*, or "changeability." This is a fairly consistent concept found in the modern study of æsthetics, and helps qualify our position.

This changeability in humans is the single, unfathomable element that keeps us from making broad, over-generalizations in æsthetic judgements, and frankly, this ability to change or adapt, is perhaps the single element that has—to-date—insured our survival as a species. Without this trait, we would long ago have set rigid æsthetic boundaries on the arts, but having done that, our artistic tastes would have become so narrow that the very nature of our beings as humans would have had to alter—to the point that we would cease to be truly "creative."

Think for a moment of the severe restrictions of some governments and reactionary groups who have tried to define and regulate "good art" and "bad art." In their attempts to control what is produced, they manage to do little more than obliterate any sense of creativity and drive the more "adventuresome" artists underground.

This changeability is the core of what—not only makes us human—but what insures that our activity in the Arts will continue to expand.

While a work may be intrinsically "well" or "poorly" conceived (*i.e.* "well crafted," *etc.*), a *misconception* of the presentation of the work (*via* cultural differences, temporal distance, *i.e.* the variable nature of the human mind) may result in a false perception or opinion of a work of art. This opinion may then change over a period of time as our understanding and familiarity increases. Good Art is constant—we (*i.e.* our perceptions of, and reactions to that Art) are the variables.

At the core of the matter, music (and for that matter, all Art), is actually a feeling (whether or not we fully understand it), evoked in us by the creator of that Art. But how does this affect us—the middle-men—the performers? The most obvious answer is that in order to correctly present the work to an audience, we need to understand it, and be technically able to present it.

This is where musicality and interpretation enter our study. We must be able to control the sound; we must make the medium of music say what we feel the composer is telling us to tell the audience. It's no easy job being the middle-man. It can result in good reviews, bad reviews, or, perhaps in the most extreme case, crucifixion... but it is a basic universal maxim that *nothing* can be brought to life without a middle-man—including music.

Æsthetics in the Studio

It is absolutely essential to begin discussing basic æsthetics with students at a very early stage and generalized discussions, such as above, will help open a student to these ideas.

The mechanics of music (*how* and *why* we play a certain way) must be the focus of most lessons, but the ultimate goal of music is to make someone *feel* something. Discussing æsthetic elements encourages students to analyze their *own* feelings which is the essential "first step" of true interpretation.

Without making excuses for wrong notes, and avoidable errors, I infinitely prefer listening to the old recordings of, for example, Jasha Heifitz or Pablo Casals—complete with their occasional wayward tuning and slips in sound, but *unbelievably* singing phrases and musicianship—than to many of the pristine, flawless musicians of today who play "perfectly," but simply sound impersonal and "cold."

As teachers we have a tremendous responsibility to instill an appreciation and understanding of *the art of making music,* not simply recreating sounds, and the basis for this understanding comes from æsthetic questioning: delving into the music and asking "why?".

In closing, let me briefly recount a story. At one of my coaching sessions with Benjamin Zander (a brilliant musician and director of the Boston Philharmonic), we began working on one of the lute suites by Bach. After playing through the entire work (without even the slightest *technical* error), he sat back, smiled and said, "Let's start again..."

I played only the first two notes before he stopped me and began "interrogation" in his striking English accent: what did I think about the first two notes?, how did they fit together?, what was the relationship between them?, the dynamics?, the articulation?, the color?, the shape of the line?, what was Bach trying to say with these two notes?, did my performance complement Bach's ideas?, did I agree with Bach's ideas?, if I disagreed with Bach's ideas, did I have a *right* to disagree with Bach since he was the composer and I was only the interpreter or 'middle-man'?

The questioning went on for over an hour, and was beyond a doubt the most enlightening lesson I ever had—*and we never ventured past the first two notes.*

Granted, this type of lesson should not happen often (because of the necessity of addressing so many other subjects in lessons), but an occasional lesson like this can be remarkable because it makes the player think through every single rationale in his decision making process.

In making these types of decisions, a player is forced to define precisely *why* he has made his musical decisions, and through this severe process—by some sort of miracle that no one truly understands—the music begins to live and breathe. This is a far cry from simply playing the notes.

Introducing æsthetic ideas into lessons will keep students thinking about the *"why."* If they never play a concert, they will at least learn to recognize other musicians who have arrived at this enlightened level. If they do aspire to a performing career, they will be even more prepared to enter the ranks of the true musician.

◇ *Suggested Assignments:*

   • Define a piece that you are currently studying in non-musical terms, and justify your definition. Do *not* use musical words. Try and decide how the piece makes you *feel* and use *emotive* terms.

   • The brilliant philosopher, George Santayana, stated that *criticism* involves deliberate *judgement and comparison* of something, while *æsthetics* involves our *perception* of something [*cf.* George Santayana, *The Sense of Beauty* (New York: Dover, 1955)].
   With that in mind, listen to a piece of music (preferably one that you do not play) and write a brief *critique* of it (what you *think* of it), then write an *æsthetic assessment* of it (what it makes you *feel*). Make a point of seeing how different you can make the two.

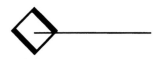

CHAPTER SEVENTEEN
PHYSICAL CONTROL OVER THE SOUND

*"Step by step, link by link,
it will be granted him to discover the work."* [1]
Igor Stravinsky (1882—1971)

In order for us to be able to convey to the audience what the composer is saying, we must have a great deal of technical and mental control over the sound. This stage of coaching is crucial because it is the first real musical freedom that the student experiences. Through dynamics, timbre changes and so on, the student's own personality and ideas will begin to emerge.

At first, this needs to be carefully guided by the teacher. This may be done by lightly marking the various dynamics, articulation, *etc.* into the music, but always explain to the student *why* something is done in a particular way. If a student has listened to a number of established artists, these techniques will come more easily. For that reason, from the very first lesson, be sure to give short listening assignments and discuss them in the following lesson.

---

1. Igor Stravinsky, *Poetics of Music* (New York: Vintage Books, 1956), 51.

Although listening to guitarists is essential, it is wise for students to listen to other instruments as well. In these listening assignments the teacher must remember the nature of the instrument and performer of a listening assignment.

For example, in teaching terraced dynamics, a harpsichord piece (which uses the upper and lower manuals) is helpful; for timbre changes, an organ piece (that uses different registration) is good; for phrasing, a slow piece on a sustaining instrument, such as violin is best. Assigned listening examples should clearly demonstrate what you are trying to teach the student.

Although a pianist may (with some success) slightly alter the timbre of the piano, it is not abrupt or obvious enough to point out the extreme timbre changes which have become popular on the guitar, so this would be a less constructive listening assignment for timbre changes.

The list of possibilities for listening assignments is endless, so be flexible. Keep in mind that if a student has shown interest in a particular style or historical period, try to assign listening examples which parallel those interests.

Obviously, a very helpful aid is to simply play the student's assignments for him, using very deliberate phrasing, dynamics, and so on. While these ideas should not be formally introduced too early, these brief encounters with control over the sound will make the elements seem much more natural to the student.

These elements of controlling the sound should only be introduced after the first year, since by that time, the hand positions will be more stable. However, if a student begins to add these elements on his own, it is time to gradually introduce these finer points of playing.

Given in the preferred teaching order, there are five basic ways that we control the sound:

1. *Dynamics* (terraced and gradual)
2. *Timbre Changes* (altering the tone color)
3. *Articulation*
4. *Phrasing*
5. *Mentally Controlling the Sound* [2]

---

2. Because of the complex nature of this subject, this will be discussed separately in the following chapter.

◇ *Dynamics*
Terraced Dynamics

If the student is given a piece, with clearly defined antecedent and consequent phrases (played *forte* and *piano* respectively), terraced dynamics rarely pose a problem. As well as giving the student aural examples of terraced dynamics, the following type of chart is often helpful.

Fig. 1   Basic Terraced Dynamics.

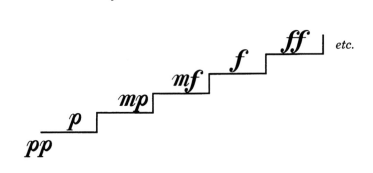

Gradual Dynamics

These dynamics are often easier to explain away from the instrument. Have the student sing one pitch, and then crescendo or decrescendo as you raise or lower your hand in the air. As always, if it can be sung, it can be played. The standard hair-pin markings for these types of dynamics are effective aids, since they visually convey the sound.

Fig. 2.   Gradual Dynamics.

In teaching gradual dynamics, it is best to use pieces with relatively fast tempi. As the guitar is not a sustaining instrument, gradual dynamics in slow pieces are more difficult, since one note will begin to fade away before the next one is played. Therefore, in a slow piece, the *illusion* of a crescendo (or decrescendo) must occur. This will be further discussed in the chapter, "Mental Control Over the Sound."

One simple way to teach gradual dynamics is to have the student crescendo as the melodic line ascends, and decrescendo as it descends. I have *great* reservations with this approach (since it can obliterate the proper phrasing) but in the beginning, it can be an effective pedagogical approach.

Timbre changes are where the true "orchestration" of the guitar is most evident. In teaching both timbre changes and articulation, a marvelous exercise is to assign a symphony or other large-scale work as a listening assignment, then have the student actually write into his guitar piece the different instruments that he wants to imitate by changing the timbre (and articulation, which we will discuss later). We will discuss these techniques at length in the chapter on "Mental Control Over the Sound" ("Mental Orchestration").

As with dynamics, if timbre changes are more extreme, the concept will be more easily understood. There are three basic types of color used on guitar. While there are several ways to achieve these colors, the easiest is to shift where the right hand plays on the strings. We will discuss this method of producing different colors first, since this is easiest for beginners.

1. *Modo ordinario (abbreviated: ord.)*

This poses no problem, since the right hand normally plays in this position (with the right hand somewhere near the soundhole).

2. *Sul tasto (tasto)*

This is the next easiest to teach, since the right hand moves nearer the fingerboard. In this position, the strings are not so taut, and require less power in sounding them. This technique is also less problematic for students since the right hand wrist position is not altered.

3. *Sul ponticello (pont.)*

This is the most difficult for students because the strings nearer the bridge (where the hand is shifted to play *pont.*) are more taut. Technically, several problems may occur. As the right hand moves toward the bridge, the length of the arm which reaches over the guitar is shortened. Thus, the wrist has a tendency to arch, the right shoulder may raise, and the right hand fingers may become too curved. All these problems can be avoided by keeping the wrist at the same angle, and *shifting the entire arm* toward the lower bout of the guitar.

---

3. I have elected to use the traditional Italian names for the various timbres. Doing so with your own students will not only help standardize this portion of the guitarist's vocabulary, but will also avoid "guitaristic terms" which are often neither correct, nor understood by other serious musicians.

This is more difficult to explain and should only be used by more advanced students. This type of timbre change is often used along with the above techniques of shifting the right hand playing position.

To complicate matters, there is no way of notating this type of timbre change beyond the terms already given (*ord.*, *tasto* and *pont.*), so this type of altering the timbre is used entirely at the discretion of the player. In spite of these complications, this method of timbre alteration *must* be learned by advanced students, since it is used (to varying degrees) by every guitarist who has attained any level of proficiency.

Simply, this technique is executed by *leaning the hand* (to one side or the other), so that more or less of the nail is used to sound the strings. The *less* nail that is used (with the wrist tilted up, away from the bridge), the brighter (more *ponticello*-sounding) the result. The *more* nail that is used (tilting the wrist down, toward the bridge), the darker (more *tasto*-sounding) the result. This is normally done while the right hand stays at the same place on the strings.

This approach should *never* be taught to a student of less-than intermediate ability, since it alters (or "tilts") the right hand position. The student's reaction to this type of timbre variation is often negative: since it is possible to achieve different timbres by simply moving the entire hand, why bother with this additional technique? The answer is simple: while subtle, there *is* a difference in the resulting sound. Obviously this technique is best reserved for small concert halls and in the recording studio since in a larger performing space these subtleties are lost.

Additionally, when this technique is used in combination with the previous techniques, a player doesn't have to move as far toward the neck or the bridge to achieve a different timbre. In particular, this is very helpful in faster passages when shifting the entire arm is impractical.

Above all, if angling the nail for timbre changes is to be successful, the nails must be filed evenly on both sides! Often a student will come into a lesson after experimenting with shaping the nails and the nails will be filed very angled, or "lopsided," which makes it impossible to play from the center of the nail or from the right side of the nail.

This angled nail shape will produce a very dark sound because of the increased nail surface releasing the string. Unfortunately, it also drastically increases the amount of time it takes to release the string. Thus, it will make fast playing more difficult, and (because of the delay in the release of the string) will often cause right and left hand coordination problems. While there are a few players who very successfully ascribe to this method of filing nails, as a general rule, it creates more problems than solutions.

Timbre Changes with Arm and Wrist Movement

As with other instruments—notably piano and the bow arm of bowed string instrumentalists—the amount of arm and wrist movement affects the sound. In guitar playing, right arm and wrist movement, when added to the normal finger movement, directly affects the attack as well as the timbre.

There are two basic ways we use the arm and wrist for effect when sounding the strings: *Opposition Movement* and *Complementary Movement*. It should be stressed that the following techniques occur at the precise moment that the fingers sound the strings.

Opposition Movement

The first way to use the arm is to move it, from the elbow, in opposition to the movement of the fingers as they follow-through (*i.e.* the arm will move slightly toward the floor). This will slightly delay the release of the string and darken the sound as well as soften the articulation. When only the wrist is pushed toward the floor the effect is essentially the same, though with a slightly more *tasto* timbre.

Complementary Movement

When the arm is raised (again, from the elbow) as the string is sounded, the release (and as a result, the attack) is more sudden. The articulation will be more "harsh" and the timbre more *ponticello*. Essentially the same effect can be achieved by moving the wrist away from the floor at the moment of release.

Both Opposition Movement and Complementary Movement (with either the entire arm or only the wrist) are *extremely* advanced right hand techniques which produce a subtle beauty in sound that very few guitarists take advantage of. In practice, Opposition and Complementary Movements with the *arm* are functional only in slower passages because of the time necessary to execute them, while Opposition and Complementary Movements with the *wrist* are often used in faster passages.

Let me stress again that this type of timbre alteration is entirely unsuitable for beginning students, but they should be aware of these techniques, since—at the very least—it will make them appreciate the finer qualities of artists who can successfully use these advanced methods of articulation and timbre alteration.

◇*Articulation*
Beginning Articulation

There are basically two types of articulation. The first, which is most applicable to beginners, is simply the technique of creating *more of less space between notes, while staying in tempo*. At the two extremes, we have *legato* and *staccato* (which are often indicated by the composer), but naturally there are innumerable degrees of articulation which must be defined by the player as he begins to interpret a piece.

Explaining this first type of articulation to a student is fairly simple. Have him play an arpeggio using the Individual Full Plant. Point out that the resulting sound is staccato, similar to Figure 3, a below. Then explain that by planting later (as in the Sequential Plant or Free technique), a more legato articulation is achieved, as in Figure 3, b.

Fig. 3.   Diagram of Articulation *a) Staccato.*

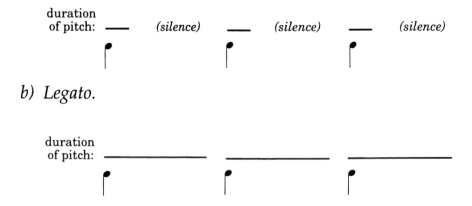

b) Legato.

Chromatic scales (using right hand alternation) are generally the best way to practice articulation. The articulation is executed by the right hand; *i.e.* the right hand finger that will play the next note is quickly planted prior to playing, creating a space of silence before the next note.

In applying articulation to pieces for beginners, works from the 19th-Century are generally most accessible. In particular, minuets or similar works in triple are effective because of the "long-short-short" character of 3/4 time, which may be articulated as "legato-staccato-staccato."

While articulation is nearly always executed with the right hand, more advanced students should be aware of left hand staccato. This is done by quickly releasing the pressure of the left hand finger, but still keeping the finger on the string (to avoid a slur to the lower note). This is the same concept as was mentioned in the Left Hand Pulsing Exercise. In performance the left hand staccato is somewhat rare, because the articulated note tends not to be as defined, or as "crisp" as it would be if it were stopped by the right hand. Nonetheless, it can be a wonderful effect.

A fascinating variation of left hand staccato (or *étouffé*) is described by Fernando Sor in his *Method*. He explains the possibility of stopping a note by placing the left hand finger directly on *top* of the fret (rather than behind it) and using very little pressure. This will slightly dampen the note, creating a more staccato articulation, though even Sor admits the difficulty of this technique.

While Sor's *étouffé* can be effective, left hand accuracy is crucial, and the resulting sound is very similar to the *appagado* technique (when the right hand leans on to the strings at the bridge to dampen the strings (*q.v. Sonatina* by Torroba or the middle section of *Asturias* by Albéniz). Normally in such instances the *appagado* technique is preferred, since it is considerably easier to execute and the sound is easier to control.

Advanced Articulation

The second, more advanced type of articulation, involves *how* the note is attacked: *i.e.* with more or less "weight." This is accomplished by changing the speed at which the finger moves when it sounds the string: the tempo of the music is the same, but the right hand finger will move across the string faster for a heavier, more harsh articulation, or slower for a softer, lighter articulation.

This should be reserved for more advanced students, because it often involves "shading" the note using one or more of the techniques mentioned in Opposition or Complementary Movement.

Practicing this is easiest using any chromatic scale and gradually changing from a heavier to a lighter articulation (or *vice versa*) within each octave.

Articulation, next to phrasing, is the most important way a soloist will control the sound and develop an individual interpretation of a piece. By-far, the most effective way for a student to recognize how a phrase should be articulated is to *sing*.

Once a student hears what he wants, it is up to him (with the teacher's help) to figure out how to play it that way—*in that order!* NEVER accept an interpretation simply because it "happens" a certain way. True interpretation is *always* a conscious, decision-making process.

◇ *Phrasing*

We will discuss advanced phrasing techniques in the following chapters. However, since these later concepts are beyond the abilities of a beginner, I wanted to briefly discuss phrasing as it pertains to younger guitarists.

The first stage in teaching phrasing is to have the student identify exactly where a phrase begins and ends. Fortunately, most pieces for beginners have obvious antecedent/consequent phrases—the consequent often being a repetition of the antecedent.

Explain to the student that a phrase is exactly the same as a sentence in language—it is a complete idea. Sometimes it helps to even have the student make up a sentence using words which fit the rhythm of the musical phrase.

With the phrase defined, have him pick the most important note of the phrase. Often (in beginning literature), it will be the highest note—usually toward the middle of the phrase. Finally, have the student "shape" the phrase toward this note by slightly speeding up (and perhaps crescendoing), then slightly slowing down (and decrescendoing) toward the end of the phrase.

While I have *great* reservations in teaching phrasing this way, for rank beginners, it is effective. Naturally the danger lies in altering the tempo, which is a problem we *desperately* try to avoid with beginners. The teacher must make sure that the piece can first be played without any fluctuation in tempo before prescribing this approach.

For more advanced students, there are a number of phrasing techniques which we will discuss in the following chapters. Nonetheless, beyond dynamics, and timbre changes, all of which can help, actual "phrasing" comes down to one thing: gently altering the articulation and tempo—whether it is within an entire line or simply between two notes (such as with a *rubato* or *tenuto*).

A good understanding of phrasing will—even at a professional level—quickly distinguish a talented musician, and a poor sense of phrasing will just as severely distinguish a mindless "note player."

◊ *Conclusion*

Throughout this section we have discussed various ways of controlling the sound. In doing this, we are attempting to make music the way we feel it should sound, rather than simply letting it "happen" any way it comes out of the guitar.

Students must always *first* decide how a piece should sound, *then* figure out how to achieve that sound. Otherwise a piece will be dominated by the limitations of the player and the instrument, and *neither* will ever reach their full potential.

You can never over-stress this with a student. The decisions are theirs (with your guiding), and those decisions are what form the basis of an intelligent, individual interpretation to which the finest players aspire.

◇ *Suggested Assignments:*

• Find one piece that you feel would be useful to teach a beginner each of the following: *dynamics, timbre changes, articulation* and *phrasing*.

• In a mock lesson, teach one of these four elements to a beginner.

CHAPTER EIGHTEEN
MENTAL CONTROL OVER THE SOUND

> *"...A slumbering thought, is capable of years,*
> *and curdles a long life into one hour."* [1]
> Lord Byron (1788-1824)

All musicianship is a result of physical action, but that action first originates in the mind. Therefore, *thinking* will ultimately dictate how a piece is played. The following subjects are key aspects in developing this ability.

◇ *Singing*

One does not need to be a singer to play an instrument, but one *must* sing! When a student is having difficulty with a musical idea, it is often because he has not made a conscious decision as to how it should sound; the fingers do their work, all the notes are there, but the piece sounds mechanical and lifeless.

Singing a phrase is the easiest way for a student to find out what should happen musically. This will also quickly distinguish the melody (the part which is sung) from the accompaniment—which can be a problem for guitarists.

---

1. Lord Byron, "The Dream," *The Poetical Works of Byron* (Boston: Houghton Mifflin, 1975).

Because most phrases are "breath-length," and singing forces the player to breathe at rational points in the music, singing will help define where phrases are, and the relationship between them. Generally, if a phrase is so long that it cannot be sung in one breath, it should be divided. [2]

Besides helping *define* phrases, singing will help a student *shape* phrases. The sense of rise and fall, articulation, dynamics and general characteristics of a phrase can be quickly discovered by singing. Quite frankly, if a phrase "feels right," when it is sung, it will almost always sound logical if it is played the same way. In short, *SING!*

◊ *Mental Dynamics*

Guitarists have a disadvantage, in that once we sound a note, it begins to decay almost immediately. In music of a faster tempo, this is a minor problem, because the notes occur so quickly in relation to each other, that they will not have a chance to decay before the next one is sounded. However, in slower tempi, our inability to sustain a note (and especially to make one note audibly crescendo to the next), is an unfortunate reality of the instrument. The most effective way to explain all this to a student is with the following drawings.

Fig. 1.   Diagram of the Actual Sound in Playing Guitar.

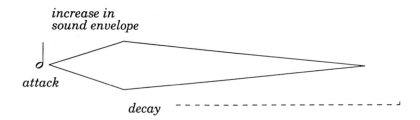

In order to play a melody with a smooth crescendo (in spite of the fact that the notes actually decay), we must *imagine* a continued crescendo from one note through the next. Each note must begin at the same volume where the previous note would have left off, *if it had actually crescendoed*. In Figure 2, the outer lines represent the imagined crescendo, the inner lines represent the actual sound.

---

2. With reference to shortening areas so they will be of "comfortable breath-length," we must *always* remember to first look at what the composer has told us to do, since a broad, extended phrase or area may be what was originally intended. Such examples occur in virtually every historical period, and should *never* be altered at the risk of minimizing the dramatic effect which they command.

Fig. 2. Diagram of a Mentally-Controlled Crescendo.

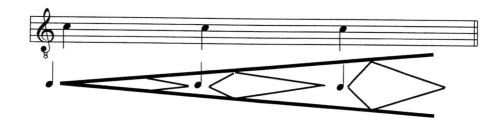

In *imagining* that each note crescendos (ignoring the actual decay), the player will create the *illusion* of a smooth connected crescendo through long, slow phrases. This is then perceived by the listener as an actual crescendo. It is also critical (assuming that this is appropriate in the given piece) that the notes be played very legato, as this will lessen the aural awareness of a break between the notes.

One of the most important elements in refining this mental technique is, again, to have the student sing. This will insure that he is hearing what he wants, rather than hearing the intrinsic decay of each note and adjusting his interpretation accordingly.

◇ *Mental Orchestration*

Heitor Berlioz described the guitar as a miniature orchestra. Fernando Sor, in his *Method*, even described ways in which he imitated other instruments on the guitar. One of the best ways to encourage a student to develop interpretive ideas about a piece is to ask him to describe what instruments might play a given line if the piece were written for orchestra or chamber ensemble.

For example in Renaissance music, if one plays the bass line as if it were being played on a viola da gamba, the line will take on a smooth, legato character. The dark, sensuous warmth of a clarinet can often be assigned to the middle voice of many Classic Period works, such as Giuliani, Diabelli or Sor, and so on.

This is another reason to give weekly listening assignments—in this case, works for small ensemble or orchestra—so the student will begin to hear different sounds he might want to incorporate (insofar as dynamics, articulation, timbre and phrasing), rather than just "playing guitar."

As I mentioned earlier, have students make a photocopy of their music and "orchestrate" the work—writing in the instrument names that might play the different lines. Then have them attempt to copy the sound or character of those instruments. The more expansive their understanding of mental orchestration, the more potentially varied their interpretations will become.

◇ *Mental Practicing—Sound and Finger Memory*

While this is an essential form of practice, it is one which is grievously neglected. A student should be able to sit quietly, away from the instrument, and play through a piece in his mind. If he is able to do this, then he consciously knows the piece. If he cannot, he is relying on either "Finger Memory," or "Sound Memory," which are two prime causes of memory lapses in performance.

Let me emphasize that in performance, playing from Finger Memory and Sound Memory is precisely what we want. However in *preparing* for a performance (or even for a lesson), this is precisely what we do *not* want because it means that the player is letting go of the music rather than analyzing each movement which is the essential first step in learning a new piece.

In practicing, we try to analyze each move and become aware of these physical aspects in order to isolate problems from a technical standpoint. Thus, at this stage (when learning a piece) Finger Memory or Sound Memory is deadly.

With *Finger Memory*, the fingers will automatically play the correct notes, while the player simply sits back and watches, but if the fingers accidently get out of position the player is lost.

With *Sound Memory*, the sound has been memorized, but if a wrong note occurs, the player will have to stop because the sound of the wrong notes breaks the concentration and he won't remember what comes next.

There are two ways to practice mentally, each of which addresses a specific problem.

1. Practicing Against Finger Memory.
Have the student sit, without the guitar, and *mentally* play through the piece. It is important that he not only "hear" the sound in his head, but that he also be able to "see" what the hands are doing at all times.

2. Practicing Against Sound Memory.

Have the student sit, without the music, and play through the piece, *using only the left hand.* This will not only point out the need for mental practice, but when a student comes to a spot where he can go no further, this will indicate an area that is not yet consciously secure; an area where the sound has been telling him what to play next.

This is *very* tedious practice, and unfortunately, it is impossible for the teacher to strictly monitor, since it all happens in the student's *mind,* but practicing like this will virtually always fix a chronic case of memory lapses in performance.

Another, almost diabolical way to practice against sound memory, is to de-tune the student's guitar so it is *totally* out of tune, then have him play through the piece as normal. Naturally the music won't sound *anything* like the original, but the fingers will make the same movements. If the student can play through the entire piece—in spite of the de-tuning—it will prove that the fingers are truly acting independently of the sound.

Sound and Finger Memory in Performance

Again, let me stress that Sound Memory and Finger Memory *are* what we want in performance—to be able to sit back, let go, and simply listen as we play. If this does not happen, several problems occur:

First, the music will begin to sound overly mechanical. There will be no "flow" or "breath" in the phrasing.

Second—and this is extremely important to remember—the player can become so obsessed with finger movement and placement that it becomes a primary source of stage fright—worrying if the next difficult passage will be correct, if a finger will make it to the next note, and so on.

On stage, a player *must* operate from Sound Memory and/or Finger Memory. However, in performance, the player must still be able to technically instantaneously "shift back into consciousness" and know exactly where he is in the piece. Therefore, until the final stages of polishing a piece (when a student is letting go and intentionally operating from Sound and Finger Memory), all finger movements must be conscious and overtly secure.

◇ *Suggested Assignments:*

• Choose one student-level piece and mentally orchestrate it (*i.e.* write in what instrument you want the student to imitate for which line).

• Choose one student-level piece and mark in the phrases. Then teach a mock lesson and explain why the phrases are where they are and how the student should bring out the phrases in his playing.

CHAPTER NINETEEN
PHRASING: THE STRONG-WEAK MAXIM

> *"The use of steam, electricity, wind water and other involuntary forces in nature is dependent on the intelligence of an engineer. Our subconscious power cannot function without its own engineer—our conscious technique."* [1]
> Konstantin Stanislavsky (1863-1938)

Often, musicians are so preoccupied with technical *playing* that it appears we have neglected the technical side of *interpreting*. A "conscious technique" of interpreting music is absolutely essential if one is to make intelligent decisions as to how the music should be played, and ultimately let go entirely of the music and allow it to live. As teachers, encouraging these skills in students is that much more critical, since it will influence their entire musical lives.

In interpretation, there are two types of musicians: those who play "from the heart," and those who simply "regurgitate" the music from the page. The problem occurs when a student relies too heavily on one attitude or the other. The player who plays *only* from the heart often has such a sporadic, idealized interpretation, that it seems he has forgotten (or worse yet, ignored) the composer's original intent.

---

1. Konstantin Stanislavsky, *An Actor Prepares*, ed. Elizabeth Reynolds Hapgood (New York: Theatre Arts, 1939), 14-15.

On the other hand, the player who, as Fernando Sor said, is merely a "note player," [2] accomplishes nothing beyond making the correct sounds at the correct time. Both approaches are necessary, but the only safe ground between the two is found in using a conscious interpretive method. Students must learn how to rationally approach the music that they play, and that can only be done through some organized interpretive system.

As we can see from the opening quote by the great Russian actor, Konstantin Stanislavsky, our subconscious interpretation is dependent upon our conscious technique. One must be able to "...*study consciously and interpret unconsciously,*" [3] in that order!

In musical interpretation, this conscious study must begin with the largest compositional unit that contains a complete idea—*the measure.* Ironically, we are raised from childhood to think in metric units, and as a result, the teacher will often find that younger students will understand phrasing more easily than older students.

For example, as children we sing songs, chant nursery rhymes, and read poetry—all of which involves a basic trochee or "strong-weak pattern." [4] In fact, we could look back even further—to the womb—where the constant pulse of our mother's heartbeat perhaps subconsciously instilled this pattern within us.

Carried even further, this strong-weak maxim may be extended to the highest metaphysical ideas of Christian good/evil, Cabalistic plus/minus, Buddhistic Yin/Yang, black/white and so on.

Regardless of our individual beliefs, it is commonly accepted that the "strong-weak maxim" is an intrinsic part of being human, and is of supernal importance if our art is to be an expansion of, or at *least* maintain a connection to that human existence. Acceptance of this maxim gives us the basis for our interpretive system. [5]

---

2. Fernando Sor, *Method for the Spanish Guitar,* (Paris 1830), trans. A. Merrick (London, 1850) (New York: published in facsimile by Da Capo Press, 1971), 10. Used by permission.

3. Carl Flesch, *The Art of Violin Playing,* vol. II (New York: Carl Fischer, 1930), 71.

4. A simple example of this is found in the nursery rhyme:

"Twin-kle, twin-kle, lit-tle star"

The concept of poetic prosody will be used throughout this discussion (*i.e.* ／ = "strong" and ◡ = "weak"). While this is not an ideal usage, it will at least keep us from thinking in the musical terms of "accented" and "unaccented," which is *not* the desired effect.

5. How directly a student can be taught this, or any interpretive method, naturally depends on his age, musical maturity and understanding of music theory. If these interpretive techniques seem too advanced, the teacher must simply "spoon feed" the student. Tell him what to do and (insofar as possible) explain why. As the student's understanding increases, gradually encourage him to make his own decisions. In any case, do not simply ignore the subject of interpretation!

Unfortunately, as a beginning student learns pieces, he is often so concerned with sounding the correct notes, that *every* note is emphasized, and the strong-weak pattern is destroyed.

Granted, every note *is* important (and, perhaps for technical development must be equally stressed), but interpretively, every note should not bear the same audible *level* of importance. Teaching students to distinguish this hierarchy of notes is essential. [6]

The example below shows how a beginner "phrases" a study by Sor.

Fig. 1.   Fernando Sor, Op. 35, no. 9. [7]
Phrasing of a Beginner.

Progressively (as shown through Figures 2-3), the student will come to understand the expansion of the strong-weak pattern until finally he is able to control entire phrases as in Figure 4.

Fig. 2.   *Advanced Phrasing of a Beginner.*

---

6. Note that in a 3/4 measure we have the pattern: strong-weak-weak, but a piece in 3/4 will *still* expand into four-bar phrases of strong-weak-strong-weak.

7. Fernando Sor, *Vingt quatre Exercises Très Faciles*, Op. 35, No. 9 (Paris: 1828), published in *The Complete Sor Studies*, ed. David Grimes (Pacific: Mel Bay Publications, 1994), 56. Used by permission.

Fig. 3. *Intermediate Phrasing.*

Fig. 4. *Advanced Phrasing.*

If we look at the progress that a student makes (from Figures 1 to 4), we find that he gradually comes to understand the music over a larger area—an augmentation of the basic strong-weak pattern which is within each measure.

If this strong-weak maxim is carried to the logical extreme, it will even dictate programing of pieces on a recital—a "strong" piece followed by a "weak" piece. One of the most blatant examples of this large-scale application is found in the movements of Baroque partitas and suites (Allemande/Courante/Sarabande/Gigue, or, slow/fast/slow/fast). It is hardly an accident that this strong-weak pattern became dominant in an historical period so obsessed with symmetry!

By using this strong-weak approach, a teacher can guide the student to intelligent decisions with regard to "conscious interpretive study," and finally, forgetting all these rules, he may begin to "interpret unconsciously." But there are factors which complicate our maxim. Some of these are actually written into the music by the composer (consciously or otherwise), some are complications due to the compositional style of a piece, and some are the result of harmonic or melodic elements within the piece.

In the following discussion, we will look at each of these factors individually, but for now, let me stress that the teacher has a responsibility to help students arrive at their own interpretations, and the concepts below provide a structured approach to that end.

Complications of the Strong-Weak Maxim

There are several compositional elements which will inherently create problems in the strong-weak maxim:

1. *Ascending lines* will cause the player to crescendo (the opposite is true of descending lines).
2. *Lines that lead to long notes* will cause the player to crescendo.
3. *Appoggiaturas*, by their nature, cause the player to lean toward, or accent these notes.
4. *Repeated notes* cause the player to push forward or crescendo.
5. *Harmonic drive* (the natural drive of certain progressions), cause the player to crescendo.

If the above items cause a student to lean or crescendo toward a *strong* measure (or beat, or phrase, *etc.*) then no problems exists. However, if they drive toward a *weak* measure (beat, phrase, *etc.*), the player must make a critical decision. Either he should:

a) give into these influences, allowing them to "break the spell" of the strong-weak pattern, *or*,

b) maintain the strong-weak pattern and view these factors as interpretive devices used to create tension and excitement in performance.

Allowing these items to break the strong-weak pattern is very easy, but more often than not, this results in the music controlling the student's interpretation, as well as making the music terribly predictable—even boring. Maintaining the pattern—*in spite of these factors*—is not only less common, but can result in unusual, original and *very* exciting interpretations.

Thus, for the remainder of our discussion, we will assume a maintenance of that strong-weak pattern. In doing so, we will hopefully arrive at a point where, as the great violinist Carl Flesch said, we may *"...study consciously, and interpret unconsciously."* [8]

Ascending Lines

A perfect example of how an ascending line fights against our strong-weak maxim is found in the popular Renaissance lute piece, *Il Bianco Fiore.*

Fig. 5.   Cesare Negri, *Il Bianco Fiore.* [9]

Because the melody ascends to the first beat of the second measure (a weak measure), many players tend to crescendo to that second measure, making it a strong measure and breaking the pattern. It is far more effective to keep the second measure "weak." This will maintain the strong-weak maxim and create a *very* dramatic line out of two simple measures.

---

8. Flesch; *op. cit.*, 71.

9. Cesare Negri, "Il Bianco Fiore" from *Nuovo Inventioni di Balli* (Milan: 1604). Transcription for guitar by Helmut Monkmeyer, (Rodenkirchen/Rhein: P.J. Tonger Musikverlag, 1953). Used by permission.

The example below shows how a melody leading to a long note may cause a student to crescendo to the E♯ in the bass, which is actually the first note of a weak measure.

Fig. 6.   H. Villa-Lobos, *Étude No. 7.* [10]

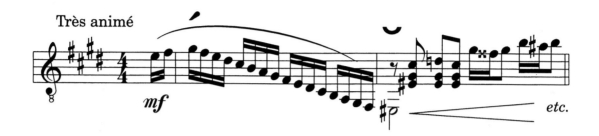

Even though the line descends (which may cause the player to correctly decrescendo), the speed and character of the piece *(Très animé)* will normally override this factor, and cause the player to crescendo.

Villa-Lobos even seems to be aware of the problem, and insists that the second measure should indeed be kept weak, since the first crescendo in the piece is *from* the E♯ in the bass, and not *towards* it!

The beautiful *Pavanas* by Gaspar Sanz contains *both* of the previous two problems: an ascending bass line (tending to crescendo) which leads to a long note (which *also* tends to crescendo). This, or any combination of items is more difficult to overcome. However, if the second measure is absolutely maintained as a weak measure, the effect on the listener is one of phenomenal excitement.

Fig. 7.   Gaspar Sanz, *Pavanas.* [11]

---

10. Heitor Villa-Lobos, "Étude No. 7," *Douze Études [Twelve Etudes],* ed. Andrés Segovia (Paris: Max Eschig, 1953). Used by Permission. All Rights Reserved.

11. Gaspar Sanz, "Pavanas," *Instrucción de Música Sombre La Guitarra Española* (Madrid: 1674). Public domain. Various editions.

By definition, an appoggiatura acts as a non-chord passing tone (either on the beat or slightly before the beat, depending on the historical period of the piece) which resolves to a chord tone. In the following example by Fernando Sor, the high B on the first beat of the second measure (a weak measure) acts as an appoggiatura to the following chord tone, A. Note also that exactly the same situation occurs on the following weak measure (the F✗ appoggiatura on beat one of measure four, to the G♯).

Fig. 8.   Fernando Sor, "Thème." [12]

Most players tend to accent the appoggiaturas, which destroys the strong-weak pattern. However, if the second and fourth measures are maintained as weak, the interpretation exhibits a great deal more excitement and control over the music. In addition, this results in a more "correct" 19th-Century interpretation of the music (if, in fact such judgements can be made).

Another fascinating situation is found in the prelude, *Lágrima*, by Tárrega.

Fig. 9.   Francisco Tárrega, *Lágrima*. [13]

---

12. Fernando Sor, "Thème," *Introduction et Variations sur un Thème de Mozart, Op. 9* (Paris, n.d.) Published in facsimile in *Fernando Sor, The Complete Works for Guitar*, ed. Brian Jeffery (London: Tecla Editions, 1982). Volumes reprinted at various dates thereafter. Used by permission.

13. F. Tárrega, "Lágrima," *Sämtliche Präludien* (Vienna: Universal Edition, 1961). Used by permission.

Again, we have a combination of problems: lines leading to long notes (quarter notes leading to the half note A in the bass), *and* ascending lines in *both* the treble and bass (implied in the bass in spite of the octave drop from the G to the A), *and* an appoggiatura (the D to the C, of measure 2) which is a chord tone of the implied iv chord.

Overcoming all three problems is *extremely* difficult, but if the pattern is carried through to the end of the B section, the return of the A section (a strong measure [*cf.* m. 5]) will have a sense of power that is otherwise lost. In addition, the intensity is magnified by the return to the E Major key center.

Repeated Notes

Repeated notes in the melody or accompaniment will tend to cause a player to push the phrase forward and often crescendo, which (as in Figure 10) would destroy the strong-weak pattern. In this study by Carcassi, the second measure should be maintained as a weak measure, which will create a far greater subtlety in the interpretation.

Fig. 10. Matteo Carcassi, "Study No. 7." [14]

An additional problem in this example is the presence of an ascending line in the bass (which tends to crescendo). As we found, any combination of items is more difficult to overcome. Yet, if the second measure is maintained as weak, the effect is one of astounding control over the music. [15]

---

14. M. Carcassi, "Study No. 7," *25 Studies, Op. 60*, published in *The Complete Carcassi Method with Twenty-five Studies, Op. 60* (Pacific: Mel Bay Publications, 1994). Used by permission.

15. I want to stress that the repeated notes of this Carcassi (even though the right hand does play *p, a, m, i*) and the repeated notes of the ubiquitous *Recuerdos de la Alahambra* are entirely different. The tremolo of *Recuerdoes* is the melody, and the intention in performance is *not* to make those repeated notes sound as such. The Carcassi is precisely the opposite.

Sometimes composers will place a *sforzando* on a weak measure or beat, and the player will tend to make the following beat a weak one. If that beat is *intended* to be weak, there is no problem. However, as in the next example, the beat following the *sforzando* is strong, and must be kept strong (*cf.* mm. 6-7).

Fig. 11. Mauro Giuliani, "Adagio." [16]

Later (in m. 9—the restatement of the main theme), we have a descending melody line (which tends to decrescendo), which is followed by the arpeggiated chord (which guitarist's tend to play "strong") on the first beat of measure ten. Measure ten must be kept "weak" in spite of these combined factors!

Another interesting problem found in the Giuliani, is that he forces the player to make the eighth measure (normally weak) a *strong* measure. He does this by the inclusion of a *forte* on the first beat, as if he is trying to fool both the player and audience into believing that this beat (or measure) is actually strong. He then "corrects" his dynamic marking

---

16. Mauro Giuliani, "Adagio," *Sonata, Op. 15* (Vienna: Richault, *ca.* 1828), *The Complete Sonatas of Sor, Giuliani and Diabelli,* ed. Anthony Glise (St. Joseph/Vienna: Aevia Publishing, 1997). Used by permission.

Another interesting problem found in the Giuliani, is that he forces the player to make the eighth measure (normally weak) a *strong* measure. He does this by the inclusion of a *forte* on the first beat, as if he is trying to fool both the player and audience into believing that this beat (or measure) is actually strong. He then "corrects" his dynamic marking upon the return to the main theme (an octave higher) with the *forte-piano*, which reestablishes the first beat of the main theme (measure nine) as a strong measure.

This gives an after-the-fact justification to the listener as to why the first measure should be maintained as strong—although still marked *piano*. Like a brilliant novelist, Giuliani has waited until the last possible moment to explain his apparently erratic behavior and the subtle confusion that ensues contributes to the excitement of the interpretation.

Harmonic Drive

From a traditional study of music theory, we know that certain harmonic progressions naturally tend to pull away from some chords, while they want to resolve to specific other chords (for example V_7 to I). As a result, the resolution (to the I chord) will normally feel like a strong beat. However, if it falls on a weak beat, and is *maintained* as a weak beat, the resulting interpretation is extremely dramatic.

In the previous example by Giuliani, the last beat of measure five (V_7/V) resolves to a deceptive cadence (V_7/V to vi/V). Because of the natural drive of the V_7/V chord, the player may inadvertently make the resolution to the vi chord too heavy or "strong." By our maxim, this is incorrect.

Giuliani even seems to be aware of this dangerous tendency, and adds the *sforzando* on the next chord. This reestablishes the next measure (measure seven) as a definitive strong measure. In short, he has played an obvious, but successful joke on the listener, but it will only work if the player does not fall into the trap of being "controlled" by the harmonic drive. Measure six *must* be maintained as a weak measure.

A more overt example of how harmonic drive can fight against our maxim is found in the following excerpt by J.S. Bach. Here, the last half of measure one (a strong measure) outlines a V_7 chord, leading to a i chord on the first beat of measure two (a weak measure). This resolution to i may cause the player to incorrectly interpret that measure as strong.

Fig. 12. J.S. Bach, "Double." [17]

It is important to notice that by strictly adhering to our pattern, measure three (which contains the transitory harmonic shift to the dominant) occurs on that strong measure, which creates a great deal more excitement. The result of that harmonic drive pushes the piece forward to measure seven, where we finally return (on beat one of a strong measure), to the tonic.

17. J.S. Bach, "Double," *Lute Suite II*, BWV 997, *The Solo Lute Works of J.S. Bach*, ed. Frank Koonce [#WG100] (San Diego: Kojos Music, 1989). Used by permission, 1995.

In this section we must address several items that not only permit the player to break the strong-weak pattern, but demand it:

1. *Sequences,*
2. *Extended Phrases,* and
3. *Elisions.*

Sequences

One of the few factors that *will* override the strong-weak maxim is a sequence. In the following example, the sequence drives the phrase forward (each measure being strong) until we reach the last strong measure (the restatement of the main motive in measure five). Then, the strong-weak pattern is reestablished by the coda, beginning with the anacrusis in measure eight.

Fig. 13. F.M. Torroba, "Allegro." [18]

---

18. Federico Moreno-Torroba, "Allegro," *Sonatina,* ed. Andrés Segovia (Washington, D.C.: Columbia, 1966). © 1966 Columbia Music Company. Used By Permission, Sole Representative, Theodore Presser Company.

This is a fascinating example because there is a crescendo written *toward* a weak measure (measure six). In instances like this, the player should still crescendo, but the following strong measure (measure seven) needs to be even stronger in relation to that previous measure. A diagram of the relative dynamics for each measure would look like this:

Fig. 14. Diagram of Relative Dynamics for Each Measure of Fig. 13.

$$\mathit{mf} \mid \mathit{mf} \mid \mathit{mf} \mid \mathit{mf} \mid \mathit{mf} \mid \mathit{f} \mid \mathit{ff} \mid \mathit{f} \mid \mathit{ff}$$

poco *a* *poco* *crescendo*

The player must always remember that the strong-weak pattern should be maintained *in relation to the given dynamics!* This way, the strong-weak maxim will strengthen and enhance the composer's original ideas while at the same time form the basis for a highly individualized interpretation.

Extended Phrases

Irregular, or non-four-bar phrases, are quite common and will naturally affect our maxim. The next excerpt by Alexandre Tansman shows three different phrase lengths (strong-weak-strong) leading to the accented B in measure 5.

Fig. 15. Alexandre Tansman, "Danza Pomposa." [19]

19. Alexandre Tansman, *Danza Pomposa* (Mainz: Schott's Söhne, 1961). © B. Schott's Söhne, Mainz, 1930, © renewed. All Rights Reserved. Used by permission of European American Music Distributors Corporation, sole U.S. and Canadian agent for B. Schott's Söhne, Mainz.

Interpreting this type of phrasing is slightly more complicated, primarily because it's difficult to recognize. Regardless, there will always be some clue. This may be an irregular harmonic movement, a disjunct rhythm or melody, *etc.*, which indicate a breakdown in the pattern between the written measures.

After the breakdown in the normal metric scheme, the pattern is simply reestablished between groups of notes that do not fit within the given measures, but the strong-weak system remains intact.

Another example of an extended phrase is found in the following excerpt by Manuel Ponce. Here, the ties (over the bar lines) are a clue to the player that the strong-weak pattern between the measures has been broken, resulting in a seven-bar phrase (all strong) leading to the *fortissimo* in measure eight.

Fig. 16. Manuel Maria Ponce, "Prelude IV." [20]

Elisions

Elisions are areas that act as the end of one phrase *and* the beginning of the next phrase *at the same time.* I would like to add that an elision—when performed correctly—is perhaps the most subtle and dramatically beautiful effect that a composer can use which creates an "aural illusion"—hearing something which is not at all what it seems to be.

Because we are hearing the end of one phrase—and do not realize *until later* that it is actually the beginning of *another* phrase—there is an astounding realization when we finally hear what has happened. Very few composers can use elisions well, and (sadly) even fewer performers, but an elision is a *magical* effect on stage!

20. Manuel Ponce, "Prelude IV," *Preludes I* (Mainz: Schott's Söhne, 1930). © B. Schott's Söhne, Mainz, 1930, © renewed. All Rights Reserved. Used by permission of European American Music Distributors Corporation, sole U.S. and Canadian agent for B. Schott's Söhne, Mainz.

In the following excerpt by Anton Diabelli, the C major chord (beat one of measure four) acts as an elision (the end of the previous phrase and the beginning of the next phrase). It is interesting to note that this C major chord is also the first chord of the returning main theme, which intensifies the effect. This is often the case with an elision—the resolution will be the main theme, a sub theme or some other recognizable motive.

Fig. 17. Anton Diabelli, "Andante sostenuto." [21]

Note also the harmonic progression : V_6/V—V_7—I. As we have already found, this type of progression tends to drive toward the final resolution (the I chord) which Diabelli permits by introducing the *crescendo-decrescendo* in measure three. He then, however, does not permit the player to overemphasize the returning main theme, by placing a *piano* on the I chord—which is a strong measure! The result is a very subtle yet dramatic effect emphasizing the elision.

Elisions, of all phrasing situations, are perhaps the most difficult to execute because they are recognized by the listener *after* they occur; the audience hears the end of the previous phrase, but does not realize that it is also the beginning of the next phrase until the next phrase has already begun.

For that reason it can help tremendously in performance if the player makes a slight *tenuto* or *rubato* at the elision point. Another effective way to stress an elision is to simply arpeggiate or "roll" the chord. These techniques draw attention to the elision, and allow the listener a chance to briefly contemplate what he has heard.

21. Anton Diabelli, "Andante sostenuto," from *Sonata in F Major, Op. 29, Trois Sonates* (Vienna: n.d.) *The Complete Sonatas of Sor, Giuliani and Diabelli (With Optional Cadenzas)*, ed. Anthony Glise, (St. Joseph/Vienna: Aevia Publications, 1997). Used by permission.

Throughout this section we have only discussed one or two phrases at a time. Naturally, interpreting larger areas is more complex, but the strong-weak maxim is still applicable and in actual practice *must* be expanded to larger areas.

In the following example by Enrique Granados, measure nine could be interpreted as *either* strong or weak (note the two options given above and below the music). While either interpretation is feasible, one should be wary of changing back and forth indiscriminately between different phrase lengths too often in a piece, since this will give a disjointed feeling in performance.

Fig. 18. Enrique Granados, "Melódico." [22]

---

22. Enrique Granados, "Melódico," *Valses Poéticos*, ed. Nicholas Petrou (London: Schott's Söhne, 1990). © 1990 Schott & Co. Ltd., London, © renewed. All Rights Reserved. Used by permission of European American Music Distributors Corporation, sole U.S. and Canadian agent for Schott & Co. Ltd., London.

It should be noted that the phrasing given below the example is the same phrasing given by Granados in the original piano version. Sadly, these phrasings appear in no guitar edition. This is a strong argument for *always* checking the earliest available edition *of the original* when dealing with transcriptions.

To find the best length into which the strong-weak areas should be divided, the player must decide how large an area the listener will be able to comprehend as a complete unit.

For example, in a binary form, it would be theoretically correct to say that the A section is strong and the B section is weak. In fact, as we shall see in the chapter "Temporal Modes in Music," this *is* the mindset which the performer wants on stage. However, it would be rather optimistic to expect the average listener to recognize such a large-scale format. To give another example, who could tell if you played the first 158.5 measures of Bach's *Chaconne in D Major* "strong" and the second 158.5 measures "weak"?

For that reason, the player must decide how large an area the listener will comfortably retain, then build his interpretation around that length. More often than not, these should be "breath-length," areas—areas that would logically be as long as you could sing in one breath. However, this length may change through the piece as shown in the following examples by Frank Martín.

Fig. 19. Frank Martín, "Comme une Gigue." [23]

---

23. Frank Martín, "Comme une Gigue," *Quatre Pièces Brèves* (Zürich: Universal Edition. 1959). Used by permission.

Fig. 20. F. Martín. *Ibid.*

In these two examples by Martín, I made the decisions as to how to divide the phrases after observing the harmonic rhythm. In Figure 19, the harmonic rhythm alternates between two measures then one measure.

In Figure 20, the harmonic rhythm simply occurs every measure. This is a cue that the strong-weak pattern will be disjunct in the first example, and more regular in the second example.

Themes or motives may also help determine the length of the pattern. In Figure 19, the first five measures could be strong, and the second five (the repetition of the main theme) could be weak. The player must decide.

One rare exception to our maxim occurs when lines lead to short notes. In the bagatelle below, Giuliani repeats the I chord in different inversions, each time leading to notes of a shorter time value. Here, the *shorter* values become strong.

In this instance the strong-weak maxim is still observed, but it is *reversed*; a result of the stagnant harmonic movement (the repetition of the I chord). This is not only true for each measure, but also for each of the four-bar phrases (the first four being weak, the second four being strong). This produces a marvelous effect and a sense of "calm" in spite of the tempo and very high level of activity.

Additionally, as we will discuss in the chapter "Temporal Modes in Music," recognizing this type of repetitive pattern in composition is extremely important in preparing a piece for the stage. These repeated motives are one of the key elements that help a player achieve a high level of concentration, which in-turn promotes the sense of "timeless-ness" that we need in performance.

Fig. 21. Mauro Giuliani, "Allegretto," Bagatelle, No. 3, Op. 73.[24]

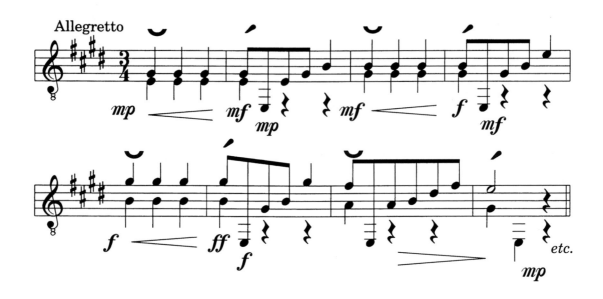

Contemporary Music and the Strong-Weak Maxim

As I implied in the examples by Frank Martín, contemporary music can present *fascinating* complications in this interpretive method. This is because the phrases are often much less defined, thus the Strong-Weak patterns may be almost totally broken down or non-existent at a recognizable level. Still, the *exceptions* to the Strong-Weak Maxim are worth noting for the simple fact that they can alert us to the natural tendencies of a compositional element which sometimes fight against the composer's original ideas.

The brilliant American composer, Daniel Pinkham, has composed a number of works for classical guitar—solo and chamber music—and given his compositional style and innate sense of line, his music often contains elements that are more easily interpreted if we keep in mind the previous discussion.

24. Mauro Giuliani, "Allegretto," *Bagatelle, Op. 73, No. 3* (Vienna: Pietro Mechetti, *ca.* 1819), ed. Anthony Glise, Anthony Glise Critical Editions, *Mauro Giuliani, The Complete Bagatelles, Op. 73* (Cincinnati: Willis Music Co., 1989). Used by permission.

For example, in "The Garden Awakes" (the first movement from *The Seasons Pass*), we have compositional bursts of energy exemplified, not only by the rhythmic movement, but by the sharp dynamic contrasts throughout the work. However (keeping in mind our previous discussion) there are interpretive complications, as shown below.

Fig. 22. Daniel Pinkham, "The Garden Awakes" from *The Seasons Pass*. [25]

In this work—although the Strong-Weak pattern is infinitely less structured—the *exceptions* to this pattern are important to consider. In this case, the repeated sixteenth note pattern tends to crescendo. This is compounded by the fact that they lead to a long note (the final cadential chord). Pinkham permits this crescendo at first (by the ***ppp*** to ***mp*** crescendo), but he then asks the player to *decrescendo* to the final chord.

Pinkham seems to be aware of the tendency of the line to push forward and uses the decrescendo to create a highly dramatic line at the final cadence, but again, it will only be effective if the player follows his directions implicitly.

I might add that this approach is what makes for brilliant composition: permitting the music to partially control an interpretation, but still fighting against it enough that there is an innate tension built into the work.

For us as performers this means we must always consider the composer's original ideas first *then* add our own interpretation. Watching for the Strong-Weak Patterns *and* the exceptions to those patterns can provide us with a solid basis from which to interpret a composition.

---

25. D. Pinkham, "The Garden Awakens," *The Seasons Pass* (Ione Press, Inc., 1988). Sole selling agent E.C.S. Publishing. Used by Permission. Ione Press, Inc., Boston, MA, 02115.

Conclusion

Let me again stress that it is essential to expand the Strong-Weak Pattern to achieve the final interpretation of a piece. Fortunately, the same rules we have already discussed can easily be extended to interpreting larger areas.

In closing, remember that this system of interpretation *is only a system*. Even the examples I've given here are open to radically different interpretations. Each player must ultimately decide how he will interpret a piece. *The key word is "decide."* Far too many guitarists allow the music to make these decisions for them, without the slightest notion of how or why an interpretation could be different.

Our final goal should never be to function as mere musicians, but as *thinking* musicians. Only as thinking musicians will we be able to *"...study consciously and interpret unconsciously."* At the very least, we have that responsibility to the music, to our audiences and to ourselves—*in that order.*

◊ *Suggested Assignments:*

• Choose one beginner-level piece and write in the Strong-Weak phrasing as it could be taught to a beginner. Be sure to keep the areas fairly small, as these are easier for a beginner to comprehend.

• Choose one intermediate-level piece, and write in the Strong-Weak phrasings as it could be taught to an intermediate student. Be sure to watch for the exceptions to this maxim, as they often appear in intermediate to advanced-level literature. With this intermediate piece, try and expand the Strong-Weak phrasing over a larger area.

• Find an intermediate or advanced-level piece that has one of the three exceptions to the Strong-Weak Maxim (a sequence, extended phrase or an elision), and write in your solution to the problem.

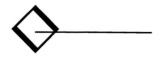

CHAPTER TWENTY
SCHENKER ANALYSIS FOR INTERPRETATION

> *"Schenker system A system of musical analysis and inter-*
> *pretation developed by Heinrich Schenker (1868-1935). It repre-*
> *sents an attempt to reveal the organic structure of music by*
> *showing that every composition is the elaboration of some simple*
> *tone structure that guarantees its continuity and coherence."* [1]

Although this is a terribly neglected subject, there are *tremendous* advantages in being able to analyze a piece for performance based on the rudimentary ideas of Heinrich Schenker. Far beyond a mere theory, this approach will give students a sense of direction in phrasing and help them decide what notes (or areas) are most important. Once those decisions are made, the phrasing, articulation, *etc.*, may be added more easily and more convincingly.

Application of Schenker's theories to interpretation is quite simple. When the performer recognizes the "simple tone structures," he has found a skeletal series of notes that are important in the music, and thus, he has found points in the music to emphasize.

---

1. Victor Zuckerkandl, "Schenker System" *Harvard Dictionary of Music*, 2nd ed., ed. Willi Apel. (Cambridge, Mass.: Belknap Press, 1969).

Emphasizing these important areas is done in much the same way as we already discussed in the chapter, "Control Over the Sound." Beginners may crescendo to the important note, and decrescendo back down to the end of the phrase. Intermediate students may do this as well as slightly altering the tempi, adding a rubato or tenuto, *etc.*, in order to bring out these important areas. Naturally, this must always be done keeping in mind the composer's own phrasing, dynamics, articulation, *etc.*

In analyzing the tone structure of a piece, we must find what Schenker calls "Scale-Steps Harmonies." [2] This is merely a recognition of the melodic direction of a line. For example, we all know that certain tones (such as *ti* to *do* or *re* to *do*) tend to "lean" toward one another, thus are important melodic moves. Naturally the same can be said of certain harmonic movements (such as V_7 to I). When we find these relationships, we have found areas that are important to stress in performance. In addition, it is possible to use this technique along with the Strong-Weak Maxim to achieve some tremendously original interpretations.

In the following example by Sor, the G♯ [beat 2.5 of measure 1 (*ti* to *do*)] as well as the D [beat 2.5 of measure 3 (*fa* to *mi of V*)] both lead to weak measures.

Because of the melodic drive of these tones, there is a tendency to push toward beat one of both measure 2 and measure 4—both of which are weak measures. Recognizing the tendency of one tone to lead to another is critical in scale-step analysis of a piece for performance.

Fig. 1.   Fernando Sor, Bagatelle, No. 5, Op. 43. [3]

2. For those familiar with Schenker Analysis, this application may seem a gross over-simplification of Schenker's theories. Nonetheless, this is still a valid method to help students come to terms with a practical interpretive method. For further details of this fascinating theory, *cf.*: Heinrich Schenker, *Harmony*, ed. Oswald Jonas, trans. Elisabeth Mann Borgese (Chicago: Univ. of Chicago Press, 1954).

3. Fernando Sor, "Andante" Op. 43, No. 5, from *Mes Ennuis, Bagatelles Pour la Guitare* (Paris, ca. 1841), ed. Anthony Glise, Anthony Glise Critical Editions, *Fernando Sor, Complete Bagatelles, Op. 43* (Cincinnati: Willis Music Co., 1989). Used by permission.

Maintaining both measures 2 and 4 as weak measures is extremely difficult because of the directional intent of the melody. However, if a player can accomplish this, the antecedent phrase takes on a power and depth that is otherwise lost.

According to Schenker, recognizing *harmonic* direction is also critical, as we see in this example by Weiss.

Fig. 2.   Sylvious Leopold Weiss, "Fugue." [4] / [5]

Here we have a fascinating problem: each four-bar unit is an alternation between the tonic and dominant chords (A major and E major). In Schenker analysis, this, or *any* type of strong harmonic movement is extremely important to recognize.

In addition (recalling our discussion on the Strong-Weak Maxim), notice in the Weiss example, that each four-bar unit which begins on the tonic is *strong*, while each four-bar unit at the dominant is *weak*. The

---

4. S.L. Weiss, "Fugue," from *Prelude, Fugue and Allegro* (Kassel, *ca.* 1719 [?]), ed. Anthony Glise, Anthony Glise Critical Editions (Cincinnati: Willis Music Co., 1992). Used by permission.

5. It is interesting to note that the first beat (A in bass) can be performed as an elision (the last note of the last phrase of the preceding Prelude). This off-sets the entrances *and* the strong-weak pattern by one quarter note. I have assumed this off-set anacrusis in the above interpretation.

In addition (recalling our discussion on the Strong-Weak Maxim), notice in the Weiss example, that each four-bar unit which begins on the tonic is *strong*, while each four-bar unit at the dominant is *weak*. The problem (as is often the case with Schenker analysis) is that there is so much activity in the piece and these strong-weak patterns are so far apart, that it may be difficult for the listener to recognize. Again, this is a primary difference between how Schenker's theories are used in theoretical analysis as opposed to how they are used when applied to performance. We must *always* think in terms of the listener.

However, in this instance, the player is aided by the fact that each time Weiss moves from I-V or V-I, there is another statement of the fugual motive. Often this is not the case.

In Schenker's theory, a great deal of time may often elapse from one important note to another. If the first important note is several phrases from the second, or if there is considerable activity in the piece, our listeners may not be able to grasp these broad relationships.

As we will see in the chapter, "Temporal Modes in Music," being aware of these broader distant areas is very important, since focusing on these can help the player to shift temporal modes. However for the sake of the listener, concentrating on smaller areas is preferable since these tones must be close enough to each other to be *aurally* recognized.

This is the primary difference between how Schenker analysis is used by theorists as opposed to performers. To a theorist, this distanced relationship would prove no problem whatsoever. However, in applying these ideas to performance, we must find important areas or notes that have a relatively close temporal proximity which our listeners will recognize.

In spite of these difficulties, recognizing these step-wise relationships and strong harmonic movements will give the player a much clearer idea of how to interpret any given piece.

On the other hand, sometimes the opposite problem may arise: if the player tries to connect too many of the step-wise notes (or important harmonic movements), the piece can have a sense of over-calculation to the point of absurdity. The example below shows the potential for an *over*-application of this theory.

Fig. 3. Anthony Glise, "Lullaby No. 3, *Con moto e leggerezza.*" [6]

As we found earlier, any pitches which outline an important harmonic center should be emphasized, yet in this case (even simply in the first measure) virtually every half measure outlines some important chordal structure. Obviously to emphasize each of these would destroy the *leggero* mood.

As for important pitches that lead to one another (also normally emphasized), virtually all of measure two falls into this category, which again, if emphasized, would obliterate any resemblance of this piece being a lullaby.

The piece above has a host of additional interpretive problems (which I will admit were mischievously added for the sake of making my students think!). The strong-weak pattern is fairly clear: the first 4 measures alternate between strong/weak. Beyond that (because of the accents), the pattern is broken and remains weak (because of the ambiguity in tonal direction). From a Schenker standpoint this is more complex.

---

6. Anthony Glise, "Con moto e leggerezza" from *Lullabies, Op. 5* (St. Joseph/Vienna: Aevia Publications, 1994). Used by permission.

In reality, the primary harmonic movement is simply a I chord (A Major) to a I suspended 4 chord (measure one to measure two). However, note the emphasis of the accented D (the 4th) over the a pedal tone (mm. 4-6). Repetition of this motive then simply calms down into a brief solo melody that calmly drifts until we have the only other true harmonic movement in this section—to the V$_6$ chord at the very end of the example.

As a result, there *must* be an emphasis on the last chord even though this is a weak measure. This is, in fact, insured compositionally by the quarter rest just prior to the end. This strengthens the resolution (giving the resolution a sense of being "strong") while still maintaining the *piano* dynamic marking.

Thus, in this example, the only true strong/weak movement is between the first I chord, (note the first *) and the very last V$_6$ chord (note the second *). The rather large section between these two points simply acts as a way to create a sense of calmness necessary for a *leggero* lullaby.

Past the Theory

Once we understand how to analyze the scale-step relationships according to Schenker, the next problem that faces the player is how to make these more important notes or areas stand out so that the audience will hear them.

At the very heart of the matter, since we only deal with sound and silence (both of which constitute a passage of time), these are the elements we must alter to stress the importance of an area or note: *sound* (including altering the tempo) and *silence* (altering the articulation).

This can be accomplished by placing a slight *rubato, tenuto* or (in extreme cases) a *ritard, marcato,* or a gentle accent on these notes. In addition, slightly changing the timbre of the more important notes can also cause these areas to stand out to the listener.

Another solution is to "push" the phrase (slightly increasing the tempo) toward an important note or area, then pull back afterwards. This method is perhaps the easiest to execute (by more advanced players), but it should be used sparingly—especially by beginners, who naturally have a tendency to alter the tempo too much. While altering the tempo can be effective, remember, this is not "correct" in the performance practices of some historical periods.

Keep in mind that students–particularly guitarists–automatically have a tendency to drastically alter the tempo, which can be detrimental to the overall performance (whether it is historically correct or not). This happens, partially, because they so rarely play with other musicians, and so, have the freedom to do what ever they like with the tempo—often with total lack of regard for the composer's original intent. This is just one of the many reasons that guitarists—even beginners—should be encouraged to play in ensemble with other musicians.

Applying the theories of Heinrich Schenker to performance offers a tremendous interpretive approach. However, it can be extremely complicated for younger students, because it assumes a fairly solid knowledge of musical theory.

Nonetheless, it can be a great help to more advanced guitarists and will provide numerous interpretive ideas that would probably not occur to many players. Frankly, when a student analyzes and successfully executes a phrase based on Schenker's theories, he will know it. It simply *sounds* right. If a student is not able to do this, it is best not to try to force it. As with many things in music—and life—when the time is right, it will happen.

• Find a transcription for guitar that is originally for solo violin or cello (virtually anything from the Baroque period is a good choice). Look at the original version (which will be written in single lines) and find the inner voices. Mark each one with a different colored highlighter. Then compare your version with a guitar transcription. Watch for Schenker's scale-step relations, note-to-note relationships and important harmonic movements.

• Facsimile editions of guitar music from the early 19th-Century are also often written in the "old style." This means they are written in "violin style" (as described above) and the different voices are not written out. Find such a piece in facsimile and compare it to a modern edition (or arrange your own edition) which shows the different voices. Discuss whether you agree with the editor's decisions and why.[7] A brief example is given below.

Fig. 4. François Molino, "Variation 12" from *Thème avec 50 Variations.* [8]
   a) Original.

   b) Possible Interpretation.

---

7. The same assignment may be done with a work in Renaissance tablature, since this method of notation doesn't show rhythmic duration and the interpretation of the different voices is at the discretion of the editor and/or performer.

8. François Molino, "Variation 12," *Thème avec 50 Variations* from *Grande Méthode Complete pour Guitare, Op. 55* (Paris: Chez l'Auteur [sic], H. Lemoine, *ca.* 1820-23). Public Domain.

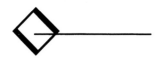

CHAPTER TWENTY-ONE
TEMPORAL MODES IN MUSIC

> *"The relation of a phantasy to time is generally very important...past, present and future are strung together, as it were, on the thread of the wish that runs through them.* [1]
> Sigmund Freud (1856-1939)

This chapter was originally written as a footnote to the chapter, "Practicing." However, as my ideas continued to grow, a separate chapter seemed the only way to sufficiently address these concepts. This was augmented by the fact that the study of time is one of my favorite subjects and the application of this study to music is a fascinating aspect of our art form.

I would like to stress that this element of pedagogy has *very* rare application for students, since they likely haven't yet experienced these temporal shifts. This is because most of these temporal modes are directly connected to performing and/or *highly* concentrated practice which younger students probably have not yet achieved or experienced.

---

1. Sigmund Freud, "Creative Writers and Day-Dreaming," *The Complete Psychological Works of Sigmund Freud*, vol. IX (London: Hogarth Press, 1959).

Often, when professional musicians get together they will talk about being "locked in" to a performance—a state of mind where they lose awareness of everything else and are totally immersed in the performing experience.

Although this sense of "timelessness" that music can evoke, is a commonly recognized phenomenon, we simply have not found a common terminology to discuss this aspect of music. This is what I hope the following discussion will resolve.

The study of time has become one of the most intricate and complicated interdisciplinary subjects imaginable, due predominantly to the fact that, as humans, we are inescapably "trapped" in time. Every aspect of our existence has some connection to time, and music is no exception.

Music is a temporal art form, and our perception of music can *only* exist within a temporal framework. Much the same concept was expressed by the psychoanalyst, Marie Bonapart, who stated, "*It is perfectly accurate to say that a sense of time can only exist where there is submission to reality.*"[2]

Accepting that music is in fact "real," and that it exists within a temporal framework, then the "reality" of music is contingent upon our perception of time. In other words, we recognize that music exists, and that it exists in time, therefore our perception of *music* is only accurate insofar as our perception of *time* is accurate. However, if time can influence our perception of music, conversely, our perception of music can influence our perception of time. This is the essence of what we need to address.

For example, all of us have attended a performance and suddenly realized that the concert is over and an hour or two has slipped away while we were lost in the euphoria of the music. Essentially the same thing happens during our own performances; we walk on stage, sit down to play, and suddenly we "wake up" at the end of the concert.

---

2. Marie Bonapart, "Time and Unconsciousness," *International Journal of Psychoanalysis,* v. 21 (1940), 468.

This type of "shift" (from our "normal" perception of time) is in fact, what we *want* to happen in a performance, but as we already briefly discussed in the chapter, "Practicing," it is *not* what we want during a normal practice session. Granted, during practice sessions, there is another type of altered perception of time, but it is not the same as during a performance and the two are highly distinct from one another.

The brilliant interdisciplinarian, J.T. Fraser (President of the International Society for the Study of Time), has isolated a number of temporal "moods."[3] For our purposes, the three temporal modes which apply are *Nootemporal* (our "normal" perception of time), *Biotemporal* (our perception of time during practice), and *Atemporal* (our perception of time during a performance). [4]

    1. *Nootemporal.* Beginnings and endings are well-defined. This is our "normal" perception of time.

    2. *Biotemporal.* A sense of "now" is recognizable, but only because of a minimal awareness of "before" and "after." This is our perception of time during concentrated practice.

    3. *Atemporal.* Absolutely no means whereby time can be defined. This includes no recognition of before/after, past/present, *etc.* This (at a fairly rudimentary level) is our perception of time when we are totally absorbed in a performance.

While his definitions of temporal modes may sound very strict, in defense of Fraser, he does acknowledge that Art can evoke an atemporal experience, though I disagree with his statement that it depends on a "degree of incoherence." [5]

For example, he cites that, being aleatoric, Alban Berg's "Desolato" (the second movement from the *Lyric Suite*), causes us to experience a breakdown of temporal awareness leading to atemporality. While I agree with him in this case, I would also like to stress that I have (as I'm sure we all have) experienced similar temporal shifts from such tonal

---

3. Although Fraser and a majority of other time researchers tend to use the more objective term "temporal mood," I strongly prefer "temporal mode," as this implies a more definable element. Whether or not this is a valid distinction rests on each individual's ability to perceive the various modes, making my definition an awareness to which we should *aspire*, rather than one to which we are *bound* by virtue of our human state.

4. J.T. Fraser, *Time as Conflict* (Basel and Stuttgart: Birkhauser Verlag, 1978), 22-5.

5. J.T. Fraser, "Temporal Levels and Reality Testing," *International Journal of Psycho Analysis* (London: 1981), 20-21.

works as those by Dufay, Monterverdi or even Bach. In short, temporal shifts seem to be dependent more on our *subjective perception* of the music rather than the specific music itself.

To clarify these three modes, we will discuss them separately. [6]

Nootemporal Mode

This is our "normal" perception of time. It is defined by a conscious awareness of *past*, *present* and *future*. All three of these are essential for us to function as temporally-bound humans. Without the presence of the Nootemporal phase, our lives would take on a chaotic aspect bordering on suicidal.

For example, imagine trying to drive a car, and (lacking an awareness of the past), not remembering if you had actually learned how to drive as you find yourself behind the wheel of a speeding car; or (lacking an awareness of the present) wondering *why* you need to put on the brakes as a child runs out in front of the car, or (lacking an awareness of the future) not recognizing that unless you turn, you will run your car into a tree.

These are absurdly simplistic examples, but realistically point out our dependence on the accurate perception of *past*, *present* and *future* in order to simply function in life.

However, as Goethe said, "Art is Art because it's not real-life!" Assuming that people enjoy art because it "takes them away" from reality, then the nootemporal is actually what we are *avoiding in* art. Frankly, if we want "real-life," we can switch on the news. *Escape* from reality is most often what we desire from art.

One of the most perceptive observations on this subject was made by Sigmund Freud, who said simply, "...many things which, if they were real, could give no enjoyment." [7] That "unreality"—which is encouraged by a breakdown of our temporal awareness *via* "Art"—is precisely what we seem to desire.

---

6. I should point out that Fraser (and others) have defined a number of other temporal modes, but these do not apply directly to our activities as artists. For those interested in further study, I suggest the following book as a primer to this fascinating subject.
   J.T. Fraser, *Of Time, Passion and Knowledge* (New York: Braziller, 1975).

7. S. Freud; *op. cit.*

Think for a moment of the worst performance you have ever attended. Recall how the minutes, even seconds, seemed to drag on and on. Your sense of temporal awareness (as well as the physical, mental and emotional anxiety) was painfully sensitized. While this heightened awareness is necessary in everyday life (in order to safely perform even the most rudimentary motor skills), this is *not* the type of temporal awareness we want on stage, since it leads, at best, to mediocre, didactic performances.

Biotemporal Mode

The biotemporal mode involves a *minimal* loss of temporal awareness, which is what we want during *practice sessions*. The concentration is very high but the player is aware of what he is doing at every moment. He is focused on the specific isolated notes or passages, fingerings, dynamics, phrasings, *etc.*, but all of which are connected to the "now" (*i.e.* each isolated point at which he is actually playing).

This is an essential mode because (with the slight loss of temporal awareness, due to the very high level of concentration on the actions being performed), the player can make rational decisions about the piece and decide what works best at the exact point he is playing *(the present)* in relation to that which he has immediately finished playing *(the past)* and that which he will immediately play *(the future)*. In short, he is "practicing efficiently."

Atemporal Mode

The modern existentialist painter, Wasilly Kandinsky, in his classic writing, *Point and Line to Plane*, makes the observation that "The geometric point is an invisible thing. Therefore, it must be defined as an incorporeal thing. Considered in terms of substance, it equals zero." [8] In other words, "point" is immeasurable because, since it exists solely on its own (with no other reference). There is nothing to gauge its existence, either in terms of size or temporal span. *It is a purely atemporal phenomenon.*

Because we often lose all awareness of time in "performance mode," it could be considered—at the very least—a low form of atemporality or a single temporal "point." Strictly speaking, atemporality

---

8. Wasilly Kandinsky, *Point and Line to Plane* (New York: 1947), reprint (New York: Dover, 1979).

occurs through a *total* breakdown of the senses (such as in cases of sensory deprivation, brain damage, or quite literally, death) or an overload of the senses (such as when the senses receive information which they cannot process). However, as we'll see below, it may truly be physically possible for music to evoke an atemporal experience.

As has been documented, any aural event of less than 2 milliseconds constitutes an atemporal event, due to our inability to consciously process and "separate" events. [9]

Our *physical* perception of music is much slower than this (*ca.* 15-15,000 cycles per second), thus, cannot fit into our strict definition of atemporality. However, we must remember that (with our *subjective* temporal experience of music) we are not only dealing with a *physical* element, but also an *emotional* one.

To explain further, since the electrons in the brain (which convey our *emotional* perceptions) operate at roughly the speed of electricity (*ca.* 386,000 miles per second), the potential for *emoting* (or "feeling") experiences is well below the 2 millisecond mark. Thus, referring to some musical experiences as atemporal may be justified.

Admittedly, this duality (of the physical *vs.* emotional perceptions of music) may stretch our original definition of atemporality, but if we assume a broader application of the postulate of E.A. Milne (which states that the proof of the Second Law of Thermodynamics depends on a hidden axiom; *q.v.* that wherever a process occurs in the universe, the universe may be divided into two specific portions, one of which *is* affected by the process, and one which is *not*), then perhaps this duality of the emotional and intellectual perceptions of music may be justified.

Acceptance of Milne's postulate also helps justify our subjective perception of time in performances (regardless of whether one is the performer or simply a listener).

For example, two people attending the same concert often have completely different reactions. One may truly slip into atemporality and become totally lost in the performance, while the other may remain in nootemporality and be painfully aware of each passing second; in essence, he is "bored."

---

9. *Cf.* J. Cohen, "Subjective Time," *The Voices of Time*, ed. J.T. Fraser, (Amherst: Univ. of Massachusetts Press, 1981), 260-1 and J.T. Fraser, *Of Time Passion and Knowledge* (New York: Braziller, 1975), 78-79.

Both of these listeners are experiencing totally different, yet totally *real* perceptions of the same passage of time—each with subsequent effects; *i.e.* the first may leave the concert thrilled and convinced that the concert was brilliant. The second listener (in nootemporality) may leave the concert bored, totally unsatisfied and convinced that the concert was inferior. If we assume Milne's postulate, *both* are correct!

Obviously the same distinction occurs between the performer and the audience. Our perception of time when we are on stage is often *drastically* different than that of the listeners.

In any case, for us as performers, the moment we have *two* points, we have "line," which helps define our perception of biotemporal, that is, a rudimentary awareness of "now" defined by a "before" and an "after."

However, with regards to performance, the level of temporal awareness to which we aspire is one of *atemporality*; a total loss of self through complete immersion in the mass block of sound that we recognize as "the entire piece." This is the stage at which we completely lose ourselves in the music. When this happens, we have the potential for the most "brilliant" performances.

When this occurs, essentially, the piece (or in the best-case scenario, an entire concert)—*becomes a whole unit*—a "point," with no reference to any other temporal aspect. With *two* points (*i.e.* awareness of the present, as well as either past or future) we have "line" and the atemporality is broken.

Atemporality and Movement

Our human concept of the passage of time is inextricably linked to that of motion since motion implies vacillation between at least two separate points (past and present or present and future). If that motion ceases, from a physical standpoint, we have "death," or "immortality." From a *temporal* standpoint, if the motion ceases, we enter atemporality.

The connection between this concept, and Einstein's Theory of Relativity is fascinating. Assuming his postulate that there is no "ether" (*i.e.* no absolute standard of "rest"), then our concepts (insofar as the variable definition of atemporality) may be quite valid given the following rationale: since electricity flows at roughly the same speed as light (again, inclusive of the electrical currents which operate in the human brain), then the connection to Einstein's theory is further solidified, and the *emoting* process potentially becomes an intricate part of the proposed fourth dimension as suggested, not only by Einstein, but numerous other physicists. [10]

The concept of movement and passage of time is also consistent with a majority of religious beliefs. For example, in the Old Testament (or Torah), when Adam and Eve were in the Garden of Eden, they were in a state of eternal (*i.e* atemporal) innocence. Thus we may conclude that there was no "ethical motion" (they were in a constant state of "good"—*i.e.* one moral "point") which secured their state of atemporality (or "immortality"). The moment that "evil" entered the garden, there were *two* moral factors (good and evil, *i.e.* two "points" which = "line"), and according to biblical beliefs, they began to "age" and entered a state of nootemporality.

A vast number of philosophies (particularly in the Far-east) consider this lack of motion or "still point" as a tool for achieving "Satori," or enlightenment, the most common of which is through meditation.

Ironically, the Medieval Cabalist, Abraham Abulafia, even makes a distinction between the enlightenment achieved through "science of combination" (which was a meditative tool from the Geonic period, used to achieve enlightenment) and music, which he says can also *"conduct the soul to a state of the highest rapture by the combination of sounds."* [11]

In any case, it is clear that the atemporal mode is one of "stillness," or only one "point." Achieving that single-minded level of concentration is precisely what we must acquire on the stage.

It is also fascinating to consider the atemporal phenomena which occur in "Near-Death Experiences." These are amazingly consistent experiences shared by those who have clinically "died," and been resuscitated.

As one might assume, there is reportedly a distinct sense of atemporality in N.D.E's, but at a more intriguing level, those experiences have been mapped to a specific region of the brain: specifically, the

---

10. *Cf.* H. Minkowski in A. Einstein *et al.*, *The Principle of Relativity* (London: Methuen, 1923); H. Weyl, *Philosophy of Mathematics and Natural Science* (Princeton: Princeton Univ. Press, 1949); L. Fantappie, *Nuove Vie per la Scienza* (Rome: Sansoni, 1961); and R.P. Feynman, "The Theory of Positrons," *Physics Review*, vol. 76 (1949) *et al.*

11. It is no accident that the highest level on the Cabalistic "Tree of Life" is the First Sefirot, "Kether," which holds the highest position, and has no beginning or end (*i.e.* is purely atemporal). Its symbol, not so coincidently, is a point.

As one might assume, there is reportedly a distinct sense of atemporality in N.D.E's, but at a more intriguing level, those experiences have been mapped to a specific region of the brain: specifically, the right temporal lobe in the Sylvian fissure (located just above the right ear). This area seems to be genetically coded for near-death experiences. [12]

Under clinical conditions, when this area of the brain is excited with an electronic probe, the patient experiences an "out-of-body" episode that parallels those of patients who have had near-death experiences (including *"...seeing God, hearing beautiful music, seeing dead friends and relatives and even having a panoramic life review."* [13]). It is not unreasonable to wonder if the close proximity of this lobe of the brain in relation to the ear and the conductive vibrations to this region as we listen to music, is a factor in our own musically-generated atemporal experiences.

Atemporality in Music

For our purposes, while we may not be able to attain a total Nirvanic or Satoric level of enlightenment through music, there are specific steps that one can practice to at least approach a minimal level of "mental stillness" and thus, a closer approximation of atemporality in performance.

First, a very high level of relaxed concentration is necessary. To the extent that, as I said in the chapter, "Performing," *nothing* exists but the sound. Second, in reviewing our Strong-Weak Maxim, we remember that the patterns must ultimately be augmented over larger areas in actual application.

In analyzing a piece, and picking out important areas that are further and further apart (and focusing our concentration on these wide relationships), our awareness of the smaller areas (or "points" in between) is lessened, thus, our temporal perception is broadened and our temporal awareness is reduced.

---

12. W. Penfield, "The Role of the Temporal Cortex in Certain Psychical Phenomena." *Journal of Mental Science* 101 (1955), 319-46.

13. Melvin Morse, M.D., *Closer to the Light, Learning from Near-Death Experiences of Children* (New York: Villard Books, 1990), 103-5. *Cf.* also B. Eadie, *Embraced by the Light* (Placerville, Calif.: Gold Leaf Press, 1992).
   I do wish to stress that I am by *no* means trivializing the concept of near-death experiences. On the contrary, I find this documentation quite uplifting, and am fascinated by the comparison of "NDE's" with the atemporal experiences evoked through music.

This is also a further argument for the application of the Schenker theories to performance. Since, as Schenker says, the truly "important" areas in a piece often tend to be basic melodic or harmonic relationships—sometimes pages apart from each other (thus, temporally displaced from one another)—if we can pick out these notes (chords, phrases, areas, *etc.*) and focus our concentration on them, our sense of temporality is again lessened.

As we continue to broaden our perception of a piece, our "points" become further and further apart, and we begin to slowly shift from the nootemporal and biotemporal toward atemporality.

A number of compositional elements can help promote this loss of temporal perception, such as repeated rhythms, ostinati, repeated motivic germs, pedal tones, *etc.* Since these elements are without tension (or for that matter, *direction*), they tend to draw us into a more "still" mental attitude, which again, encourages us to focus on one "point," propagating a sense of atemporality.

Conclusion

Because we are dealing with an art form which is radically bound by time, and yet so conducive to temporal shifts, we should try and take advantage of this marvelous aspect of music. It is one of the true wonders of music; one which we have all experienced, and one which we should continually try to expand and develop. This is necessary because it enables us to focus more intensely on the music which enhances our ability to musically communicate with an audience.

◇ *Suggested Assignments:*

  • In a written assignment, explain how you feel differently when you practice as opposed to when you perform.

  • Mark in your music target "points" (based on either the Strong-Weak Maxim, Schenker's theories or other interpretive methods) and focus your concentration on these areas when playing. At first try this only with points a phrase or less apart. Then gradually find areas further and further apart until you hit your "limit" of concentration. Over time, try to extend these areas further and further apart in order to lower your sense of temporal awareness.

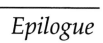

Epilogue

In closing, I would like to take the opportunity to challenge the future teacher. Music is one of the most miraculous gifts on earth. Thus, the ability to recreate music (as we feel the composer intended) puts us in a position of astounding responsibility and power. The ability to teach someone *else* to do this literally doubles that responsibility.

As you interact with your students, please never forget this. What they learn from you—good or bad—can alter their lives, and they will pass on these traits to *their* students.

Constantly check your words and actions. Constantly prove to yourself that you deserve this responsibility, and always act out of love.

Constantly act out of love.

Repeat that sentence to yourself before every lesson, and *whatever* level you reach in your career, it will be correct for you. This is perhaps the one and only thing of which I am truly sure.

There are thousands of things which make a good teacher—some of which I've included in this book—but beyond all things...

"...the greatest of these is love."

Anthony L. Glise
Ingolstadt, Germany
14 February, 1997

APPENDIX I
TROUBLE-SHOOTING CHECKLIST

While it may seem negative to list all the things that could go wrong in a student's playing, the following checklist will prove helpful in isolating general problems.

Included are a majority of common problems. Still, nearly all problems, if traced to the core, are simply a result of a lack of technical control. While any of the problems cited could be due to an unfamiliarity with proper guitar technique (as with absolute beginners), or the typical problems associated with learning a new piece, *etc.* this checklist assumes this is *not* the case.

Teachers should always be wary of trying to correct more than one problem at a time, since remedial work on two or more problems can be counterproductive. Additionally, some students can be very sensitive and may feel "persecuted" if the teacher oppressively lists all the things which need to be corrected; this is especially true if a student has come to you after playing some time. In any case, use tact. You will ultimately get more response and develop a stronger rapport with your students if problems are approached gently.

The following list should be consulted to determine which problems need immediate attention, and those which can be dealt with over a period of time.

1. Critical. If a problem could have serious physical consequences: *i.e.* a problem that might lead to tendonitis or other debilitating conditions.

2. Moderate. If a problem can be corrected easily (*i.e.* with one or two weeks of practice).

3. Casual. Problems that simply need to be brought to the student's attention and corrected. These may require a longer period to correct and can often be combined with problems that require moderate attention.

Remember that each student and remedial situation will vary. A teacher must be guided by his intuition, his concern for the student and his love for the guitar.

• *SITTING*

1. Check chair height.
2. Check footstool height.
3. Check the position of the guitar.
4. Check position of the arms and legs.
5. Check for twisting of the back, collapsing or arching the lower back, raising shoulders, twisting the neck, *etc.*
6. Make sure the student is practicing in playing position at home.

• *RIGHT HAND*

1. Poor Hand Position.
   a. Check sitting position.
   b. Check position of the arms.
   c. Check that p is extended away from the hand.
   d. Check that the fingers are not falling underneath the strings while playing.
   e. Check nail length.

2. Improper Finger Movement.
   a. Practice Scratching Exercise.
   b. Practice Moving Exercise.
   c. Practice Moving Exercise with release.
   d. Practice Individual Full Plant.
   e. Check that the fingers are not falling underneath the strings.
   f. Stress a wider follow-through with exercises.
   g. Check nail length.

3. Lack of Finger Independence.
   a. Practice Scratching Exercise.
   b. Practice Moving Exercise.
   c. Practice Moving Exercise with release.
   d. Work on the following right hand arpeggios progressively:
      i. Individual Full Plant
      ii. Full Plant
      iii. Sequential Plant
      iv. Free

4. Lack of Control.
   a. *Cf.* 3, a-d.
   b. Check music for "cross-fingerings" and if possible, correct.
   c. Play through pieces slowly, making sure right hand fingering is consistent each time the student plays. If not:

    i. have student write in right hand fingerings, *or*,

    ii. if fingering is consistent through each playing, isolate the problem (between which fingers does the lack of control occur?), and make a right hand study out of the problem section.

5. Inability to Develop Speed.
   a. *Cf.* chapter "Developing Speed."
   b. Practice nos. 1 & 2 of "The Basic Seven" Exercises playing staccato.
   c. Isolate different areas to see if the problem occurs in similar places.

6. Bad Sound.
   (Bad Sound in General)
   a. Check angle of the nail as it releases the string. Often this is due to playing too close to the tip of the nail. If so, tilt the hand slightly to the player's left side.
   b. Check nail shape. Make sure the shape of the nail follows the natural shape of the finger at the fingertip on both sides of the finger.
   (Worsens as the Player Crescendos)
   a. Check 6, a & b.
   b. Practice diatonic or chromatic scales (across all six strings) using a gradual crescendo as the scale ascends and decrescendo as the scale descends.
   c. Practice arpeggios with crescendo and decrescendo.

N.B. It is important to determine if the bad sound occurs in melodic lines, or only in arpeggios, as it is often only one or the other, and once isolated, is easily corrected.

7. Incorrect Finger Placement.
   If the pad of the finger touches the string before the nail, there will be a momentary break in the sound before the next note is heard. There will also be a "click" as the string slips from the flesh of the fingertip to the nail. On the contrary, if the nail touches the string before the fingerpad, the nail will rattle on the vibrating string. In either case:
   a. Practice touching the string, alternating fingers (as in a chromatic scale on one string), but do not sound the string.
   b. Practice touching the strings in an arpeggio pattern, but do not sound the string.
   c. Practice 7, a & b, but release the string.
   d. Practice chromatic scales slowly (listen for a break in the sound or a "click" or listen for a rattle from the nail on the string).

N.B. In all the above solutions, make sure the finger placement is obsessively precise in the exercises. If a student can conquer refined finger placement in exercises, it *will* eventually filter into the student's regular playing with virtually no extra effort.

• *LEFT HAND*

1. Poor Hand Position.
   a. Check sitting position.
   b. Check position of the arms.
   c. Check that the left hand thumb is correctly positioned at the back of the neck.
   d. Check that fingers are staying properly curved. If not, work on a piece that uses the "Fourth-Finger Approach."

2. Joints Collapse.
   a. Check left hand finger nail length. *Cf.* 1, d. If nails are too long, the finger will naturally collapse at the first joint when the nail presses against the fingerboard before the fingertip. With more advanced students, use No. 6 of "The Basic Seven" Exercises (the ascending and descending slur).
   b. Check hand position.

3. Improper Finger Movement.
   a. Practice Scratching Exercise with left hand.
   b. Work on finger placement, pulse and release.
   c. Work on chromatic scales and nos. 1 & 2 of "The Basic Seven" Exercises.

4. Lack of Finger Independence.
   a. *Cf.* 3, a–c.
   b. Make sure that in exercises, fingers are not being held down when not in use, as this can reinforce independence problems.
   c. Work on nos. 3, 4 & 5 of "The Basic Seven" Exercises.
   d. Isolate the specific passage and make a study out of that movement.

5. Lack of Control.
   a. *Cf.* 3, a–c.
   b. Practice slowly.
   c. Isolate the problem area and use it as a study.

6. Inability to Develop Speed.
   a. *Cf.* Chapter "Developing Speed."
   b. *Cf.* 3, b. Practice staccato. Use various dotted rhythms.
   c. Practice No. 6 of "The Basic Seven" Exercises and accent the ascending slur.
   d. Isolate the problem area and use it as a study.

7. Difficult Reaches.
   a. *Cf.* 3 & 4.
   b. Practice Nos. 1 & 2 of "The Basic Seven" Exercises, and alternately skip a fret between fingers on each playing (*i.e.* skip a fret between ① and ② and play through the exercise; skip a fret between ② and ③ and play through the exercise, *etc.*).

8. Difficult Shifts.
   a. Practice diatonic scales (the Segovia edition or similar fingering that includes shifts).
   b. Make sure the student is not starting to vibrato prior to landing securely on the target note.
   c. To isolate and practice the actual shift, break the shift into three segments:
      i. start at the original position (before shifting) and sound the note,
      ii. shift quickly to the new position, but wait: do not sound the note, *then*,
      iii. sound the note.
   Gradually decrease the "pause" before the note is sounded until the section can be played in tempo. This exercise conditions the left hand to stay *ahead* of the shift, and is extremely constructive.

• *RIGHT AND LEFT HAND COORDINATION*

Work through nos. 1-4 of "The Basic Seven" Exercises, in order (Individual Full Plant, Full Plant, Sequential Plant, Free), with the following steps:

1. Practice touching the string with both hands at exactly the same time. Listen for simultaneous "click" of the right and left hand fingers on the string.

2. Practice pulsing both hands at the same time.

3. Practice *touch, pulse* and *release* with both hands at the same time.

4. In the context of pieces, isolate specific areas that seem to be problematic, see if there is a consistency, and make a study out of those movements.

• *GENERAL OUTLINE OF STUDENT LEVELS*

As a general rule, students usually pass through three phases in studying the guitar. Naturally these overlap, but the categories below (and the various subjects that pertain to each category) may help the teacher to more accurately define a student's level which can make teaching more effective.

The most beneficial way to approach these phases is to make an adaptable list of pieces (suitable for each level) which introduce these techniques. Obviously this list should include pieces in all historical periods to insure the student has a well-rounded understanding of period performance practice and historical literature.

Beginner
    Right & left hand finger movement
    Notes in first position
    Dynamics
    Articulation
    Beginning bars (across 2 and 3 strings)
    Basic analysis [usually only phrase recognition, basic compositional forms (two-part song form, rondo, *etc.*)]
    Basic research skills

Intermediate
    Upper position notes (shifting)
    Intermediate bar techniques (across 4, 5 and all 6 strings)
    Slurs (first ascending, then descending)
    Harmonics (natural)
    Vibrato
    Phrasing
    Tone color changes *(ordinario, tasto, ponticello)*
    Basic stage presence/etiquette
    Intermediate research (This could include writing brief program notes for a joint recital, *etc.*)
    Intermediate analysis (discussion of basic harmonic movement, tonal centers, application of an interpretive method, *etc.*)

Advanced

    Harmonics (artificial)

    Special effects (appagado, subito piano slur, specialized
      fingering, *etc.*)

    Tremolo

    Tone color changes with Opposition and Complementary
      Movements

    Advanced bar techniques (Angle Bar, Hinge Bar)

    In-depth research (Usually choose one piece per year which the
      student is playing. This could culminate in a written paper
      presented to the other guitarists in a studio class.)

    Prepared guitar techniques

    Transcribing tablature (lute, Baroque Guitar, *etc.*). Be sure to
      explain the different types of tablature notation for Renais-
      sance tablature (Spanish, French, English, *etc.*).

For truly serious advanced students (who appear to be headed for a career in music), I've found it beneficial to take them on as unpaid "assistants" assigning them to one beginning student. As the teacher you should still teach the lessons, but the assistant is encouraged to attend the lessons, help the younger student with research, *etc.*

This serves a number of positive interests. The assistant begins to learn how to teach (in some cases they may even act as a "substitute" for you if you are away on tour). This will also give the assistant a "younger peer" to which he will have to "live up to" which can be highly motivating.

For the younger student (assuming you have paired an assistant and student who are compatible) having a rôle model (who is reinforcing the ideas you teach) can be highly motivating.

This can also give you a chance to watch the interaction between the assistant and younger student and perhaps gain new insight into your own teaching. In short, everyone benefits; you, the assistant and the younger student.

Professional-Level Student

This is the final stage (beyond "Advanced") that occurs at the graduate or post-graduate level of study—as well as in extended masterclasses.

The relationship between the teacher and a professional-level student is a rare and *fascinating* situation. In lessons, the teacher obviously works more as a coach and "mentor," since the student will already be aware of all the technical and musical possibilities on the instrument. In lessons, rather than saying "...*do it this way...*", the teacher uses inquiry, such as:

    1) "...what do you think about the timbre you're using here?"

    2) "...I don't understand what you want to do with this phrase."

    3) "...are you sure the audience will understand this dynamic change?"

    4) "...I'm not convinced that the shape of the line works here. Convince me."

In defining this phase, European study has an innate advantage, since a student will often begin very young, and stay with a teacher for many years, which makes the progression into this final stage more logical. Another advantage in Europe is that the formal version of "you" (in French "vous," in German, "Sie", in Italian, "lei," *etc.*) is always used between the student and teacher. When the *teacher* decides that they should begin using the familiar form of "you," this final stage of the relationship has formally arrived. This is such a monumental "shift" in the relationship (particularly in German), that it is not uncommon for the teacher to bring a bottle of champagne to the lesson, and they spend the lesson talking, and for the first time the student/teacher will use their first names when talking to each other.

In English, this phase is more ambiguous since we don't have a linguistic distinction in relationships. When I teach in English and this final stage arrives, I usually invite the student out for a coffee or a glass of wine, and explain that he has arrived at this level. He should be encouraged to begin moving out on his own (musically and professionally) and use the teacher as a "sounding board" for his ideas.

Be aware that the student will—from here on out—have the right to disagree with you, which some teachers find threatening, and (much like an adolescent rebelling against his parents) you may have confrontations; but there is no other way for the student to earn his "independence." If the teacher has carefully guided the student's musical and personal growth, the relationship will be secure enough to withstand these slight differences.

APPENDIX II
SAMPLE 16-LESSON OUTLINE

Since every student and situation varies, the outline below is intended to be only an example. Nonetheless, the order of teaching these various subjects has proven very successful.

Past the 16th lesson, there are naturally innumerable subjects that need to be taught, such as upper position playing, harmonics, *etc.,* but these should be applied to specific pieces being studied, rather than haphazardly thrown at the student for no apparent reason.

For very young students each of these suggested "lessons" may take twice as much time. As long as the student is having fun in the lesson, the fact that they are not progressing one lesson per week is never a problem. *Never* try to rush progress with the younger students.

For these (as well as the older students), I've found it helpful to keep several pieces "active." At the same time that they are learning the "next piece" have them memorize the previous piece. This not only gives them more repertoire (even at the beginning stages) that they can play, but will accustom them to memorizing music.

I usually make a game out of this by creating a "concert list." Once they have a piece memorized, they can write that piece onto the list. In a lesson, I go through the list and, on demand, have them play through any of the pieces on the list. This encourages them to keep the pieces ready to perform and inadvertently encourages more practice. Astoundingly, I have had some young students for only one year, after which they could perform from memory over 45 minutes of music.

• *Lesson 1*
    • *Introduce:*
—Briefly discuss the anatomical function of the hands, and the reasons that we play as we do.
—scratching exercise
Particularly if the student is non-classically oriented, explain the vast advantages of having a classical background: establishing a solid technique, familiarity with note reading (necessary for any type of commercial or studio work, *etc.*) familiarity with varied literature, and so on.

Write out anything the student should bring to the next lesson (method book, blank staff paper notebook, *etc.*) but avoid a long list of expensive items—remember, often a student has just bought a guitar so finances may be a bit low. Be sure to mention buying a new set of strings to have on hand, and show him how to change a string. This can save a wasted week if a string breaks between lessons.

Finally, if you are responsible for collecting the lesson fee, explain this as well as your absentee policy. Generally, the best payment schedule is at least one month at a time (this insures a minimal commitment to the assigned lesson time). For missed lessons, normally a 24-hour advance notice can be rescheduled, otherwise, the teacher should be under no obligation to refund a fee or reschedule a lesson.

On this subject, it is wise to have a printed handout or "contract" with all these details (as I discussed in Chapter 15,—*Arranging a Private Studio*) to give to first-time students and signed by either them or the parents. A dated "sign-in book" is also helpful, since this will verify when and how many lessons a student has had which can help in scheduling make-up lessons as well as help you organize your gross income.

• *Lesson 2*
• *Review:*
—anatomical function of the hands
—scratching exercise
• *Introduce:*
—names of right hand fingers
—sitting
—introduce note reading and basic rhythms (on open strings)
—listening/reading assignment
    While the first two lessons give a student little to actually work on, stress the importance of the scratching exercise. One or two weeks on this exercise will usually insure good basic right hand finger movement.

N.B. For guitarists with little musical background, a guitar "note speller" is often helpful. *Cf.* Appendix III, "Suggested Methods, Studies and Pieces."

• *Lesson 3*
• *Review:*
—all previously introduced material
• *Introduce:*
—further music reading (notes on ① [*i.e.* first position, E, F & G])
—moving exercise with various right hand finger patterns (this can be a good time to introduce the Giuliani *120 Studies for the Right Hand, Op. 1, A.*

One interesting approach to right hand arpeggio studies is to use Giuliani nos. 25-35, rather than nos. 2-10. These later studies include *all* the right hand fingers instead of only *p, i,* and *m,* and these usually pose no additional problems. If the teacher decides to use the earlier Giuliani, make sure that the student goes back and relearns each study using *p, m* and *a* (in addition to *p, i* and *m*). This will insure that the *a* finger begins to develop along with the others.

If the student is *very* young (*i.e.* if you are avoiding using material with notes) another effective approach is to simply give them different right hand arpeggio patterns to use as warm-ups such as the following four patterns:

p, i, m, a
p, a, m, i
p, m, i, a
p, a, i, m

Design a practice schedule! Actually sit down with the student and write out a half hour/hour long schedule of what is to be practiced every day. Simply having this sort of regimented daily practice schedule on paper can promote more consistent practice habits. A sample practice schedule is given below.

Fig. 1. Sample Practice Schedule

• *10 Minutes:* Warm ups (usually technical exercises) *i.e.* scales (diatonic or chromatic) and arpeggios.

• *5 Minutes:* Study the music (without the guitar—*cf.* chapter on "Mental Practice"). This not only accustoms the student to this type of quintessential practicing, but will also give the hands a slight chance to "cool down" after the initial warm up period.

[Fig. 1. Sample Practice Schedule, cont.]
   • *15 Minutes:* Play/practice new material.

   • *5 Minutes:* Warm Down. Play through old material from previous lessons and end the practice session with a few technical exercises. This time of the practice session is actually the most beneficial, since the student will invariably get "carried away" and end up playing for a much longer period of time "for fun," because he is playing through pieces he already knows. [*Cf.* Appendix III "Suggested Methods, Studies and Pieces" which lists a number of collections (even for beginners) which have pieces easy enough to use as a daily "reading-for-fun" time.] This can include the "concert list" that I mentioned previously.

•*Lesson 4*
• *Review:*
—material from previous lesson
• Introduce:
—release of the string
—new lesson (notes on ②)
—introduce the first Giuliani Right Hand Study #2, using only Individual Full Plant. I have deleted using #1 of the Giuliani, since this is not actually a right hand finger pattern, but to simply accustom the left hand fingers to the notes. If a student is not familiar with the chords in the Giuliani "120," use open strings.
—listening/reading assignment

•*Lesson 5*
• *Review:*
—material from previous lesson
• *Introduce:*
—new lesson (notes on ③)
—Giuliani Right Hand Study #3 [Individual Full Plant]
—listening/reading assignment

•*Lesson 6*
• *Review:*
—materials from previous lesson
• *Introduce:*
—new lesson (notes on ④)
—Giuliani Right Hand Study #4
—listening/reading assignment

•Lesson 7
• Review:
—material from previous lesson
• Introduce:
—new lesson (notes on ⑤)
—Giuliani Right Hand Study #5
—reading/listening assignment

•Lesson 8
• Review:
—material from previous lesson
• Introduce:
—new lesson (notes on ⑥)
—Giuliani Right Hand Study #6
—listening/reading assignment

N.B. By this time, depending on the chosen method, the student will normally have learned the diatonic notes on each string in first position. Begin working immediately on a piece (presumably from the method) which has a melody line on the top and a bass line with open notes. If the method doesn't have such a piece, find a supplementary book. This will keep up the momentum of the lessons and heighten the interest of the student.

Sometimes it can be best to have the student spend one week playing the melody and the following week add the bass line (perhaps as they are learning the melody line of the next two-part piece).

This may seem overly cautious (to those of us who already play guitar), but for students, playing two voices at once is an extreme and sometimes traumatic event.

•Lesson 9
• Review:
—previous lesson
—all notes
• Introduce:
—Giuliani Right Hand Study #7
—listening/reading assignment
—new piece

• *Lesson 10*
• *Review:*
—previous lesson
• *Introduce:*
—Giuliani Right Hand Study #8
—begin working on dynamics within the new piece
—discuss methods for learning/memorizing [*cf.* chapter "Memorization"]
—listening/reading assignment

• *Lesson 11*
• *Review:*
—piece with dynamics
—review discussion of the different methods of learning/memorizing
• *Introduce:*
—a new piece
—Giuliani Right Hand Study #9
—listening/reading assignment

• *Lesson 12*
• *Review:*
—both pieces
• *Introduce:*
—Giuliani Right Hand Study #10
—dynamics
—Chromatic Exercise #1 from "The Basic Seven" or a similar exercise
—listening/reading assignment

• *Lesson 13*
• *Review:*
—both pieces with dynamics
—chromatic exercise
• *Introduce:*
—Full Planting Technique (*N.B.* At this point go back to the first arpeggio study, and rework the right hand study with Full Plant. When this is accomplished with all ten, again, go back to the beginning and rework all the studies with Sequential Plant, then finally with the Free Technique. Since each planting technique is considerably more complicated than the previous, using familiar arpeggios will ease the transition.)
—Chromatic Exercise #2 of "The Basic Seven" Exercises or a similar exercise
—listening/reading assignment
—new piece

•*Lesson 14*
• *Review:*
—old piece
—both Chromatic Exercises
—check Giuliani Right Hand Study with Full Plant
—continue to discuss various musical elements (dynamics, articulation, timbre, *etc.*)
• *Introduce:*
—the next Giuliani Right Hand Study with Full Plant
—new piece
—listening/reading assignment

•*Lesson 15*
• *Review:*
—old piece
—check Giuliani Right Hand Study with Full Plant
—continue to discuss musical elements
• *Introduce:*
—the next Giuliani Right Hand Study with Full Plant
—new piece
—listening/reading assignment

•Lesson 16

The 16th lesson will normally take a student through the first semester of study. Thereafter, the student will probably be finished with the chosen method book, and may either continue with another volume of the method, or be slowly introduced to individual pieces.

I would encourage teachers to make up some sort of curriculum—a list of graded *(but adaptable!)* pieces from which the student can choose. If the selection is varied enough, this not only gives the student a feeling of being in control of his musical direction, but is also a way to gently monitor what he is studying and make sure that he is being exposed to different historical periods.

In any case, beyond this point, each lesson should *always* include the following three elements:

• *Technical Study*
    Review or introduce an arpeggio or scale (diatonic or chromatic).

• *Musical Study*

Review or introduce a new piece or section of a piece. Always include some musical element in the discussion such as dynamics, timbre changes, articulation, phrasing, *etc.*

• *Educational Study*

Some sort of brief discussion relating to the reading/listening assignment, a recent concert, guitar history, *etc.* Ironically, students who do more research on their own are the same ones who tend to practice more.

APPENDIX III
SUGGESTED METHODS, STUDIES AND PIECES

Because of the vast amount of literature printed in the last 50 years, and the continuing amount of literature arriving on the market almost every day, a list of suggested pedagogical works is nearly impossible to compile.

For that reason, I have listed only those most readily available, and those which tend to have a high level of scholarship. In many cases, there are numerous editions of the same works. In these instances, I have tried to list those which are the most true to the original intent of the author/composer.

**Methods
(For adults)**

Carcassi, Matteo. *Method for Guitar.* Various Editions.
I list this method because, in the original, each lesson is in a different key, (in virtually every "common" guitar key center) and each has an entire multi-movement suite in that key. This method also has separate lessons in each major position, as well as lessons on harmonics, and special effects (tamboura, *etc.*).
All these factors make the Carcassi *Method* a phenomenal supplementary method. The Carcassi is, however, less practical as the primary method because all the music is written by Carcassi and students are not introduced to different styles or historical periods.
While there are many modern editions, most have bastardized the original beyond recognition. Be careful of the edition, but even in its worst form (at the hands of murderous editors) this method is worth having and is a marvelous pedagogical tool.

Parkening, Christopher. *Classical Guitar Method, Vol. 1.* Chicago: Sherry Brenner, 1972.
This is one of the finest general method for adults. It moves quickly, is interesting and reads easily.

Pujol, Emilio. *Escuela Razonada de la Guitarra.* Buenos Aires: Ricordi, 1952-55.
While the text is in Spanish and French (there is an English translation, but it is *very* difficult to find), the studies and exercises in

vols. 2-4 are exceptional for added assignments if a student is having particular technical problems. Pujol was very much a "closed hand player," so some of the illustrations may not be applicable, but this is a solid supplementary method for ultra-serious players.

Glise, Anthony. *Classical Guitar Method for Adults.* St. Joseph/Vienna: Aevia Publications, Ltd., 1998.

In English, French, German and Italian, this is a good method, though it was written for college music majors who are taking guitar as a secondary instrument, so it assumes a *very* solid understanding of music and moves too quickly for most beginning guitarists.

Methods
(For children)

Glise, Anthony. *The Child's Guitar, A Rote Approach.* St. Joseph/Vienna: Aevia Publications, Ltd., 1994.

A method based on rote learning. In three volumes. Includes a cassette.

_____. *Guitar Note Speller, First Position.* St. Joseph/Vienna: Aevia Publications, Ltd., 1994.

A valuable book for beginners. Essentially a workbook where students are given a note and they must write in (on a fingerboard picture) where the note is to be played, the name of the note and *vice versa.* Rapidly solidifies note/fingerboard recognition.

Michaelson, Sonia. *New Dimensions in Classical Guitar for Children.* Pacific, Missouri: Mel Bay Publications, 1991.

This work includes many musical "games" that can help with children. Some ideas are direct from the teaching methods of Zoltán Kodály but applied to guitar. A solid method.

Studies
(Technical Studies/Scales & Arpeggios)

Barbosa-Lima, Carlos. *Arpeggio Studies.* Pacific, Missouri: Mel Bay Publications, 1995.

These are *left hand* arpeggio studies (as opposed to right hand, such as the Giuliani, 120). While somewhat stylized (they do not stick to the standard major, minor, *etc.* arpeggios), they are a fine collection of exercises that fill a need in technical development.

_____. *Guitar Scales*. Pacific, Missouri: Mel Bay Publications, 1995.

These give the standard Segovia fingerings as well as some slight variant fingerings. The primary advantage to this, is that it also gives various modes and some fun altered scales. Suggested for more advanced students.

Barreiro, Elias. *Diatonic Scales (Major & Minor)*. Cincinnati: Willis Music Co., 1980.

This edition gives the traditional fingerings (*i.e.* the "Segovia" fingerings) as well as first position scales which are more suitable for beginners.

_____. *Diatonic Scales in Thirds, Sixths and Octaves*. Cincinnati: Willis Music Co., 1981.

Upper position studies good for beginners/intermediate students. Similar to the "Studies for the Left Hand" found in the Giuliani Op. 1, A (*cf.* below), though these are written simply as scale studies, and are more suitable for beginner/intermediate students.

Berg, Christopher. *The Elements of Classical Guitar Technique*. Pacific: Mel Bay Publications, 1996.

This is a marvelous "sleeper" originally written by Mr. Berg for use with his students. This book covers a number of technical facets of classical guitar rarely addressed. Well-written, logical and applicable to different schools of technique. Highly recommended.

Dodgson, Stephen and Hector Quine. *Progressive Reading for Guitarists*. London: Ricordi & Co., 1975.

This is a graded book of sight-reading studies. Virtually no fingerings are given (to prohibit the student reading the "fingering" rather than the notes). Valuable if a student is having trouble sight-reading.

Giuliani, Mauro. *120 Studies for the Right Hand, Op. 1, A*, ed. Elias Barreiro. Cincinnati: Willis Music Co., 1982. Also: *Studies for Guitar*, ed. Dieter Kreidler. Mainz Schott, 1981.

Both these editions are true to the original, though the Schott edition uses the old German fingering (with dots), while the Willis uses letters (*p, i, m, a*). The Schott edition also includes "*Studies for Left Hand*" (studies in thirds, sixths and octaves which are written as etudes). For more advanced students. This collection of right hand arpeggios has never been equaled and is the standard collection of right hand studies for classical guitarists. Highly recommended.

Glise, Anthony, ed. *Chromatic Exercises ("The Basic Seven") and Arpeggio Studies, Op. 2, A.* St. Joseph/Vienna: Aevia Publications, Ltd., 1994.

Good preparatory studies for scales (upper position). The section on arpeggios includes detailed instruction on Individual Full Plant, Full Plant, Sequential Plant and Free right hand techniques. Included in Chapter 7 of this book.

Segovia, Andrés, ed. *Diatonic Major and Minor Scales.* Washington: Columbia Music Co., 1953.

This is the "standard" edition of scales, though (because of the upper position work) they are less suitable for beginners.

Sagreras, Julio. *Lecciones de Guitarra* (7 vols.). Buenos Aires: Ricordi Americana, n.d.

While these volumes are perhaps not so practical as the main method, they contain hundreds of exercises that are useful as supplementary assignments. Written in Spanish, there is an English translation, but is difficult to find.

Concert Studies

Brower, Léo. *Études* (4 vols.). Paris: Max Eschig, 1972.

A brilliant series of contemporary studies. Similar to the Glise, *Unterwegs* (below), but for intermediate to advanced level students.

Carcassi, Matteo. *25 Studies, Op. 60,* ed. Miguel Llobet. Buenos Aires: Ricordi, 1974.

This excellent edition can be *very* difficult to find. There are several newer editions, *Melodische und Fortschrittende Etüden,* ed. Anton Stingl. Mainz: Schott, 1971, and *The Complete Carcassi Guitar Method (including the Op. 60 Studies).* Pacific, MO: Mel Bay, 1994. Both the Schott and Bay editions are similar to the Llobet—which is brilliant, but very difficult to find.

Glise, Anthony. *Unterwegs, I & II* (2 vols.) *(Twenty Progressive Bagatelles for Beginners).* St. Joseph/Vienna: Aevia Publications, Ltd., 1994.

Both volumes introduce students to various aspects of contemporary music (*i.e.* mixed meters, contemporary harmonies, prepared guitar techniques *etc.*). Good supplemental pieces for beginners and intermediate students interested in contemporary classical music.

Sor, Fernando. *Complete Sor Studies*, ed. David Grimes. Pacific,
      Missouri: Mel Bay Publications, 1994. *also*

_____. *The Complete Studies for Guitar*, ed. Brian Jeffery. Published in
      facsimile. New York: Shattinger, 1978.
      Both these editions of the Sor studies (Ops. 6, 29, 31, 35 & 60) are
valuable for different reasons. The Grimes is a modern edition (which
also includes op. 44) and are graded. The Jeffery is in facsimile, thus
reliable from an historic standpoint, but ghastly to try and read. Teachers should have both, while students are probably best to stay with the
Grimes edition.

Collections of Pieces for Beginners

Bay, Mel. *Editiones Classicae*, (numerous editions). Pacific, Missouri:
      Mel Bay, 1995-present.
      This is a new series of editions published by Mel Bay Publications.
They are easy to read, and many come with a cassette or CD which can
help with less advanced students. Repertoire ranges from traditional
classical literature to "gig" music. Especially worth attention are the
editions from:

      David Grimes: Historically correct, and while scholarly, still read-
able for the student. Highly recommended are the *Treasures of the Baroque*
series (three volumes to-date) which are good for beginner's repertoire
or for more advanced students to use as sight-readable "gig" music.

      Carlos Barbosa-Lima: Some well-written and creative technical
writings for more advanced students.

Examination Repertoire for the Royal Conservatory of Music—Toronto, 8
      vols. Toronto: Frederick Harris, 1990.
      This is a marvelous collection of general repertoire for guitar.
Logically graded, and easy to read. For intermediate students and
beyond.

Goetz, Walter. *Die Stunde der Gitarre*, in three vols. *(An Hour With The
      Guitar)*. Mainz: Schott, 1925, 1953.
      This edition uses the old German right hand fingering, but is a
good collection of original guitar pieces, predominantly from the 19th-
Century. It can be highly unfaithful to the originals, but is *extremely* well-
organized. These are good for the student to read "for fun," or to
supplement weekly assignments.

Michaelson, Sonia. *Easy Classic Guitar Solos for Children.* Pacific,
Missouri: Mel Bay, 1991.

Exactly what the name implies. Well designed, and suitable for
students up to about age 8. Good supplementary pieces if the regular
method seems to be moving too quickly for a student.

Music Theory
(Beginners)

Goldsmith, Rob. *Easiest Guitar Theory Book.* Pacific, Missouri:
Mel Bay Publications, 1992.

A *very* basic theory book applied to guitar. Explains half steps,
whole steps, scale construction, *etc.*

(Intermediate)

Cimino, Basil, Robert Lilienfeld. *The Guitarist's Harmony.* Melville,
NY: Franco Colombo, 1965.

Very difficult to find but highly applicable to more advanced
guitarists. Traditional music theory applied to guitar and with musical
examples from the standard repertoire.

N.B. In addition to these few listed works, publishers are constantly
releasing graded collections of music. Students should be encouraged
to periodically visit their local music store and simply "browse" through
the available materials, and bring what they find to lessons.

APPENDIX IV
SUGGESTED MAGAZINES

The following magazines include articles, information, lists of current events and activities in the classical guitar world. Because addresses sometimes change, students should consult *Ulrich's Guide to Periodicals* (available in any general library) for a current address. *Ulrich's* (which is updated annually) will also list any newer magazines that appear in the future.

Those magazines marked with asterisks should be available in any music school library which has a guitar program.

• U.S.

* *The Soundboard* [in English]. Published by the Guitar Foundation of America. This is the largest and perhaps the least biased and most scholarly of any classical guitar magazine available. Also lists festivals and masterclasses world-wide. Highly recommended.

Guitar Review [in English]. Published in New York, and very closely associated with the New York guitar scene. Contains principally information regarding that area, though some articles and general information often appear.

Guitar Player Magazine [in English]. Traditionally a pop/rock magazine, though periodic articles about classical guitar do appear.

• GERMANY

* *Gitarre und Laute* [in German]. The principal magazine for German-speaking countries. Contains scholarly articles, but also a good source of information for the entire European guitar scene including festivals, masterclasses and concerts.

Zupfmusik [in German]. This publication is not terribly scholarly, but is a *highly* reliable source of information for masterclasses, concerts and guitar festivals in Germany, Austria and Switzerland. Also includes information on activities for mandolin, which is still very popular (and very active) in German-speaking countries.

• FRANCE

* *Les Cahiers de la Guitare* [in French]. The principal source of guitar information for French-speaking countries. Strongly associated with the activities in and around Paris, but also includes information regarding all of France, Belgium, French-speaking Canada and the French Caribbean.

• CANADA

Guitar Canada [in English]. Primarily a source for Canadian guitarists. Canadian activities are generally well-documented as well as some of the major activities in France and the U.S.

• ITALY

* *Il Fronimo* [various languages]. An excellent source of information for the Italian guitar world. Scholarly articles which are generally not re-translated from the original manuscript submissions. Thus, an issue may contain articles in English, French or German as well as Italian.

• ENGLAND

Classical Guitar [in English]. Occasionally nationalistic, though a reliable source of information for guitar activities in London.

APPENDIX V
SELECTED SECONDARY RESEARCH
SOURCE MATERIALS

Most of the sources below should be available in any university or conservatory music library. Non-reference books may be obtained on "inter-library loan." Some of the sources listed are "primary" (*i.e.* they are actually written in the specific period), and are available in facsimile or in modern editions. The remainder are "secondary" sources (*i.e.* written by someone else [usually contemporary] *about* the given period). All sources are in English unless otherwise indicated.

I cannot over-stress how important it is for students to become familiar with these materials! Research will help them grow into solid, thinking musicians—which are virtually the only type who ever develop beyond the beginning stages or survive the business at a professional level. From a practical standpoint, they will need to be familiar with these materials in order to write their own program notes, find composer's dates (for programs), and to simply acquire the historical background of a given piece or composer to insure the correct interpretation, *etc.*

Secondary sources and encyclopedias have become fairly comparable from country to country, so I have tried to list only those in English, though some foreign sources are well worth the attention of multilingual students.

Beyond the materials listed here, magazine articles are an important source of information on the cutting edge of research, which often do not appear in books until years later. These are most easily located through one or more of the listings under "Research Options."

Computer internet services can also be useful in tracking information. While still in its infancy, this can be a valuable tool. If you are unfamiliar with this high-tech aspect of research, talk with the music librarian at your school. They are there to help you and are trained professionals in research.

◇ Research Options

Bibliographies. Bibliographic references are best found in books that are exclusively bibliographic listings (*Cf.* McCutcheon below).

Other options are the bibliographies from various encyclopedias. The entries are usually listed chronologically. *Cf.* for example "Guitar" bibliographies in *The New Grove,* and its offshoot, *The New Grove Dictionary of Musical Instruments,* written by Dr. Thomas Heck.

The International Index of Music Periodicals. This is exclusively a Web database for which institutions can purchase passwords for their students and faculty. Available through Chadwyck-Healey.

Music Index (1949-present) is a good source and is found in music libraries as well as on CD-ROM in selected libraries.

Repertoire International de la Littérature Musicale (RILM). RILM is available in printed form and also located on internet on OCLC FirstSearch. This includes periodical articles and documentation of various scholarship activities.

◇ Encyclopedias

Atlas zur Musik, ed. Ulrich Michels, Munich: Deutscher Taschenbuch
    Verlag, 1995.
    This is a *brilliant* two-volume general theoretical and historical dictionary over music that can be helpful if the student is trying to learn musical terms in another language (to prepare for study overseas, *etc.*). There are translations from the original German edition into the languages listed below (the publishers are given in parenthesis):
    Danish (Munksgaard, Copenhagen); *French* (Librairie Arthème Fayard, Paris); *Greek* (Nakas, Athens); *Italian* (Sperling & Kupfer, Milan); *Japanese* (Hakusuisha Ltd., Tokyo); *Dutch* (Bosch & Keuning, Baarn); *Polish* (Editions Schubert, Breslau); *Portuguese* (Editorial Comunicação, Lisbon); *Spanish* (Alianza Editorial, Madrid); *Hungarian* (Hungarica, Budapest).
    Sadly, there is not yet an English translation of this work, but if students have studied the basics of one of the above languages, they should be able to fight through this writing and glean a considerable amount of musical vocabulary.

Dictionary of Contemporary Music, ed. John Vinton. New York:
    E.P. Dutton, 1971.
    A good source for recognized contemporary composers and their works. Gives composer's dates which can be difficult to find for program notes, *etc.*

Encyclopédie de la Musique, eds. F, Michel, F. Lesure and V. Fédorov, 3
    vols., Paris: 1958-61.

This is a good standard reference source in French. As with
virtually all French publications, this is insanely expensive, but should
be available in a university or conservatory library.

*Handbook for American Musicians Overseas with The Dictionary of
    Contemporary Musical Terms (in English, French, German and
    Italian),* ed. Anthony Glise. St. Joseph/Vienna: Aevia Publica-
    tions, 1997.

There are hundreds of dictionaries which give the "standard"
musical terms in foreign languages *(i.e. forte, ritard, etc.).* This dictionary
is precisely *not* that. It gives music-*related* terms *(i.e."* articulation,"
"make-up lesson," "stage fright," "microphone stand," *etc.),* in French,
German and Italian. Highly valuable since most of these terms are never
taught in foreign language classes, but are necessary in a musician's
daily foreign vocabulary if he is studying or working overseas.

Also includes the *Handbook for American Musicians Overseas,* which
gives various details of studying and living overseas as an American
citizen.

The New Grove Dictionary of Music and Musicians, ed. Stanley Sadie, 20
    vols. London: Macmillan, 1980.

This is probably the single-most important secondary source
available in English. While it has limited entries regarding guitar, it does
list exceptional bibliographical information for expanded research, and
a vast array of subjects that supersede any other source in English. A
revised edition of *The New Grove* is slated for publication by roughly
1998.

The New Harvard Dictionary of Music, ed. Don Michael Randel. Cam-
    bridge, Massachusetts: Belknap Press of Harvard Univ. Press,
    1986.

This is the most standard music dictionary available in English
and it should be a fixture in every musician's personal library. While it
has limited entries regarding guitar, it is a reliable source for musical
terms and general information.

Die Musik in Geschichte und Gegenwart, ed. F. Blume, 17 vols. Kassel:
    Bärenreiter, 1986.

This is the German language equivalent of *The New Grove.* Scholarly and very reliable, this is strongly recommended for students who
speak German and aren't afraid of losing their eyesight to unbelievably
small print.

◇ General Music History

Grout, Donald J. with Claude Palisca, *A History of Western Music, 4th ed.* New York: W.W. Norton, 1988.

This is the standard music history textbook used in most colleges, universities and conservatories in the U.S. A very reliable source, which is far more readable than any previous attempt to compile nearly 3,000 years of musical history into one volume.

Prentice Hall History of Music Series, ed. H. Wiley Hitchcock. Englewood Cliffs: Prentice Hall.

This series of small books offers a good general history of music with each historical period published in a separate volume and written by a specialist in that period. Covers Medieval through Contemporary music as well as separate volumes for ethnic musics. A good inexpensive introduction for the uninitiated but serious student.

◇ Specifically Guitar Sources

Bone, Philip J. *The Guitar and Mandolin, Biographies of Celebrated Players and Composers.* Temecula, Calif.: Reprint Services, 1988.

This contains inaccuracies (this is a reprint of the original 1954 edition), but it lists many players long forgotten today. A valuable source for tracking information about relatively unknown guitarists and music.

Chiesa, Ruggero, E. Allorto, M. Dell'Ara, A. Gilardino. *La Chitarra.* Torino: EDT [Edizioni di Torino], 1990.

This is a good general book on the guitar. Written in Italian by four of that country's leading guitar scholars. It has good historical documentation and information on various playing styles, techniques and methods.

Grunfeld, Frederick. *The Art and Times of the Guitar.* New York: Collier Books, 1969.

This is probably the most readily available "general" history of the guitar. It is a questionable source to quote, due to some inaccuracies. Nonetheless, it was one of the first attempts (in English) to compile a general history of the guitar and worth overlooking the occasional problems.

Manuale di Storia della Chitarra (2 vols.)

Gilardino, Angelo. *La Chitarra Moderna e Contemporanea.* Ancona: Bèrben, 1989, *and*

Dell'Ara, Mario. *La Chitarra Antica, Classica e Romantica.* Ancona: Bèrben, 1988.

These two volumes comprise a good general history of the guitar. Unfortunately, it is available only in Italian, but full of documentation, information facsimiles and opus listings for composers. This along with *La Chitarra* (above) is the standard text for Italian conservatories.

McCutcheon, Meredith Alice. *Guitar and Vihuela: An Annotated Bibliography.* New York: Pendragon Press, 1985.

This is a good bibliography for our repertoire. Note that many bibliographic guides can be found in encyclopedias. (*Cf.* "Research Sources" above.)

Powrozniak, Jozef, ed. *Gitarren Lexikon.* Berlin: Verlag Neue Musik Berlin, n.d.

Written in German by the Polish guitar historian, Powrozniak, this is in dictionary format showing entries for virtually every guitarist that he could come up with. With his death several years ago it is likely that there will be no revised editions, but for information about guitarists up to *ca.* 1985, it is a fascinating and predominantly accurate source.

Turnbull, Harvey. *The Guitar from Renaissance to the Present Day.* New York: Charles Schribner's Son's, 1974.

This is probably the most accurate and readily available "general" history of the guitar. Somewhat dated due to recent research, and written in a rather dry style, but a well-rounded book.

Tyler, James. *The Early Guitar—A History and Handbook.* London: Oxford Univ. Press., 1980.

An extremely well-written and reliable source on the early guitar and plucked instruments. Gives many primary sources that are in facsimile reprint, and a good bibliography.

Zuth, Josef. *Handbuch der Laute und Gitarre.* Vienna: Universal, 1926.

This is a fairly reliable source in dictionary format written in German. As with the Bone and Powrozniak, this lists famous guitarists as well as relatively unknown guitarists and repertoire. It is important to keep in mind the date and the national background of the author to compensate for his zealous attitude toward Germanic guitarists/composers.

◇ Performance Practice
(General)

Brown, Howard M., and Stanley Sadie, eds. *Performance Practice—Music after 1600.* New York: W.W. Norton, 1989.
    An intriguing series of articles by leading musicologists covering music from 1600 to the 20th-Century. Most articles also give valuable primary and secondary source bibliographies.

Crocker, Richard. *A History of Musical Style.* New York: McGraw-Hill, 1966.
    This is a wonderful "historically-oriented" book which crosses the tenuous boundaries between music history and performance style in the various periods. While the guitar is not addressed, the information is invaluable.

Donnington, Robert. *The Interpretation of Early Music.* London: Faber & Faber, 1963.
    A somewhat dated study, due to the amount of research in the field since its publication. However, this has been a standard source for years and is still a good general overview of performance practice.

Keller, Hermann. *Phrasing and Articulation*, trans., Leigh Gerdine. New York: W.W. Norton, 1965.
    A good general study of the options which lie before a performer.

Tonazzi, Bruno. *Liuto, Vihuela, Chitarra e Strumenti Similari Nelle Loro Intavolature, con Cenni Sulle Loro Litterature.* Ancona: Bèrben, 1974.
    Besides having an impressively long title, this book is invaluable in deciphering the various tablatures used for guitar and guitar-related instruments through the centuries. Sadly, it is available only in Italian, but fairly easy for non-Italian speakers due to the many examples and facsimiles of tablature. Essential for any research in pre-traditional notation.

Vinquist, Mary and Neal Zaslaw. *Performance Practice: A Bibliography.* New York: W.W. Norton, 1971.
    A good source listing for performance practice of various instruments and historical periods. Also lists articles (international) in nearly 100 publications up to 1971.

◇ Performance Practice
(Specific Periods)

Medieval Period

Aspects of Medieval and Renaissance Music—A Birthday Offering for
Gustave Reese, ed. Jan LaRue. New York: W.W. Norton, 1966.
A monument of research written by various musicologists as a
birthday present for the giant of musicology, Gustave Reese. Good for
serious readers.

Bukovzer, Manfred, *Studies in Medieval and Renaissance Music.* New
York: W.W. Norton, 1950.
One of the milestones in period research. Highly recommended
for anyone interested in serious research and detective stories.

Hoppin, Richard. *Medieval Music.* New York: W.W. Norton, 1978.
Very comfortable to read and highly informative, this has become
a standard text for graduate school studies in the U.S.

Renaissance Period

Dowland, Robert. *A Varietie of Lute Lessons* (London, 1610), facsimile
edition, ed. E. Hunt. London: Schott, 1958.
This is a tremendous work written by the son of lutenist John
Dowland. As well as being a marvelous historical document, this
volume contains an impressive compilation of well-known pieces by
various composers (in English lute tablature) which may be given to
more advanced students when they begin learning how to transcribe
tablature.

Ganassi, Sylvestro. *Regalo Rubertina* (Venice, 1542-43), modern edition, ed. Hildemarie Peter, trans. Daphne and Steven Silvester.
Berlin: Robert Lienau, 1977.
A fascinating method for recorder with good information on
period performance practice. Also gives many examples of Renaissance
improvisation.

Reese, Gustave. *Music in the Renaissance* (New York: W.W. Norton,
1959).
This is the standard text in most U.S. universities and conservatories for classes targeting the Renaissance period. A tremendous source
of information.

Simpson, Christopher. *The Division Viol or The Art of Playing Extempore Upon a Ground* (London, 1659), facsimile edition. London: J. Curwen & Sons, 1955.

Similar to Ganassi, but with more details on Renaissance improvisation.

Baroque Period

Bach, C.P.E., *The True Art of Playing Keyboard Instruments* (*Versuch über die wahre Art das Clavier zu spielen*, Berlin, 1759), modern edition, ed. William Mitchell. New York: W.W. Norton, 1949.

An excellent primary source for Baroque music and performance practice. Includes explanations of period Northern Germanic ornaments.

Baron, Ernst Gottlieb. *A Study of the Lute* (*Untersuchung des Instruments der Lauten*, Nürnburg, 1727), modern edition, ed. Douglas Smith. Redondo Beach, Calif.: Instrumenta Antiqua Pub., 1976.

A wonderful book, similar to Bach but written from a lutenist's standpoint.

le Huray, Peter. *Authenticity in Performance—18th-Century Case Studies.* New York: Cambridge Univ. Press, 1990.

A bit weighty to read, but a marvelous source of information although the guitar is neglected.

Quantz, Johann Joachim. *On Playing the Flute* (*Versuch einer Unweisung die Flötetraversiere zu spielen*, Berlin, 1752), modern edition, ed. Edward Riley. New York: Schirmer Books, 1966.

Similar to the C.P.E. Bach, though with a different slant because the flute is a sustaining instrument. Remember that both C.P.E. Bach and Quantz were in the same court (under Frederick the Great in Berlin), as was Sylvious Leopold Weiss. Thus, for guitarists, this information is directly applicable to Weiss' compositions and indirectly to those of J.S. Bach.

Classic Period

Glise, Anthony, ed. *The Complete Sonatas of Sor Giuliani and Diabelli*, (St. Joseph/Vienna: Aevia Publishing, 1997).

I list this, not only because of the sonatas (which are published as an urtext edition in *all* the original versions), but because the preface is the first (and to-date) the only extensive treatise on 19th-Century performance practice for guitar. It covers a wide gamut of subjects including general performance practice, special effects, ornamentation, improvisation and cadenzas.

Heck, Thomas. "The Birth of the Classic Guitar and its Cultivation in Vienna, Reflected in the Career and Compositions of Mauro Giuliani (d. 1829)." Unpublished Ph.D. dissertation, Yale University, 1970.

This is the definitive writing about Giuliani. The second volume is a cataloging of Giuliani's works, which was the basis of the *Complete Works* of Giuliani reprinted in facsimile by Tecla Editions, 1984-87. (A more complete checklist of the earliest editions of Giuliani's works is found in Heck's 1995 book cited below.) While this dissertation gives little insofar as period performance practice, it is a fascinating and readable study of the father of our modern concert guitar.

_____. *Mauro Giuliani: Virtuoso Guitarist and Composer.* Columbus: Editions Orphée, 1995.

This is the culmination of 25 years of further research by Dr. Heck following his monumental dissertation on Giuliani (*cf.* above). Highly informative, easy to read and above all, *highly* recommended for any guitarist who plays Giuliani.

Jeffery, Brian. *Fernando Sor: Composer and Guitarist*, 2nd ed., Soar Chapel, Penderyn, South Wales: Tecla Editions, 1994.

This is a *marvelous* biographical source, including a cataloging of Sor's works, which is updated from the first edition of this work from 1977.

Mozart, Leopold. *Violin School (Einer Gründlichen Violinschule, Augsberg, 1756)*, modern edition, trans. Editha Knocker. New York: Oxford Univ. Press, 1985.

A milestone in performance practice of the early Classic period, written with a charming dry sense of humor. Easy to find and fun to read.

Neumann, Fredrich. *Ornamentation and Improvisation in Mozart.* Princeton: Princeton Univ. Press, 1989.

Marvelous ideas on interpretation and ornamentation for those playing 18th and early 19th-Century works.

Ribouillault, Danielle. "La Technique de Guitare en France dans la première moitié du 19e Siècle." Unpublished doctoral dissertation, University of Paris-Sorbonne, 1980.

This is a *brilliant* dissertation on the guitar and technical development in France in the 19th-Century. Written in French, this work is highly practical for information on France at the time of Sor, Carcassi and Carulli. Full of marvelous documentation.

Rosen, Charles. *The Classical Style.* New York: W.W. Norton, 1971.

This is a brilliant writing which has no direct connection to guitar, but since it deals primarily with the music of Haydn, Mozart and Beethoven, it focuses (for our purposes) on the music of Vienna at the time of Giuliani and inadvertently to the music of Sor, *etc.* Well worth reading.

N.B. There are also numerous guitar methods from the Classic/early Romantic periods (notwithstanding those by Sor, Aguado, Carcassi, et al), which are worth studying. Most are available in reliable editions and many in facsimile.

It is also important to point out to students that many modern editions of music and CD liner notes may contain biographical and historical information.

Romantic Period

Czerny, Carl. *Systematische Anleitung zum Fantasieren auf dem Piano-forte* (Vienna, 1829), facsimile edition, ed. Ulrich Mahlert. Wiesbaden: Breitkopf & Härtel, 1993.

Improvisation in the late Classic and early Romantic periods was considered a critical aspect of the performer's rôle and there were many books published to teach musicians these skills (*i.e.* C. Czerny, *Die Kunst des Präludierns in 120 Beispielen...*, Gétry, *Méthod simple pour apprendre á préluder..., et al.*). This art has sadly died out, but considerable information on 19th-Century performance practice is to be found in these improvisation methods. I list the Czerny above because it is probably the most readily available, though obviously written in German.

Czerny, Carl. *Über den Richtigen Vortrag der Sämtlichen Beethoven'schen Klavierwerke* (Vienna, 1842), facsimile edition ed. Paul Badura-Skoda. Vienna: Universal Edition, 1963.

Contains Czerny's "On the Correct Performance of the Complete Piano Works of Beethoven" along with his "Erinnerungen an Beethoven" [*Memories of Beethoven*], both of which are invaluable sources for information on performance practice during the transition between the Classic and Romantic Periods. Difficult to read, since it is in 19th-Century German, but well worth the effort.

Flesch, Carl. *The Art of Playing the Violin, Vol. II.* New York: Carl Fischer, 1930.

While not a true romantic (by date) Flesch is a tremendous source of information for performance practice on music from the Romantic Period.

Many of his ideas on phrasing, articulation and general interpretation can be applied to late 19th and early 20th-Century guitar repertoire.

Deri, Otto. *Exploring 20th-Century Music.* New York: Holt, Rinehart and Winston, 1968.

This is one of the best general histories of 20th-Century music. A difficult subject to analyze, since we are still in this period, so our views are not yet terribly objective. An enlightened discussion of styles, composers, and compositional trends, with many references and a valuable discography.

Elgart, Peter and Matt Yates. *Prepared Guitar Techniques.* Upland, Calif.: California Guitar Archives, 1990.

This is the definitive booklet describing various techniques for prepared guitar. Highly recommended.

◇ Materials for Dance and Dance Inspired Music

N.B. Much of our guitar literature (in particular, music from the Renaissance and Baroque) stems from dance music. While it is unrealistic to expect a student to study dance simply in order to understand this music, it is essential that they be familiar with the basic elements of various dances in order to properly perform the music on the guitar.

Needless to say, tempo, mood and articulation of dance and dance inspired music are strongly dictated by the dance itself and performers should be at least minimally aware of these aspects.

Arbeau, Thoinot (pseud. for Jehan des Preyz) *Orchesography* (Langres, 1587), ed. Dr. Julia Sutton. New York: Dover Publications, 1967.

This is a period instruction manual for basic dances in the Renaissance. Readily available, informative and fun to read, this will give students background on some of the more popular Renaissance dances as well as a feeling for how important dance was during the Renaissance. Edited by Dr. Julia Sutton, who is one of the world's leading authorities on pre-classic dance.

Caroso, Fabritio, *Nobiltà di dame* (1600) trans., ed. Dr. Julia Sutton. New York: Dover Publications, 1995.

This is one of the most informative dance manuals from the Renaissance faithfully translated from the Italian (including numerous works for lute accompaniment). Highly recommended, not only for the insight into period dance, but because in this period the dancing master was usually also the fencing master and also responsible for teaching court etiquette and manners to the children. Thus, it gives considerable insight as to daily activities in the Renaissance Italian court. Highly informative and enjoyable reading.

Congress on Research in Dance (CORD), [later titled Committee on
    Research in Dance]. Proceedings of various conferences on
    dance research.
    These reports from the various meetings of CORD are valuable for more scholarly research.

Glise, Anthony. *Performing Dance and Dance Inspired Music—A Hand-
    book for Instrumentalists.* St. Joseph/Vienna: Aevia Publications,
    Ltd., 1999.
    Currently in preparation, this book is designed for instrumental-ists who want to know the tempo, mood and the basic steps of pre-classic dance forms such as the pavan/galliard, allemande, sarabande, courante, gigue, minuet, *etc.*
    In dictionary format which covers most dance forms from the Renaissance through the mid 19th-Century. An extremely valuable secondary source which lists bibliographical sources, photos of basic dance steps and other general information for musicians who want to learn more about the dances in order to perform the music more authentically.

Horst, Louis. *Pre-Classic Dance Forms.* Brooklyn: Dance Horizons,
    1937.
    A somewhat dated but available source for determining the style of a dance, though actual steps are rarely given. Accuracy of some of the entries is questionable as are the "Hollywood-type" photos of the dances. Still, this is one of the few contemporary sources on pre-classic dance forms.

◇ Additional Subjects

Barlow, Wilfred. *The Alexandre Technique.* New York: Knopf, 1976.
    A good overview of the Alexandre Technique of relaxation and physical balance. This technique has become very popular for actors and performers in Europe (especially England) and is slowly making deserved headway in the U.S.

Helm, Eugene and Albert Luper, *Words and Music.* Clifton, NJ: European American Music, 1971.

The correct written format and style are essential for any writing on music (from program notes to term papers). I *strongly* recommend this booklet as the reference for any such documentation. Newer editions appear periodically which update changes in accepted means of musical documentation in writing.

Larayne, Harry and Jerry Lucas. *The Memory Book.* Briarcliff Manor, New York: Stein and Day, 1974.

Good general overview of the basis for memorization.

Matthav, Tobias. *On Memorizing.* London: Oxford University Press, 1979.

Similar to Larayne (above). Valuable reading for any performer.

Newman, William. *The Pianist's Problems.* New York: Harper and Row, 1974.

A very insightful book suitable for intermediate students who have shown aptitude and interest in truly expanding their musical abilities.

Ortmann, Otto. *The Physiological Mechanics of Piano Technique* (Baltimore, 1929), reprint. New York: Dutton, 1962.

A good study of the physical aspects of playing piano. Very applicable to guitar technique.

Salmon, Paul G. and Robert G. Meyer. *Notes from the Green Room (Coping with Stress and Anxiety in Musical Performance).* New York: Lexington Books, 1992.

This is beyond question the best book written to-date on how and why performers experience anxiety in concert.

It offers numerous suggestions and could easily be adapted as a workbook for performance classes or in a studio class. *Highly* recommended—not only for those who suffer from performance anxiety, but for those of us who *don't,* to help us understand what some of our students may be experiencing.

Author's Biography

Anthony Glise is a product of the *Konservatorium der Stadt* (Vienna) and the *New England Conservatory* (Boston) with additional studies at *Harvard University*, the *University of Vienna* (Austria), the *Université Catholique de Lille* (France), and the *Academy for the Study of 19th-Century Music* (Italy) where he periodically teaches summer courses on the Italian Riviera.

He has been awarded additional diplomas at *Festival Ville Sablé* (France), *Nemzetközi Gitárfesztivál* (Hungary), *ARCUM* (Rome), and the *Accademia di Studi Superiori* (in Stresa, Moneglia, Verbania, Intra, Brezzo di Bedero and Pieve di Teco, Italy).

A Pulitzer Prize Nominee for composition, Anthony is the only American-born guitarist to win First Prize at the *International Toscanini Competition* (Italy), an honor which included an unprecedented unanimous decision by the jury.

Host of the world-wide syndicated radio program, *"Glise on Guitar,"* Anthony records for Dorian Recordings (New York), and is head editor of *The Anthony Glise Editions* of guitar music published by Willis Music Company and *The Anthony Glise Urtext Editions*, published by Mel Bay. His original compositions (for guitar solo, chamber music, ballet and orchestra) are published by Aevia Publications, Ltd.

Anthony is Artistic Director of the Summer Festival of the *Southern German Guitar Academy* and when not on tour, he teaches and lives part-time in the U.S., part-time in the Flandres region of Northern France and part-time in the Black Forest region of Southern Germany.

Mr. Glise proudly endorses:
E&O Mari—LaBella (guitar strings), New York
Gioachino Giussani (guitars), Anghiari (Arezzo), Italy

"...Glise has produced (re-discovered?) a radically different way of playing the guitar. His constantly evolving articulation makes every phrase a revelation. His fastidious attention to phrasing creates a 'chiaroscuro' effect that I have only heard from the very best pianists or lute players." "...a revelation, and should be heard by any guitarist who wishes to play 'expressively'."

The Soundboard—Guitar Foundation of America (U.S.A.)

"The playing and sonority of Glise is not only clear and varied: it's a highly individual and spirited voyage. His style is not only that of power and decisive virtuosity: Glise seduces us by the grace and emotional intelligence of the phrase. His is a language of delicate effects, pure sensitivity and contemplative emotions."

Le Diapason (Paris, France)

Classical Guitar Pedagogy
A Handbook For Teachers
◇ Classical Guitar Technique
◇ Classical Guitar Pedagogy
◇ Musicianship

Anthony L. Glise

In spite of the tremendous popularity of the guitar—until now—there has never been a university textbook written for guitar professors and guitar pedagogy classes.

Whether you're an established classical guitar teacher or an aspiring student, the ideas and techniques in *Classical Guitar Pedagogy* will help expand your ability in the teaching studio and organize your teaching more efficiently.

Designed for use as a university-level textbook, *Classical Guitar Pedagogy* is the ideal text if you are teaching a course on classical guitar pedagogy. Each chapter has suggested weekly assignments, and the book is designed to be completed in one semester.

If you're already teaching—privately or in a conservatory—*Classical Guitar Pedagogy* contains numerous ideas for expanding your teaching studio as well as tips on career development as a classical guitar teacher and performer.

Complete Catalog of Books and Music On Request:
Mel Bay Publications
#4 Industrial Drive, Pacific, MO 63069-0066
Toll Free 1-800-8-Mel Bay
(1-800-836-5229)

Great Music at Your Fingertips